KT-197-615

Venice
Revealed

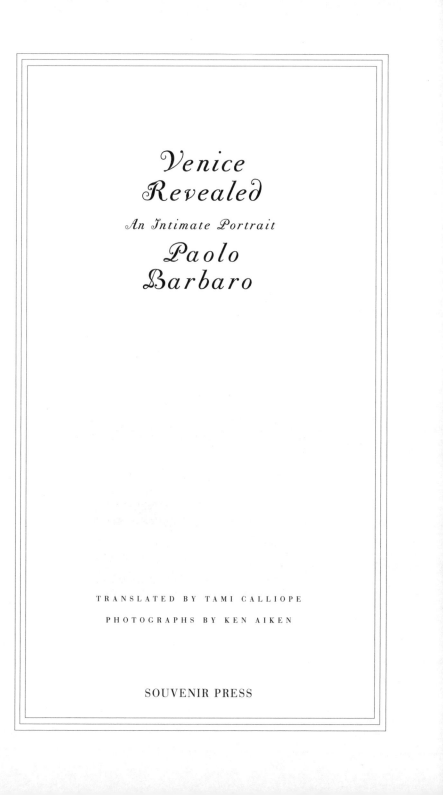

Venice Revealed

An Intimate Portrait

Paolo Barbaro

TRANSLATED BY TAMI CALLIOPE

PHOTOGRAPHS BY KEN AIKEN

SOUVENIR PRESS

Venice Revealed (La citta ritrovata) was written by Paolo Barbaro at the invitation of the Consorzio Venezia Nuova, which published it in December 1997 in a nontrade edition. The original publishers, Marsilio Editori, wish to thank the Consorzio Venezia Nuova for having permitted this new edition with amplified text.

Copyright © 1998 Marsilio Editon

English language edition copyright © 2001 Steerforth Press

The right of Paolo Barbaro to be identified as author of this work has been asserted by him in accordance with the Copyright, Designs and patents Act 1988.

First published by Marsilio Editori, Venice

First British Edition published 2002 by
Souvenir Press Ltd.,
43 Great Russell Street, London WCIB 3PD
Reprinted 2005

All Rights Reserved. No part of this publication may be reproduced, stored in a retrieval system or transmitted, in any form or by any means, electronic, mechanical, photocopying, recording or otherwise, without the prior permission of the Copyright owner.

ISBN 0 285 63635 9

Printed and bound in Great Britain by
Creative Print and Design Wales, Ebbw Vale

To everyone who asks me about Venice,
everywhere in the world:

> if it still exists, if it's sinking,
> if she's alive, if she's dead.
> Whether it's truly a city
> or whether the other ones are.
> To all who attempt or who dream,
> in whatever way,
> of returning
> to her.

PART ONE

The Days of Reentry

"We are approaching our landing in Venice," they repeat, "*Venezia, Venise, Venice, Venedig.*" In fact, what immediately appears, instead of Venice, is Marghera. Oil tanks, hangars, cranes, loading docks, power plants.

Seen from above, the powerful industrial zone stretches endlessly alongside the fragile and imperiled water. Concentrated, spreading, grandiose, a vision of hell rises up from the slender strand where earth meets lagoon, a hell with its own eager and sinister beauty.

I recognize the enormous factory gliding beneath the descending plane, and follow the shadows of wings over its warehouses and towers. For years I have worked, all over the world, in great industrial centers like this one: Marghera has been their model. How much human labor, effort, money, thought. And now worries, anger, and problems: so many more than we had ever thought possible — in the waters, on the earth, among peoples. The shadow of the plane passes swiftly away, as do the factory, the power plants, the plane itself. As do the years.

I glimpse an oil tanker in the lagoon — slow, almost motionless — arriving from the Canale dei Petroli. It plows stolidly into red and yellow waters spitting out effluents-discharges-arabesques, a profound and seasoned pollution. And who will ever wash it

clean now? Soon the tanker will moor itself to one of those white
wharves. "Like a toy!" they shout in the airplane, laughing.
Maybe; but for me, remembering what this expanse of earth-
water-world was like only a few years ago, it's no toy; it's no joke.
Instead, it's a deadly trap between shoals and sandbars, a few
inches of water — I can see it clearly from here. And it's all so
close to the waiting houses, the tiny gardens — to Marghera, to
Venice. And yet it all continues, as if the years weren't going by:
the protests against the oil in the lagoon, the agonizing over red
pollution or yellow waste, visible or invisible, are words in the
wind, useless.

Early evening and we're already on the runway, or maybe still
over the water; but Venice is there, in the fog on the other side of
the plane. I glimpse the puffs of distant cupolas — or clouds, perhaps — and the spires of bell towers like the masts of ships: the
other part of the world. In the pale winter light, more moon than
sun, we begin to invent Venice.

—◌ 2 ◌—

And yet today, as the family comes back home to stay, we're in
luck: there's traffic between sky and earth, so the plane is making
a slow descent. "A minute or so more," they repeatedly assure us,
"a moment or so more to wait." We wheel in the air, over islands,
coasts, and tracts of ocean. They are giving us a small gift of time
— right here, in the airplane, one of the great time-destroyers. But
how can I get this across to the kids, who are ever more impatient?
They want to "arrive."

Thomas Mann was right, Venice should be approached from
the sea. But now there's the sky; millions of beings drop down
every day from the clouds. Today we're arriving at sunset, sliding
through tremendous rents of light over the waters, from one
horizon to the other. The kids crowd together on the other side of
the airplane, piled up on top of the Japanese, the Brazilians, the
Americans . . .

But here it is, at last, appearing suddenly and in its entirety: the long, rose-colored island in the perfect form of a fish, immersed and emerging, born in this moment for us. "What is it?" asks a little boy, sprouting up out of the front seats, seeing and not seeing.

A city I don't know, I should tell him. I don't know what to call it, since "Venice," by now, is a thing that gleams on the glossy backs of a million postcards.

"What is it?" he insists, "what fish is it?"

"It's the Venice-Fish," I say. "Don't you see it?" He seems happy enough.

I look down on it again myself: Venice, mysteriously interrogatory and enchanted, tranquil and troubled. Pathetic, motionless, delicate — sailing, maybe. But who put it together, this living event at once minuscule and enormous, this impeccable shape built of infinite, shapeless scales? Is it a miracle of human life? A random act of nature?

Island upon island, dusky molecules, houses great and small, compact, solid, dreaming, waiting; rare the empty spaces, the piazzas, the gardens. Canals, banks, mirrors and more mirrors: clear or opaque, reflections of reflections, dazzling. And the great blue-green expanse that reassembles, recomposes everything. There is a moment of silence in the airplane, our fraction of eternity. Japanese, Brazilians, Venetians . . . who are we, really, in here, but a group of individuals, big and little, young and old, spying on the flower of stone in the sea from on high?

An instant later, it's there, in the center of the island: a black hole, a square piazza — Piazza San Marco, hollowed out from the heaped-up cluster of houses, brushed ever so lightly by the lagoon, which now has begun to rise and fall like the plane in the gusts of wind, in the heart of the Venice-Fish. The nearest surrounding islands tilt and press toward the center for safety; the farthest begin to cast off their moorings, to depart even as we arrive. The plane drops and wheels, the lagoon changes color with every turn: green-lagoon among the curls of white

foam, green-yellow-blue, green-rose-lagoon. The sunset intensi-
fies, streaking the sky with violet and orange.

We've arrived at low tide, that's easy to see now. How many
possible Fish, how many versions of Venice, are under us here?
They are being born and reborn in the water and mud, ready to
replace ours, now that it's starting to vanish . . . appearing perhaps
one time only in the history of the world.

At almost the same moment — on the islands, in the water, on
each smallest scale — the streetlamps come on, doubling the reflections, the season, the hour, the evening, the strangeness of this
beauty. In reality, we realize, thinking back for a moment to the
metropoli we've lived in, Venice is small, Venice is very little. It's
tiny and fragile, this flower of stone. In contrast the lagoon is so
big; the sea is so big; and the cities we've loved in our life disappear, are destroyed.

By now we can hardly see anymore, can just barely feel, barely
perceive a reflection within us. Our sliver of metal gets ready to
land: the city reappears, returns, vanishes, seeks a place on the
horizon in the last, suspended light.

And here we are on the runway — it's really earth, a sudden
strip of earth. But we don't want to land, to return to the planet;
miracles are brief, especially celestial ones. Set foot in Venice? I
still hesitate to say it, even: Venice, *Venezia*. I only know that I feel
doubly alive, between the rediscovered earth and the waiting
water. And so do they, the little band that's following me.

"Have we arrived?"

"Yes, we've arrived."

—◦ 3 ◦—

On the water, sitting in the barge bearing our furniture, we
breathe in water as if it were air as the continuous aggregate of
houses and canals slips silently beside us between the banks, beneath the rain that changes octaves with every bridge. Here and
there I recognize particular banks, portici, arches, the narrowing

funnel of a *calle*.* Stone after stone, I begin to rename her: Venice. Here in the center she is neither pathetic nor postcard-glossy, but gray, hard, flaking, and restless, like an old scratched film.

Then up and down on the boat called *vaporetto*.† Such a strange word — it makes us laugh a little, coming back from the outside. And it's an empty vaporetto, only a few people and almost all of them old, almost all old women, actually. In the evening purple lamps come on in the cabin still full of old people. Maybe they're the same ones, and they just leave them there for the night. Happy thought.

Back on the barge: our furniture wanders through the canals, appearing and disappearing between smaller and larger bridges. The film becomes complicated, everything is more and more arduous; the transportation of four pieces of furniture is a *puzzle*. Exactly so, a "puzzle," repeats the skipper. Now we're in *acqua alta*, high water, now *in secca*, scraping the bottom, now *in dosana*, being pulled back out to the sea. And now *al morto d'acqua*, dead in the water, caught between tides. "*Al morto d'acqua*," repeats the skipper, without looking at me but in the appropriate tone of voice. The boat is slow, the men are slow — my fellow citizens, after all, but they seem hostile, crafty, even sly to me. The one wearing mirrored sunglasses is particularly equivocal and unenthused about working, yet he's in charge. The dialect, or rather *la parlata*, the talk, sounds funnier than ever to me, even worse than when I hear it on TV: drawled phrases with that falling cadence that never ends, followed by sudden, quick, doubled syllables (*"mi-te-te. . . , ti-ti-me-vòl"*) spewed out in an anguished stammer. It will take some getting used to. Does one change so much in a few years of absence, of exile?

"It depends," answers one of them, who has the same first and last names as I do. "It depends on what kind of idiot you are," he clarifies peevishly. He stares at me and says, not stammering or

---

*Venetians call their innumerable narrow streets *calli* (*calle* in the singular) rather than *strade* or *vie*. — TRANS.

†A *vaporetto* is public transportation in the form of a water bus. Various *vaporetti* crisscross the lagoon and growl up and down the Grand Canal, zigzagging from bank to bank. — TRANS.

drawling: *"Zitto, eh"* — shut up. For an instant my mind flashes on *il morto d'acqua,* but in another sense — maybe it's me, in this film, who's the designated victim. Where is the sweet temperament that Venetians used to have, the smiles we remember, the joyful spirit always so noted by visitors, diarists, writers?

—❧ 4 ❧—

A rain so light you can barely feel it, barely hear it hit the water; it is all you could ask of a rain, gentle, gracious, Goldonian.* Insistent and implacable, however: it drips straight down our necks and wreaks havoc with the furniture. And now we hear the Word, dreadful, absurd, typically Venetian: destiny,*"Fatalità."* They repeat it over and over, Caronte with his mirrorlike glasses and all his companions: *"Fatalità–fatalità."* I don't recall it being used so frequently when I lived here before. Was it used less, or was I just younger? Certain words and thoughts don't exist when you're young — other ones do. Certainly I hadn't taken it, *Fatalità,* into consideration in this matter of moving furniture.

It was swiftly followed, as I had expected, by the other Word: *"Combàtter"* — to struggle, to fight. Which in this case means *not* to struggle, *not* to fight: What are we working our butts off for, why should we bust our balls over furniture, or the world? A variation of *Fatalità.* And in fact: Enough already, let's go for a drink, everyone go for a drink. The usual *spritz,* a little wine and water. I'll pay, you'll pay, the other guy will pay. It ends up, every time, that I pay — *Fatalità.* The trip takes three days of maneuvering between rain and high water, and countless spritzes alternated with *ombre.*† Notwithstanding the number of bars and shadows there is little gaiety; although the furniture movers, bartenders, and their clients are never truly angry, they seem always irascible

*Carlo Goldoni, 1707–93, native Venetian and world-famous playwright, whose masked characters derived from the ancient tradition of Commedia dell'Arte and whose plays were written and are still performed in the Venetian dialect. — TRANS.
†*Ombre,* often called *ombrète,* are "shadows," the Venetian term for a quick glass of wine, usually red. — TRANS.

for some fundamental reason that escapes me at the moment.

At high tide we can't pass under the bridges with our over-loaded boats. At low tide we can't go forward because our over-loaded boats scrape the bottom. Et cetera. However, every once in a while someone leans out a window overlooking the canal — from the kitchen, I realize — and calls out or waves to us. They still do that here, I think with joy, they still lean out the windows. But it's not for us; they're just keeping a domestic eye out on the water level and this damnable weather, using the canal under the house as a barometer.

We spend angry, arduous days and nights trying to make the house we left a few years ago at least a little more livable. "And you're lucky," everyone tells us, "very lucky." Carpenters are not to be found; or, if we find them, they vanish immediately, always stacked up with work as if there were millions of people moving house on these four tiny islands. The blacksmiths are gone. Those hell-fired caverns of my childhood, homes to untold marvels, are now closed down and locked up. All the smiths are in Mestre,* the people on our calle explain; or else they're too old, vanished, who knows? "Flown up there," says the old woman in Corte Re-diva, waving her arms like wings. On the other hand, the painter Boschìn, nicknamed Lightning, whom we hired months ago when we were still in Milan, is always late. He's an *artist*, he ex-plains, not just a painter, and he shows me miles of pictures he's painted. He'd like me to buy a couple — what a nightmare — for the house when it's put back in shape, and is unpleasantly insis-tent: "Buy two, pay for one."

I lose three kilos in a few days. And I don't have that many of them — kilos, days, or banknotes. But we're lucky, everyone tells us again and again, "lucky beyond belief."

The Words are repeated continually, in the most astounding combinations and arrangements: destiny; it depends; (don't) fight it; lucky, unlucky; "shadows" and more "shadows" — all of it stuff that would make no sense in the more Cartesian places we've

---

*Mestre is the larger municipality on the mainland surrounding the industrial port of Marghera. — TRANS.

come from — that is, in the cities that are actually cities. Fog after rain and rain after fog do the rest. Not only dead in the water, but dead from exhaustion; in Venice you risk being on your feet, walking, carrying, moving for hours, one bridge after the other, without ever stopping at all. It's as if we were back in the Middle Ages, before the advent of machines, cars, hoists, elevators, none of which exists here. It's obvious, too, that Caronte and his companions aren't about to put themselves out. Perhaps it's just the exhaustion, but I feel that I've failed, been mistaken about everything. Especially about coming back.

I telephone my engineer friend Sara, who works at the Port. I haven't heard from her for a few years: "Are you still at the Port?"

—❀ 5 ❀—

"In what's left of the Port," clarifies Sara. She's happy, extremely happy that we're here. "Returned at last," my wife and I. "Reunited," she repeats, as if she can't believe it's true, "back together again," as if we were family. "But what crazies," she adds absently. Right. "So now you're all nearby," she says, "and *I'm* far away."

"Far away?" I ask. Ah . . . she works in Marghera; the Port is no longer located in Venice. "Why in the world?" I ask. "Where has the *Port* ended up, isn't it still there on the Riva delle Zattere?"

There was a time when I was always looking for her, right there on the Zattere — Sara of the golden skin, the ever-ready smile, the energy of a stevedore. And now I even have to look for the Port.

"But the Maritime Station," I ask, "that beautiful villa on the riva, that narrow, narrow calle right beside it, remember? With the little wild roses cascading down the wall . . ." I wax romantic.

"The station's still there, at least most of it . . . the villa, half and half . . . the administration is sort of there and sort of not there, but there are no more ships. The calle has lost its wild roses, it's exploding with underground cables, but . . . the way it seems is . . . that in Venice they're useless. All the work's in Marghera and the bank is in Graz . . ." She pauses. "But what crazies!" she concludes. "What crazies you are! I'll call, I'll call," and she's gone.

Crazies-crazies, I'll call–I'll call: key words with which to hang up quickly, *addio.* I try calling a few other friends, but half the time the phone is busy; they're already talking or faxing. Or they're on the computer, watching the TV, scanning the Internet — all these infernal new gadgets that are emptying the *campiello,* tolling the death knell for the old conversations from window to window, from one bank to the other. It seems to me that I can even measure the phenomenon around here: Every evening there are fewer people on the streets, while those blue lights flickering from the windows expand the empty space between houses. The old greetings, the old cries and calls, have been extinguished one after the other — you don't hear them anymore, you don't *see* them anymore — that magic made out of the infinite sounds, voices, and echoes of the calli, large and small, each of which inhabited, in my memory, a precise body and soul. Instead, more or less *virtual* contacts are growing to find an ever-greater share with the water and stones; perhaps the soul was not so deep, and it was enough to change the signals. Soon we'll be saved from our endless heaps of disasters — *combàtter* or *non combàtter* — by the underground and aboveground cables, the coaxial cables, the yellow and blue pipes, the new "highways" as they call them, that even now are swarming and exploding through even the narrowest calli with their frenetic good works.

Just as long as all this work actually accomplishes something . . . But it seems that there's always something *newer,* more *advanced,* arriving our way from the outlying headquarters; always something new under the sun, everything keeps changing faster and faster.

Except for those smallest of signals, the whispers of lovers — even tonight, accompanying the last of the footsteps right here under the house.

—◦ 6 ◦—

I climb up into the attic and glance out the window, a ship's port-
hole overlooking the centuries-old roofs. A sea of roofs: brown-
yellow-ash-coffee-iron-soot-mold-gray-purple-violet-lead . . .
also rose, red, and blue. Shadows, repetitions, arches, stairways,
geometries, chasms, all merging for as far as the eye can see beneath the most uniform sky in the world, endless and indifferent.
And under me is water, *perpendicularly*; I can see it by leaning
out. The wall is about to fall forward and so am I. The attic walls
are wavy, in tune with the water. Who knows if they'll last for as
long as we're here, these walls, portholes, and roofs, these delicate
equilibriums?*

I descend the steep little ladder, prehistoric wood and trembling rungs that shake me off; I slide and go flying away, landing
on the so-called staircase riddled with gaps, under the row of
enormous, exaggerated windows. Drafts blow through the glass
panes, the ruined plaster has fallen out in chunks, and I seem to
be staggering through the ruins, buffeted by the gusts. But again,
it's the water giving me this sensation; on the far side of the
stairway windows is a sheer drop-off, straight down into the canal
— the *rio* is directly beneath me. In this stretch it's neither large
nor small, just gray-green and crafty, disappearing a little way off
and then returning. Beside it I glimpse a garden, or a kind of
garden, half vegetable patch and half rubbish heap.

On the other side of the house everything changes: a calle
about as narrow as they come, a black wall three feet or so from
my nose with a good view through the windows of the opposite
house: kitchen, parlor, bathroom. The shutters are closed —
there's no way around it — as soon as dark falls. Imprinted on my
retina — in memory or perhaps in absence of memory — is the
continuous impression of *water*, both inside and out; and on top

---

*In awful fact, the author's attic has *not* lasted as long as he had hoped; in June 2000
the ceiling caved in, burying his study and half of the kitchen. Luckily no one was
home when it happened, but the cost and labor involved in renovations will be extreme. — TRANS.

of that, the sudden wall, the aperture onto such narrowness, the opposite window slammed suddenly shut on my nose. Who's in there behind it, and what is that stifled sound? Even here in my own home, I'm going to have to get used to it all over again.

The elements, so far, are at play: water, sky, almost-sky, empty walls, sheer vertical drops. Of earth, very little; of solidity, none whatsoever. A bit farther on it's water again: a meeting of differently colored canals, one limpid, the other filthy. After the curve, they make an exchange: filthy to limpid (actually more filthy than not, right there at the crossroads, where the current accumulates; but after that it clears, and after that . . .)

—⌀ 7 ⌀—

Never before had it seemed to me so much an *island.* Maybe that's because this time I've come back from such earthbound places; or maybe because years before, years ago, I had lived in an absolute labyrinth of calli, filled with the good healthy odor of cats, rubbish, and so on; although the water was around somewhere, it was hidden, out of sight. Also because Venice in those days was still full of people, local people, whereas now there's no one out on the streets, not here on the outskirts. Or maybe it's only (once again) that I was younger; we mythologize the places that belong to our childhood, to our youth; filling them — crowding them — with faces, words, friendships, nostalgic appeals. This time it seems to me that it's *them,* the places, that are searching for *me,* calling to me in their low voices out of the water.

There's no doubt, however, about my friends at that time; I remember them perfectly. My schoolfellows were the sons of men who worked at the Arsenale, the huge naval dockyard; or were employed by Mulino Stucky, the big industrial mill that made all kinds of pasta; or who owned small businesses or worked in them. Pino's father varnished and painted boat bottoms; he was a kind of magician with submarine paints. Ughetto's father was one of a group of Venetian-mosaic workers; Gianni's worked in the *fabricòn*, brewing beer. Where they all ended up I have no idea. I *do* know where their businesses went: the beer to Friuli, the mosaics to Zelarino, the submarine paints half to Marghera and half to Australia. The gigantic Mulino Stucky, as big as a small town, is completely shut down; the ancient Arsenale, as big as a city, is closed and in ruins.

The tugboats that towed the big ships — I realize it only today, standing on the riva — have also ended up on terrafirma. How I loved those tugboats, as a child, and later still as an adult! The *Ursus*, powerful and splendid, and its almost-twin the *Titanus*, both of which my friend Guido and I planned to skipper one day . . . what competitions *in laguna* we had! When Guido's *Ursus* passed by at full steam, the bridges and shores shook and trembled, as they did for my own *Titanus*.

Even the boats' winter storage places are now on dry land. All winter long, Venetian boats sleep, as they say, "in the country."

In the evening we can't even breathe: stuck on an island, without *Ursus*, without any boats.

—◦ 8 ◦—

My wife, my friends, and I are perpetually trying to compare "then" and "now."

Everyone here has more money than they used to — we all agree on that. But how many of the old trades, crafts, businesses large and small have vanished!

"Did they make less money than a souvenir stand full of postcards?" someone asks.

Probably; and perhaps by now the idea of industry on the islands is absurd. So everyone's richer, but also — it seems to us — more restless.

"Unhappier?"

"'Fulfilling yourself' by selling postcards is a contradiction in terms," someone answers.

You can measure the death throes of a city, and of a whole human psychology, by the gradual disappearance of these occupations.

"Maybe it's the beginning," says my friend Martino, always the optimist, "a slow, even painful beginning, continuously shoved down into the subconscious, of another city we don't know yet."

But what's happened, what's changed so fundamentally in just a few years?

In brief, basically *everything* has changed. A bit like the two of us, who returned believing we were the same people who had left; yet there are tracts of body and soul missing, lost, we won't find them again. She, the city, is the same, dreaming of what she used to be. It can seem that nothing has happened; the external structures remain, which is a lot in itself — they wait, call out, remember and remind, these surfaces of houses and things (and even of us? More or less). But no one, or almost no one, is inside them. How many trades, how many crafts that were ours alone, maritime, *lagunari*, I find only in slivers, fragments of memory ever more rare; how many "industries," as my grandfather called them, have ended up somewhere between memory and oblivion? Hundreds? Thousands? We should try to count them up sometime, if possible: a terrible inventory of lost activities, a record of the men lost along with them. The very thought suspends thought inside me and catches at my throat. It's true that there's more money floating around now; tourism is a fountain of it. But it's too little to compensate for the loss of so many kinds of work, so many faces, hands, diverse tasks — choices that were always difficult, certainly, but up until yesterday still *possible* — our varied "vocations" of days gone by, our hopes.

Our friend Sara, who works ten hours a day in Marghera, seems not to realize any of this. "Everything's changed? Well, maybe some things," she admits. But — I say — a hundred thousand people have left in the past few years, only around seventy thousand are still living here, they're ebbing away, the numbers decline every day. And she . . . she talks about the *long wave*: "These few years," she says, "count but they don't count."

"Everything *has* changed," I insist unsuccessfully. "We're talking about an exodus of people from Venice, a continuous exodus during all the years of our lives, it's like we're emptied, we don't make sense anymore. It's only the old people who stay here, the old who come back . . ." It's as if she were deaf.

What was I thinking about, coming back here?

But this evening a desk calendar for the current year arrives at the house for my wife and me, filled with beautiful photographs of Venice and of the lagoon. One is lovelier than the next, not too mannered; they look timeless. It has been sent to us by Sara, who has written on it, "To your return to Venice, this year and xñ."

The symbol *xñ* means, to engineers, infinity, forever . . . and yet here we are, in this city that might not have much longer to live, in this most precarious and fragile of places. "Forever": an idea that otherwhere, in other cities and towns . . . I don't know, maybe doesn't exist anymore, is absurd. "What crazies" is buzzing around in my head; but I go out and decide to pick up a couple of notebooks, just generic graph-paper notebooks so I can jot down a few notes — what am I thinking? — about these first days back on the island, the better to ponder them. So that something tangible, who knows what, will remain from the Return of the Crazies. The Venetian calendar is too beautiful to use — Venice is always too beautiful.

I begin my notebooks with Sara's symbol: xñ, forever. More absurd than ever, on a graph-paper notebook. At least for a while, though, for as long as we stay here. Will we stay here?

―༄ 9 ༅―

The city reduced by half, the island syndrome, its galloping difference from the rest of the world, its growing *emptiness*, the refrain of the absurd . . . and now this continuous *forever*, not only on Sara's calendar, but haunting you on every wall, every stone, even the oldest ones, crumbling with age. Strange, the blend of first impressions and memories. I wonder if the young people here feel anything of the kind. "Are you staying here or thinking of going someplace else?" I ask Marco in the vaporetto. We're all constantly meeting up with each other — *per forza*, there's no way around it — on the vaporetto, which always seems like yesterday's or the day before yesterday's vaporetto, always the same one.

Marco is aware of me right away, naturally, as soon as I set foot on the boat; but like all good Venetians, he sees and doesn't see. And I see and don't see. He was a skinny kid yesterday, running down the calli; now he's a young man playing on the rugby team. I was more or less his age when I left. "Will you stay here," I ask, "or are you thinking of leaving?"

"We could at least have a discotheque," he says, avoiding the question. "If not, if we can't even have a *discotheque* in Venice . . ." Evidently we can't; it's forbidden by the neighborhood associations, the *Superintendenza*, the town council . . . who knows?

"And if not?" I ask.

If not, he and his friends go to the moon. La Luna. The biggest of the discotheques, out in the country somewhere on the Romea, the renovated, ancient pilgrims' route to Rome. It's just a bunch of kids, he says, nothing wrong with it. "There's also La Marmellata, which is closer, full of kids from the nearby towns, gangs of friends in competition with La Luna."

"Do you have fun?"

"So-so," he says, measuring his words, a true Venetian. "It depends." But it's clear: there's a sort of city made up of discotheques over there, and that's the city of the young. "You should come see it," he says. I promise I'll come. Then he tells me, as the vaporetto chugs ever so slowly from one landing to another, that he, Marco, lives here in "Calle della Scimmia or delle Scimmie, monkey or monkeys, no one knows for sure." But he works as an assistant concierge in a tourist hotel in Marghera, on a month's contract at a time.

"Whyever in Marghera?"

"Don't you know that there are more hotels and tourists in Marghera than in Venice? Or else they're in Mestre, on the *autostrada*, that damned superhighway . . ."

Yes, I knew, I know, but I hadn't given it much thought.

"They've sprung up like mushrooms," he explains, "every-where over there, exploiting the image, the name."

"Whose name?"

Ah, Venice's name. A name, an image; the city itself doesn't count.

"Everything costs less on terrafirma, the hotels are a lot cheaper and so are we. And everything's more practical. The Japanese arrive and think they're in Venice; they stick them back in a bus as soon as they get here and take them on a quick little tour, a couple of hours in San Marco, half an hour in a gondola, then they smile and kick them back out. Arrivals and departures at fixed hours every day, millions of Japanese, all exactly alike."

Which high school did you go to, I ask.

"The *liceo classico*," he says, "but you don't learn languages there." That is, you learn Latin, Greek, even Italian, "all really useful stuff," he snorts, "really useful with the Japanese."

I get off with him, I've forgotten at which stop, and go to see his Calle delle Scimmie. We enter it through the PORT . . . DELLE SCIM . . . , DO . . . OF THE MONK . . . The name makes me hopeful, puts me in a good mood, although it's almost illegible on the crusted walls among the crumbling bricks.

"We just have to imagine them," I say, "your monkeys."

"There are as many as you could want around here," he replies. "Monkeys and bigger monkeys."

We pass under a low, dark, stinking portico and follow a narrow calle funneling into deeper darkness, Calle Prima. The whole complex is clearly a place designated for ancient and modern pissing of the human variety, rather than for monkeys. Streams, rivers of international pee a step away from the Accademia, the Museo del Settecento, the Guggenheim . . . "In a city," I say, "without public toilets, I haven't seen even one."

"Yeah, think of London," laughs Marco. "So many, *too* many, it makes you want to go all the time just to give them a try . . ."

We reach Marco's: a little room and a half on the ground floor looking onto the calle, almost completely without light. A bath-room with a rust-streaked shower, an extra-poor antique; walls crumbling into dust, permeated with the stale smells of cat, must, graveyard, rotten food.

"This is where we live," says Marco, "all the young people, all my friends, in all the calli and *rami** around here, on the ground floors and in the basements, rooms squeezed under the stairwells, dark, pissy cellars." He corrects himself: "Old people, too. At night *we* all come out of our dens and go to La Luna. The old people stay here, and sometimes in the summer they wait for us on the riva."

"But then who are they for," I ask, "these restorations I see happening everywhere?"

"Every once in a while," says Marco, "I sleep in the hotel in Marghera just so I can breathe. But then I miss," he adds without laughing, "the smell of the cats."

We sit down for a moment — he on the bed, I on the creaking chair.

"In the morning," he says, "there's the *other* river, the stream of kids from the country arriving in squadrons: waiters, errand boys, cooks, since there's no other kind of work here. Thousands of waiters ready for Venice — it's all one big constant coming and going. Only the old people stay put. Every once in a while they watch us, tell us there used to be real work in the old days."

A great blow to the door makes the house shudder. It could be a monkey, an orangutan, an elephant. But instead it's Manuela.

—⌒ 10 ⌒—

Manuela still lives with her family. She's a waitress *ai piani*, meaning that she speaks several languages, at the Grünwald, but her contract is precarious, good for only a day, not a month. She studied sciences and wanted a career in research biology.

"And the others who were at school with you?" I ask.

"They're studying in Bologna, Ferrara, Milan . . . but they all

---

Rami are calli so narrow that they can accommodate only one person at a time. In many rami even a small person can easily touch the opposing walls without stretching her arms to full length. — TRANS.

come back every Saturday, all the Venetians come home."

"Because their mothers' fish or risotto is the best?"

"No, because they get fed up, they can't take it."

"Can't take it?"

"They can't stand being *out there*, they have to be here at least one or two days every week. Everything's different *out there*, too different. Actually, even I," she admits, "stay here because of Marco and because I've found a job . . . But it's not just that. I don't like the job and as for Marco, well, I don't know," she laughs. "I stay here," she says, making an all-encompassing gesture, "because we're in Venice, in a place that's crazy, different . . ."

"But do you all work in the hotels, in tourism?" I ask, skirting her statement.

"Almost all of us, if we want work. It's an army of young men and women," she says, suddenly serious, "who could give a shit about the tourists, who treat them badly, *pesci in faccia.** They accept tourism because there's no way around it, under any condition, and they come by the thousands from the terrafirma every day, just to work by the day."

"That's what Marco was saying," I venture. "The great stream, the great human river from the terrafirma."

"What stream? What river? They're exiles," she says, "ex-Venetians, almost all of them. For years they work here by the day, then by the month, then if they're lucky by the season . . ." She sighs. "You can make money, it's true, but only if you're very, very good can you finally — whether you're an exile or from the country — can you be *in pianta*, with a solid contract, a permanent position in Venice."

"Why are you calling them 'exiles'? After all, terrafirma is only a step away."

"What do you mean, 'only a step away'? It's a whole other thing, it's as far away as America. *Anyplace* is different from here — it's *terrafirma*, country, continent . . . Mestre or Milan, Italy or America . . . it's not *here*."

---

*"Fish in the face," meaning a person so rude he would slap your face with a fish. — TRANS.

She must know at least a couple of languages. But "in reality," she says, "I don't know the language that's called on for work. I only know that the work is hard and that we're free only one out of every three evenings."

And what are the languages, I ask, that she'd need?

She'd need them all: English, Spanish, Russian, Arabic, Japanese . . .

"The Russian and Arab tips," she says, "are the highest. Marco and I put them away for a whole year, and then when they fire us . . . they always fire us, every month, every winter . . . well, the day after, we fly to Nepal."

"Nepal?" I ask.

"Nepal, you got it. Twenty days. And anyway," she says, giving me a look, "what's farther away from Venice, Nepal or Marghera? Every year we take a little trip somewhere over there in the Orient, twenty days or a month — it depends on the tips, it always depends on the tips. Sometimes, if we pool them together, they come to two or three times more than our paychecks. Other times . . . You never know, you just hope all year long. One winter in Nepal, one in Malaysia, one at home."

"In Malaysia?"

"Malaysia, Indonesia, whatever."

Perhaps geography is not her strong suit; but the longing is certainly strong, every once in a while, to "get out of these catacombs, both of us together. Then we come back hoping they'll hire us again. If they don't, maybe we'll stay in Malaysia. We'll see; it's all ups and downs. We seem," she concludes, "to be always in Venice and never in Venice all at the same time."

We walk out of the catacombs together. "And this evening?" I ask. "Where are you going?"

"This evening," she replies, looking up at the sky and smiling, "the moon must be up there somewhere . . . Can't you guess where we're going?"

"To La Luna," I say, happy to be in the know. "To the discotheque next to the Marmellata."

"Don't be an idiot. This evening we're going out in the boat."

She shows me the old *topo** sailboat, rocking gently under the moon; it looks like the one I used to have. Just as rickety as mine was, and as leaky as a sieve; but hey, they're young, it doesn't matter.

"Are you going out fishing?"

"No, it's not the season. We're going out to see, *a vardàr.*" There's no need to explain any further.

"Tonight," confirms Marco, "we'll sail around the Terre Perse, the Lost Lands, and the breakwater at Alberoni." Eyeing the world from the water.

I turn back toward home. On nights like this we, too, when we were young, never questioned where we were going; we were going out fishing. With the moon or with a lantern, *in laguna* or *in mare*, depending on the month and the fish. But when it wasn't the season for fishing, we went just to *see*, to see the miracle we can never get enough of. During the war years we waited under the moon for the planes in boats without lanterns; not a light shone in the city, only a blue glimmer here and there on the waters. But who knows if that was me, if that was really us? Even then, exactly as now — just as my two young friends put it — I feel that I've always been in Venice, and that I've never been in Venice at all.

—∾ 11 ∾—

Tonight I'm here for sure and always have been, deep in the Venetian night at the beginning of winter, which gusted in all of a sudden after endless warm, still evenings. It's cold and dark; only a few lights gleam on the water, as if lit by the wind. The lights are hidden in the calli, reflecting here and there on the facades, and a pallor lies on the bell towers. I take in the white of San Giorgio

---

*Topo, literally translated as "mouse," is a Venetian flat-bottomed boat measuring anywhere from six to twelve meters in length, commonly used for fishing both in the shallow waters of the lagoon and in the Adriatic Sea. Until a decade or two ago, it was generally graced by a large, trapezoidal, vividly colored sail, which has been replaced, for the most part, by a motor. — TRANS.

in Isola, the livid gray of San Moisè, the solitude of San Nicolò dei Mendicoli.*

You can feel something arriving in the air, a shiver, a thrill: the stars pursued by the *bora*.† From the apex of the Accademia Bridge, overlooking the most fairy-tale stretch of the Grand Canal, the archetype of a thousand postcards, human beings are watching intently as the last few wisps of fog dissolve in the dark of the sky, loosened and scattered one by one by the wind. And as each whorl of fog disappears, the flash of the constellations opens and dazzles above us, white, silver, and blue.

Other beings are toiling up the great dark bridge step by step without saying a word, looking reduced and foreshortened. The youngest ones arrive at the top and head back down the other side. But nothing is more moving than to see certain old people — rich or poor, or whatever — climb up this bridge in the night with their shadows, in the most beautiful labyrinth created by man in the world. They come up here and stand still, as if to see and understand it for the last time, and they speak — at least a few words — to the first person who comes along. Then, sometimes, even the youngest will stand still beside them. Among them I encounter Paolo, who comes straight to the point.

—◦ 12 ◦—

"There's Sirius," he shows me, "splendid, right on the tip of the bell tower of San Vidal." Arcturus, instead, is uncertain, hanging over the water without a bell tower. "Vega's lower down," he assures me, although I don't see it. "But if we walk down the bridge toward the riva, it will come meet us."

Paolo-the-astronomer is an engine mechanic, an "engine repairman" on the boats that crisscross the lagoon. In his underwater office all day long, at night he occupies himself with the

---

*All three are Venetian churches. — TRANS.
†The *bora* is the cold northeastern wind that blows from the northernmost stretches of the Adriatic across the lagoon and into the city, heralding winter. — TRANS.

stars. He has a telescope (I don't know whether it's little or big) at home on his terrace. "It's a good period," he insists, "the best period of the year *for them.*" And he points them all out to me as we walk, expanses of sky shifting with the street, stars and planets, visible and invisible; it's an effort for me to follow him. I suspect that at certain moments he tells me one name, at others another, for the same star, but I don't say anything as he attempts to follow them, to reach his nocturnal certainties — my friend the astronomer-mechanic, sequestered by the sun in his submarine engine rooms. Besides, who else in the world talks about stars anymore, who else sees them? It's as if they weren't there. Somewhat like the dead — the thought crosses my mind — whom no one remembers.

And he's off, scooting along sideways as if blown by the wind, *via di bolina* as they say around here, with the lilting, disjointed gait of an old sea dog, looking a little demented — *bagonghi.*

And I'm right behind him. "Venice changes so much from one night to another," I venture, "that it seems impossible . . ."

"It seems impossible that the stars and planets," he breaks in, returning the conversation to its lofty heights, "Venus, Mars, and the others, that they should all come back on these different nights," he says, suddenly stopping midstep, "to their exact same places.

"I mean," he clarifies, "into their precise orbits, to their expected, imaginable, calculable spots." And let us not forget the moon, which is vaulting up into the sky. "Also the moons," he says, for the moon is doubled, tripled, in the high tide; here in the long shudders of the racing water, there motionless and serene. I look as intently as he does: double, triple . . .

"It's the perfect moment," he breathes, "because the air is light, 'rare,' and the sea is high but happy — quiet down underneath."

I understand that there's no stopping him tonight. There's nothing to do but follow him — a series of steps over here, one over there; he's steering forward, under way, accelerating — as they, the constellations, emerge one at a time from between the profiles of the palazzi on the anonymous firmament. Called by name, hailed happily, discovered abruptly and maybe mistakenly. One after another, behind the bell tower of the Frari, above Gastone the newspaper vendor's bridge (an extraordinary observatory), beside Trattoria Sportivi, in the shop windows of the Pettenello toy store in Campo Santa Margherita, all over the city. It's as if we were racing between the mirrored expanses of the lagoon, rounding the bends of streams meandering through the marshes, newly emerged from the engine room onto the decks of the boat. Who can stop him by now? The bora is at its lightest and "Vega is at the height," Paolo assures me happily, "of its splendor."

—◌ 13 ◌—

Suddenly, from the Riva delle Zattere, all of them appear to us together, "in one fell swoop," according to Paolo: stars, planets, moons, constellations, galaxies. A random window or two is still lit on the island of the Giudecca, which seems to be a scale model of itself at this hour; but the luminaries, dazzling in their immensity above the dark lagoon, are not threatened by these few human lights. The same marvel, the same miracle that enchanted our ancestors for millennia, everywhere in the world — from the deserts of Asia to Stonehenge, from the Druids' woods to the coasts of America — still, in those rare, ever-rarer times we chance to see it, moves us to our depths. Tonight the miracle hangs suspended over Venice, reflected back to itself from the waters. We stand for a long time, watching — *seeing* — on the endless riva, we two alone. For the moment this entire spectacle is for Paolo-*bagonghi*, leaping up and down the bridges, and for me, racing along in his wake.

Except that we can't keep it up; we're unable to look at them for long. "We're not able to *sustain* them," says Paolo, "while they're looking at us like that, all of them together." We have to keep moving; we can't manage to stay still for a moment under the stars. We've forgotten how to look at them, how to contemplate them.

From the Ponte Lungo to the Fondamenta degli Incurabili, from the Ponte dei Saloni to the Magazzini del Sale,* we finally wend our way toward that magic point, the customs house or Dogana da Mar, which cuts the lagoon in two like the prow of a ship. Each of our footsteps feels light, everything's in its place — even our most earthly thoughts, now and forever so tangled — all in tune with the stars, each inhabiting its exact spot in the skies.

Yet here come two beings with great black beards and diabolical eyes, hurtling down toward us from the top of the bridge, swooping by us, brushing us with their arms . . .

They pass by as if we did not exist: young men still, but grave, serious, heavy, with loud voices in complete disharmony, it seems to us, with the dreamy night and our own peculiar dialogues. In reality, they're talking to each other in somewhat low voices, but in the silence that surrounds us it's as if they were shouting, the echoes of their words distorted and jarring.

"By this time," reasons one of them, "there are no more *things*." He stresses, *"things*, in the skies or on earth, not even the names of things . . . Maybe their shadows, their refractions, their virtual images."

"So we don't even know," echoes the other, "if speaking is speaking, if seeing is seeing." They glance over at us, who are gazing up at the stars. But they are not done. "Those are satellites," they hiss alarmingly, "artificial moons, space probes, vectors, signals, weather stations, luniks, or voyagers, temporary and permanent satellites . . . anything but *stars*." Their eyes flash like lightning at us from the dark. "The stars, friends . . ." They make a gesture of farewell: "You can kiss them good-bye, what are you standing there looking at? There are no stars anymore." They move away, saluting us — *salve!* — and disappear into a nearby calle.

"That's never happened to me before," says Paolo, "to run into two philosophers in the night, here in Venice where there's never

---

*From the Long Bridge to the Quayside of the Incurables, from the Bridge of Rooms to the Salt Stores . . . The names of every bridge, calle, alley, campo, riva, canal, and rio in Venice evoke the rich history of its thousands of years as a proud, self-sufficient, thriving republic and throng with the ghosts of lost activities and forgotten souls. — TRANS.

been a single philosopher (except for the mayor),* discussing
under the stars — what was it they said? — whether things are
things, whether speaking is speaking . . . And their gravest doubts"
— he starts laughing — "are actually launched toward the *firma-
ments*, spreading out all through the heavens tonight here above
us, shining so splendidly down on us and in the waters they could
even give you a headache . . ."

We start walking again, in our same curious gait, as if were
sailing close to the wind; but the conversation has left us with
some doubts and we turn toward home in silence. Perhaps Paolo-
the-astronomer is in crisis.

"But that's *Vega* over there!" he bursts out suddenly, pointing
to the sky. "Don't you see too that that's Vega?"

"Certainly it is." But the others?

"Some yes," he admits. "Others no. It's all out of whack here in
Venice, it's harder to find certain stars here than at sea." It's true:
our labyrinth of streets, canals, footsteps, and dialogues affects
even the stars.

"Seen from the curves of the calli," he confides to me under
his breath, "or from the bends of the smaller canals, they're continuously changing positions and names, above us and even inside, in the brain . . . You end up confusing them, even if you
know them really well, you invent them, you lose them . . ."

So now I understand why you can make mistakes with their
names: between our personal labyrinths and these labyrinths of
stone, the stars are always changing, above and within us.

"Maybe it's the two of us who are crazy," bursts out Paolo, "wandering around at this hour only a couple of years away from the
millennium, searching out the stars and guessing their names . . .
Or maybe it's the city that's gone, gone away . . ." He looks at me.
"A couple of years before the millennium, when everyone else, in
every other city in the world, is placidly driving home in their au-
tomobile . . . here we are walking around like two madmen. And
yet we know very well," he continues, looking back up at the stars,

---

*The mayor of Venice, Massimo Cacciari, is professor of aesthetics at the University of
Architecture. He is well known as a philosopher and has always united his theoretical
researches with his political responsibilities. Among his published works are *Krisis*,
1976; *The Critical Dialectic of Politics*, 1978; and *The Necessary Angel*, 1986. — TRANS.

"that in reality they're all fiery balls, a bunch of boiling cauldrons, and we even know the exact temperature of each of those cauldrons — soon, one by one, we'll probably be able to *control* them . . . It's a long way from my engine rooms." He stares up at them from the riva. "Certainly it's possible," he admits, "that a few of those lights tonight may be artificial satellites; there are so many of them and they wax and wane every night. Maybe tonight there's a double Sirius up there, an Arcturus that isn't Arcturus, a Vega that maybe is already dead and replaced . . . But those over there," he encourages himself, "are stars, by God, they're stars for sure, don't you see how they . . . how they *pulse*, how they *beat?*"

I see, I see.

"Tonight they're calling us," he insists. "They're making us drunk." He drifts a bit more as he walks, entering and departing the dream.

I attempt to shake off the dream myself. "What about the constellations, though?" I ask. "You have to admit those are false."

"They're false and they're true: stars that seem a certain way, are arranged a certain way — it depends on how we see them, whether we're looking at them from San Vidal or from the Dogana. It all depends on us, even meeting up together tonight, seeing and not seeing . . ."

So even the two bearded philosophers on the bridge were partly right, and Venice complicates everything: We don't know where to turn anymore, between island and island. We wander continually under the wheeling stars, and no one knows where it begins and nobody knows where it ends.

And yet they move us so that we keep on walking, one step after another — and our dialogue by now is utterly senseless — but we're unable, by now, to go home.

"It's almost the hour," whistles Paolo, "for the early shift."

They move us and that is enough, whatever their names are, whatever we whistle or see. They hang suspended over the waters, the gardens, the houses beginning to come back to life, a rare light shining out here and there once again from a window. They sparkle as if they were ever the ancient, the true constellations, telling stories of madness and love — and they disappear.

PART TWO

Toward the Roots of the Water

They are vanished, closed, undiscoverable: there's no longer a sign, not a trace of the offices Martino and I are seeking so desperately. The centuries-old walls swiftly erase those superimposed traces and return to being themselves, laughing at the metamorphoses that we attempt to impose on them over and over.

On one creaky front door we find written, between two antiques dealers' doorbells: OFFICE LIQUIDATED (*liquidated* — what a horrendous word). On others it's the agency, company, annex, or branch office that's been liquidated. HEADQUARTERS ARE IN MESTRE, FOR FURTHER INFORMATION APPLY TO MESTRE. HEADQUARTERS ARE IN MILAN, FOR FURTHER INFORMATION APPLY TO MILAN. That's a shame, since I just got here from Milan. Martino even glances down into the canal; you never know. But in the motionless water, the color of ash at the moment, the walls have returned to being themselves alone, even more so than their counterparts on earth (is it earth?).

The strangest part is that, as we pass from one "liquidation" to another in search of phantom offices, everywhere we look we see large- and small-scale restorations, nonstop reparations all over the place. Emptied, Venice is much cleaner and cared for, on the face of it, than it used to be. Underneath in the foundations, of course, it's another story. Certainly the city is losing that crumbling, flaking, melancholy-interrogative face that had remained imprinted on my soul, in order to assume another, less pathetic, less typical one. Perhaps it's only an outward image, but it does make you hope. I note that the new plaster jobs tend more toward white or off-white than toward Venetian red and its shadings. Venice in white? It works better in the darker calli (I think about Marco's black catacombs) but facing the water . . . I don't know, but it doesn't look right. What counts is the whole juxtaposition, the composition of all the colors together; and this insipid, wan white over the gray-green water doesn't make it. Then the water changes, so the white changes; nuances of color and architecture change; vision and moods change. But here we are at Rio Nuovo, where a great undertaking is under way — magnificent, I think — on the water, embracing canals, bridges, banks, docks, and quays. Out of the water and under the water everything's *in restauro*, and it's all the same color.

In search of lost activities, I wander among the Calle delle Bande, Rio della Guerra, Calle dei Bombaseri, Cassellerie, Ponte delle Cererie. *Le bande* were sheet-metal workers; *i bombaseri* once worked the *bombaso*, or cotton. *Cassellerie* were workshops specializing in furniture, *cererie* the wax factories and warehouses. In those days references to work were ubiquitous, as omnipresent as references to the saints. Administration, production, handcrafting — they were all here on the island. A little farther on lies the factory of all factories: we wander around the Arsenale, once the world's greatest shipyard, for hours, losing ourselves in this city within the city.

A great desire to see/see again/see anew springs up in Martino and me. Everywhere we go we stretch things out as long as we can, hoping to rediscover her, to recognize her, "like a person who's waiting for us," says Martino: the city and the lagoon. Unfortunately, I realize, our time for this is limited; these days we always have something we *must* do. This period of readaptation to work, both in and out of the office, is more difficult here than in any other place we've ever been. And then Venice, for as small as it is, is so big. Big or little? We must readapt both physically and psychically, with our eyes, our thoughts, our frames of reference. By nightfall it's the legs, most of all, that protest: Venice is hard, literally, to get around in for anyone used to a car. We don't have legs anymore; they may have gotten lost in Milan, or . . . who knows where?

The tremendous scatteredness of the place we need to reach in order to work constrains us to march and countermarch all day long. The municipality, the *Comune*, is dispersed into I don't know how many seats, often listed in the directories, manifestos, and beautiful official logos without any address whatsoever. According to *them*, the name of the *sestiere** or palazzo is enough: Farsetti, Loredan, Marcello, Zen, and so forth. But there are thousands of palazzi in Venice, and thousands of names, often the same ones or only slightly different. Certain names make us laugh: Ca' di Dio, for example, Ca' Boldu. But we discover that the very ones we're laughing about are places of sorrow: in them we find the aged, the drugged, the infirm — all of whom welcome us ecstatically, don't understand us very well, yet accompany us back "just to the bridge." From there, they say, you can walk directly to the palazzo . . . although I don't, we don't know what it's called . . . Or they give us some incomprehensible name. But it's always *"sempre dritti,"* just go straight forward — as we head once again down the twisting maze of ever-more crooked calli.

The university seems designed as a tease. It's tiny, they tell me, compared to the ones in Rome or Milan, but from *our* point of view it's infinite, dispersed as it is in at least forty different locations, secreting itself in the most unimaginable, well-hidden, and camouflaged places — enough to call for a specialized guidebook all its own. Almost all of these premises are extraordinarily beautiful and some of them truly splendid: romantic palaces, ancient Gothic houses, intriguing inner courtyards full of fascination. The walls tremble with beauty and cracks; the pavements are unable to support libraries with too many books.

I find Ca' Foscari, its central and most ancient seat, on the edge of ruin. No one is in the beautiful Gothic courtyard. There's not a sound, not a footstep.

---

*A *sestiere* is one of the six distinct districts of Venice. — TRANS.

"However, everything's ready," says the surveyor, popping out suddenly from behind a column. "It's been ready for restoration for quite a while now. I've been here waiting," he adds, looking at me kindly, "for the past three years."

Huge, black steel reinforcements uphold the facade, and powerful silver-and-yellow scaffolding supports every window and arch: a fearful file of prostheses on the giant wounded to death. Meanwhile, from the palazzo on the far side of the canal, the firemen every so often sound off with their trumpets and sirens: *Ready! Ready!* screams the loudspeaker — readier all the time.

"Every afternoon," the surveyor assures me. "You can find me here every afternoon." He arranges and rearranges the four signs — DANGER, FALLING STONES — looks around, and whistles. And now I see why he's here, as he modulates his whistle and they finally appear: two little white rabbits, leaping and lunging out of their little surveyor's house, built just beneath the arch of the library. They're stunted, savage, ferocious; there's no grass in the Gothic courtyard, and in the library, only books.

"It's been three years," he explains. "I raise a pair every year." Rocki and Becki hurl themselves at him, making stones fly in every direction; the courtyard resounds. "Here's your grass," he says. "And now for a little cleanup, a little restoration to your house." He disappears with them.

An immense amphitheater of ancient stone, a surveyor with a human face, two white rabbits, happy for the moment. And over there, the firemen, with their trumpets and sirens, are ready again, ever more ready. Then comes the good silence and the curtain falls.

—❀ 15 ❀—

We walk from one palazzo to another, from one university or municipal seat to another, or to some sort of "underseat," covering kilometers by foot. The numbers of the addresses reel as if crazed; there are thousands and thousands of numbers, door after door and often even window after window without the slightest order, totally at random. Why do they keep changing like that, making vast numerical leaps forward and backward from one step to another? We've never known.

"Maybe," ventures Martino, "the oldest houses have the first numbers and the newest the last numbers, and the ones in the middle . . ."

The numbers here probably follow time, not space, or else some mad combination of the two systems — try to figure it out. Time or space, in Venice there's nothing surprising in that: The combination is part of the picture, the fascination, the curse. And of a second, necessary memory that begins to take form in the substratum of consciousness and to reascend, and little by little stabilize. Everything here, even house numbers, must always be held in the mind in some *other* way, even if you don't know what way that is.

An added complication is the names of the streets, since they correspond neither to those written down on the maps nor to the names we remember.

"What's *Ospeaeto?*"

"Ah, it means *Ospedaletto*, the old hospital."

And *Marzaria* would be *Mercerie*, the haberdashery shop. *Ogi* is *Olio*, oil, maybe oils. But why have they changed the street names like this in the past few years; what could be the reason?

"They're *Venetianizing* them," people explain. Important authors — they insist — professors, even world-famous architects, are taking this in hand; also specialized painters. Since all the names of the streets, of course, are painted onto the walls, they vary according to the whim or fancy of the writers and painters, not to mention the humidity and wind, which change or erase names and pictures according to the vagaries of the walls themselves.

The city is world-famous, it's true, while the writers, the professors, the toponymic architects, and the artist-painters are provincial; still, this *worldwideliness* — I say — depends on them, too. Stop: Do you know how many place-names there are here for the *piazze, campi, campielli, calli, callette, sottocalli, rami, rive,*

ponti, ponticelli, portici, sottoportici?* Thousands, tens of thousands; there's no way to count them. "Almost the same number as
the inhabitants," laugh my friends. "They die down or spring up
with them, with us, with the foreigners, the *foresti*." During certain months in winter, everyone can have his or her own calle and
name of calle, bridge, bank, or canal.

And into this elusive, ungraspable number steal, like sudden,
malignant spirits, the names that everyone on the street continues
to call them, even though they're not written down on the walls.
These are the names that have vanished with time, that great
sculptor, painter, and prestidigitator; but above all they're the
ones that have disappeared under the plaster, the repairs and
human restorations.

Last of all, damn it, are the names repeated in one quarter or
another, on both sides of the water. I hadn't remembered how you
think you're over there and you're really over here. Now you find
them, not only repeated but also written differently according to
the interpretation or moon of the writer or painter whose turn it
has been, now Venetianized and now not; mistaken, half erased,
and uncertain, like the Venetians — or like me, in Venice, among
all the footsteps and names.

—⌒ 16 ⌒—

Both Martino and I do miss one thing, though, and we laugh
about it together: traffic lights. We feel the lack of what, otherwhere, were our continual master compasses, and of our own recurrent tics (remember?) as we checked to the front, to the side,
here, there: red-yellow-green-doublegreen-arrow-doublearrow . . .
It's hard to lose the tics; we dream of traffic lights at night — red,
yellow, green, or maybe white-gray-black.

There are no traffic lights here; and — it seems incredible —

---

*The piazze, the campi, the intimate little campi, the calli, the little calli, the tiny
calli, the final, even tinier branches of calli that only one person can possibly walk
down, the banks and shores, the bridges, the little bridges, the porticos, the under-
passes beneath the porticos. — TRANS.

no motorscooters, motorcycles, cars, buses, exhaust pipes under our noses, roar of traffic in our ears. There are none of those damned trucks, no pullmans full of tourists pulling right up under the house, running over our feet, parking in the courtyards. It's true, we've actually lived that way. We've exchanged it for this trickle of water beside us, flowing now more, now less toward other banks and thoughts. The motorboat traffic in certain canals is no joke; but we have seen only one traffic light, only one, and that one's gigantic, planted where Rio Nuovo crosses Rio Santa Margherita, a spot where there's no traffic at all. Traffic by water (as I came to understand during our furniture voyage) takes its own routes, its own shortcuts; who knows where it will come out? It follows its own surprising circuits of the canals, and arrives. Human traffic is by foot, which is more of a miracle with each day that passes, if you think about the rest of the world. Encounters, greetings, halted gatherings, accelerations, resumptions — all are by foot. Certainly if you're carrying papers, shopping bags, books, and so on (and especially if your feet hurt), it's a drag. But as long as you can, you walk. The truth of it is that in Venice you can lose your head, but never your legs. Bit by bit we're rediscovering our feet, a certain sense of balance, "the pace," says Martino.

"And our heads?" I ask.

"We'll see about our heads. We'll see about everything in the end."

—❦ 17 ❦—

The bank of the Cannaregio canal, or *fondamenta* as it's called around here — that hasn't changed. I follow Martino up and down the north bank, in search of I-don't-know-what other offices he has in his head; maybe they're all hallucinations. One after another — people tell us, laughing — they've been "transferred." The city has been sucked dry of its businesses, right down to the last riva, and they laugh. We end up traversing the whole fondamenta, with its various ramifications (from San Leonardo all the way to the Penitenti, and after that I don't even know where we are), a couple of kilometers. Returning along the southern bank (Savorgnan through San Giobbe to the railway station), we clock at least a couple more.

Martino has just returned from Rome, which is the most beautiful capital in the world (as far as capitals go). I've lived for years in Milan, London — even, unhappily, in Johannesburg. He's spent his in Los Angeles and Sydney. "Even in Adelaide, hah hah," he sneers. "How did I ever stand *that?*" These were all places we went to for work, to earn our livings; neither of us has ever traveled around as a tourist. But for now there is nothing more beautiful — both of us are suddenly washed with happiness at the same time — than a Venetian fondamenta full of people like today, under the winter sun.

Nothing more beautiful or more arduous: we can hardly manage to squeeze through the people conversing and chatting out here as if they were in their own homes, beside the water repeating and blocking, flowing and multiplying everything. And nothing could be gayer than these two banks, one facing the other across the canal, watching, hailing, ignoring, and answering each other, tracts of one sparkling in sunlight while the other is steeped in blue shadow, between eleven o'clock in the morning and noon. For a moment, despite the lost offices, we forget why we're here; we're here, and that suffices — also despite our shoes, which are still hurting us on these inexorable *masègni.** (Our shoes are as unaccustomed to this environment as are the feet within them.) We're here, and that suffices; we don't ever want to leave again — just as we never want to leave the earth, whether the shoe fits or not.

At noon the two banks are strained to their limits, to the absolute maximum of their capacity. At this hour they must support and uphold an incredible weight of human beings along with an infinity of cats, dogs, pigeons, and seagulls, all crowded together right on the edge of the water. And the water is very high today; it bulges against the banks and swells the canal, green and blue,

---

*The great trachytic stones with which Venice is paved. — TRANS.

moving, restless, superbly beautiful. The banks are as devoid of bulwarks or railings as they are of warning or danger signs. An inch or two more, a pushier wave, and the water will flood banks, houses, and feet alike, but it doesn't seem to matter to anyone. People walk, stop, talk, load and unload, call out to each other, hug and kiss each other . . . all on this strip of white stone between water and earth, as if balancing on a thread.

Now the motorboats, the *motoscafi* as we call them, begin to arrive — to moor, load up, embark, and go on their separate ways. A rhythm establishes itself, composed of arrivals, dockings, departures, returns, embarcations, loadings, and unloadings — and also of humanity's motion: late, waiting, calling, smiling, shouting, cursing, greeting each other. The *osterie*, the bars and *caffè* are crowded with men and women (lots of women, a rarity in Italy) going in and out of the bars and shops continuously, as if in a film about people who rub shoulders gladly together — in the world, on the boats, in the streets, at the bars, in the city of Venice. How many bars or quasi-bars there are, one right after the other! Tourists are filing into the Ghetto, which is only a few steps behind us, and kids are bursting out of school. Boats of all colors pass by, exchanging whistles and greetings in an air — for us, who have come from *outside* — of recurrent madness, in waves like the tide that's arriving, arriving. A crowd of faces, eyes, hands, and human cries fills water and earth. Can it really be that Venice is so terribly reduced as they say, so emptied of people?

—◌ 18 ◌—

Up until that point, there — Martino tells me — on either side of the canal. At that point, we realize, both banks curve slightly to accommodate the bend of the canal where it once was a river. We saunter over to look at it with the sensation, as *ex-milanesi*, of wasting our time; that is, we have no real reason to do it. But we do, squeezing our way through the crowd. It is truly the bend of the ancient river, turned into a canal between houses uncountable centuries ago. On the other side of the bend toward the lagoon, on both banks, all animation ends. We see only a few individuals scurrying along on their own, hurrying and not-hurrying at a pace somewhere between sane and reckless, feet stammering on the stones.

An imposing, squarely planted palazzo rises up from the point of the curve. But it's only a facade, we realize, or almost only facade from where we're standing to look at it, just a long stone face on the river-canal. Its design is strong, almost excessive, almost distorted. Is this another touch of madness, a new level of it, or is it simply meant as a signal, a reminder? Behind the facade . . . We stand there, staring. There must be a room or two behind it, I imagine, but you never can tell. The few passersby stop and look, not at the palazzo, but at the two of us who are looking at it: continuous theater. The great palazzo becomes the fantasy of all palazzi, the ambiguous finale played out on the great stage in front of the lagoon (which is nearby, but you can't see it, you have to imagine it). This is the quintessence of the spectacle always under way, more crucial than any architecture or urban phenomenon: this evasive situation at the point of the curve becoming stone-almost-stone, without weight. While we two, without wishing it, find ourselves in the scene without parts, feeling very insecure, wondering whether we've forgotten them. Our parts.

—❦ 19 ❦—

A few steps farther along on our fondamenta and there's even a change in the air, the humidity, the climate, the microclimate. It's the *salso*, as we call it, air loaded with sea salt, and it's arriving little by little from the lagoon, swirling into our eyes, into our noses, into our lungs until it's so strong we can feel its touch on our clothes. It smells also of moss and musk, and of the grasses in the lagoon — according to Martino, the "algae" — although the lagoon is invisible from here. "You can glimpse something," he says; yes and no, in a way: a brief glimmer of gray water at an indistinct distance, but the time is soon coming when there will be enough of it to empty the calli and banks, the streets and the rive, and unhinge what little remains of our foothold in space and in time.

As we walk on the air is laden less with lagoon and more with trees and earth. By chance, strolling along a small, isolated facade and rounding a cloister, we discover two gardens, very large and filled with the most splendid plants: Savorgnan Park and San Giobbe Garden (once the old Botanical Garden) sandwiched between power plants, both old and new. A whole other city: workshops, machines, and gardens.

Then we feel it coming toward us, here it is: the light wind off the lagoon, the light wind and the sense, almost, of a void given off from the horizon. Now we can see a bit more — be calm, my heart, be calm: the great green and azure mirror that is, in this moment, also rose-orange and red-blue. Our hearts must be calm to accustom themselves to the shock: on the far side of the water, on the horizon, the factories of Marghera begin to appear between jets of black smoke. The palazzo-facade, that great face of stone that is still following us, signals the danger, cries out from this side.

Martino tells me that for years it housed the French embassy and hosted poets and writers such as Montaigne and J. J. Rousseau. It was a *casino,* in other words, a Casino of the Spirits. In Venice that's what they're called: a Casino is a place of reunion, and Spirits are poets, philosophers, and the like. But was it only a facade even then? Even then, surely; there are lots of facade-houses in Venice, for spirits and other sorts, too — more facades than houses, actually. But where did those Great Men stay, where did they sleep? Perhaps they were always on their way out somewhere, partying, making the rounds, out day and night *a far casino,** taking part in the scene themselves.

But suddenly spirits, footsteps, casinos, all are suspended, interrupted by the hour of noon. An uproar of bells burst out in the air on both sides of the canal. On the Bridge of Spires, Ponte delle Guglie, there are those who stop at the sound and those who rush forward. On the rive, inside and outside the taverns and shops,

---

*A play on words: *a far casino* means "to kick up a row, to get rowdy." — TRANS.

this is the moment of uncertainty, the renewal of greetings and the last calls good-bye. Even the white clouds above us are moving, traveling somewhere else. It is the moment of deceleration, the instant in which anything can happen. Out of somewhere, nowhere, the beloved of our youth will appear: tall, blond, sure of herself; or dark, mysterious, with deep, sparkling eyes . . . all that we could desire. She will descend from that strange bridge with three arches, put there on purpose to allow her just this entrance on stage. Or she will emerge from one of those tavern doors that open mysteriously onto the canal. Here we are once again, as always, waiting for her.

—❧ 20 ❧—

On Sunday my rediscovered friends invite me over to their house, to their "Little Theater."

"We do it for ourselves, the grown-ups," they explain, "and for them, for the children as long as they're still living with us."

In the damp little front room by the entrance (it seems to me they used to call it a *pòrtego* in the past) there's a crowd of people, some in costume, some not, reading or performing passages from Goldoni and other playwrights I don't recognize. The costumes are simple, the readings informal, the cadence completely Venetian. How incredible! I think — that in 1995, on a Sunday afternoon, there should still be a place in the world where reunions like this one occur; in a way, it breaks my heart. But then I recall that only a few weeks ago in Basilea some friends invited me over and immediately asked if I knew how to play an instrument. I didn't, I don't. But they formed a little orchestra there — the players all dressed in black — and here there's the theater. In Basilea they played Handel and other well-known composers; here they recite Goldoni and other unknown playwrights. Two civilizations: the first offered music, without a word spoken, while here all is words, chatter, talk — theater. Those simple costumes.

—◌ 21 ◌—

All the cracked, flaky, peeling walls form a sharp contrast to the restored facades, large and small, that I keep seeing wherever I go. These rows of walls, wounded and abandoned to time, seem almost human; they strike us immediately upon our return from *out there*, and the impression they make on us grows ever stronger the longer we see them.

"They imprint on the retina," says Martino. "You accumulate them, you carry them with you . . ."

By a process of attrition they bring back to mind the cities in Switzerland, the "European" cities, elucidates my friend. So what is this one? Thinking about them from here — we both laugh — Basilea and the others, they all seem overpolished, painted and repainted each morning, insufferable.

The fact is that here, with all the humidity, plaster runs swiftly to ruin. But there are modern methods, too, we tell each other: insulators, waterproof repellents. The catch is, they're expensive. And if you don't use them, you need to leave the bricks uncovered so that they can breathe. Then again, there are different ways of preparing the plaster: it should be made of crushed bricks mixed and kneaded together with the desired color, not painted afterward, since the paint peels off right away.

We turn into Calle San Domenico — Giacomo, Martino, and I, in the midafternoon. It's a poor and beautiful calle, still paved with bricks as it was time out of mind, in the most ancient Venice of all, and almost all of it winding through hidden orchards and gardens. Forsythia, elderberries, and wild roses rise above the walls that enclose them, and they emanate the perfumes of grasses, the fragrance of strawberry shrubs. The flaking walls reveal their ancient brickwork and remaining patches of plaster in every possible color, from deep red to spring green, from ash to ochre. Variations, curves, strata, compositions, and shadings: these are all to be studied, point by point, in these patches of plaster. Certain stretches remind me of Pollock, others of Rothko. Only here, on the ancient wall exposed to the damp and the sun, each tiniest daub of color varies continuously in time, even with the simple passage of hours on a common gray day like today. Walking toward home, it seems to us that variations of red are predominant; walking back, we see mostly grays, blues, and a soft confusion of yellows.

We pass by the same place a few other times, with shopping bags, without shopping bags, in rain or wind . . . and slowly but surely realize that everything around us — every stone, every wall that had appeared insignificant until now — has acquired meaning from its most minimal essence, from its flaking scales, from its colors in decomposition. These walls are no longer walls, more or less solid erections-enclosures, but exchanges of colors, permeable diaphragms in the infinite shadings of nuance within this labyrinth of calli. Their substance is no longer static, but follows us wherever we go, its long natural history always in movement as it becomes, again and again, color.

Those perfect white cities, painted, repainted . . . I think we should leave them to Switzerland where they belong.

A bit farther on the undermined paint, the ravages of the damp, the peeling plaster and salt-laden air are implacably corroding the little houses that overlook the canal, on this bank and the other; disastrous stains and blotches, deep streaks and cracks — the signs of degradation are everywhere, in the water, in the air. And who can guess how it is underneath, among the foundations? Now the colors disquiet us, no longer just colors but wounds, lesions, craters — "signs from the deep," says Giacomo. And all the questions fall open again: how to help, intervene, what to do. What *can* you do in this continuous water-soaked fabric that is Venice? For that is what Venice is, above all, now that her center is lost, San Marco taken by tourists.

Here and there someone in one of the little houses has tried to resist the inevitable and has recently replastered and repainted their home. Unfortunately such houses now look *too* new, too shiny in comparison to the others, waiting for their turn on the edge of the water. Here an entire facade gleams in uniform yellow — too gleaming, too uniform; a little farther on, a terrible ivory

white glares from another facade in the full sunlight. The house
on the corner is in the middle of being refinished and given a pathetic soap-bar-pink face-lift, being "revived" by a fresh coat of
paint for the umpteenth time because of the salt in the air. In
Venice every intervention is a problem and an adventure. These
facades move us, being brave attempts to stave off degradation
(destiny), yet they no longer seem to belong to Venice at all. Now
they could be anywhere, in any other city; they have become ordinary. "They could be in Mestre, Milan, wherever," says Martino. They've lost their true colors, the mutability of their plaster,
their rapport with the environment, the centuries, the passage of
time; they will never find them again. And the old walls adjacent
to them suffer in comparison, visibly crumbling, desperately dissolving, casting their skins.

Later, with the first fall of darkness, both old and new walls become the emanations of their contrasting reflections, submerged
little by little in the inexorable damp of the night, until the last
confused and tenuous lights yield to the darkness around them,
finally dissolving into the silent death of all colors. They will live
again tomorrow, subject to the whims of the sun, the rain, and the
wind. According to how well we notice them, whether more or
less attentively, or with an ill grace.

—❍ 22 ❍—

We ourselves are noticed much more attentively. People are
aware of us immediately, whether we like it or not, even if we
duck away *per le fodre*, by the hidden back alleys. Everyone knows
right away if you're here or not here, if you've come back or not.
Between casual encounters, friendships, cousinhoods, nodding
acquaintances — that is, as we say, acquaintances "by sight" —
this whole choral life, there is no escape. "Brodsky was right, it's
an incestuous city," insists my wife, who hails from cities where no
one knows each other. Above all, they don't know each other "by
sight" there; the expression doesn't exist in those metropoli, at

least not anymore. Here it lives on; and I have to say that I like it: "by sight." However, you have to be careful: it can also mean watched, "in sight."

So we're very much in sight, but there's not much solidarity to show for it, I say to my friends. No one, in fact, has given us much of a hand during these first hard days, burdened as we were with small children and the awesome number of things we had to get done. Maybe there *was* more sense of solidarity in the old days, they admit, as there was everywhere in the older, poorer world. Are there volunteer organizations? Well, there's a little of that, but a lot more is needed; it's a drop in the bucket on these islands, where 50 percent of the population is old. Above all what I see is curiosity, gossip, backbiting, the telephone ready to hand. There's very little culture; it's a city of *commercianti.* But something good remains, some kindness, some courtesy, some bonds forming, yearning to grow. Superficial? Almost always; but in these days, even reduced to their minimum, we must hold them dear.

What's certain is that you'll always run into someone on the street with whom you must exchange greetings, at least a couple of words. Sometimes this is annoying, at other times vital — by which I mean it nudges you into awareness, makes you remember that a greeting, a couple of words could be the last (of the day, of your life). It's usually some elderly man who will greet you, even if you don't know him, who has need of a sign, some minimal human rapport, to sustain him through the isolation of his days and nights. One of these men warns me each morning at about eight o'clock that it's getting hotter. Or colder. The fat woman at Caffè Poggi advises me on my life. Another repeats, "But where are we. . . where are we . . ." The solitary boy who plays the violin greets us with a half smile — *salve* — and offers to give us a hand on the bridge as we struggle to carry our damned packages home after shopping (good-bye, back!). This morning the fat woman's friend was on the same bridge, telling her about some friend of the night, saying over and over, *"El me piaxe, e no'l me piaxe,"* I liked him and I didn't like him. And the fat woman: "*El te piaxe, e no'l te piaxe, capisco, come ti capisco,*" you liked him and you didn't like him, I understand, oh, how I understand you.

Worst of all, on the street, insists my friend Paolo, you're always running into someone when you don't want to; when, damn it all, you want to slink off with your girfriend. (Is this Paolo-of-the-stars? Perhaps the stars are friends of his girlfriend.)

Still, in an ever-more self-vaporizing society, even this little, very little bit on the streets, even when you don't want it, ends up by counting, lending you a hand . . . I don't know. . . before the end, as I said, of the day, of your life.

—◌ 23 ◌—

Today — I read in the chronicles of the *Gazzettino* — two babies were born in Venice, and six people died. Yesterday eight died, and only one was born. Soon our population, already halved, will be reduced to a third, a quarter of what it once was. The city is packed with strangers, of course, but they're all passing through; very few stay. Reading these two simple lines in the paper scares me; a number or two, a statistic can pierce to the quick where words fail.

If things keep going this way, even the places that are always crowded with people — the many *rioterrà* of Cannaregio, the mythical *campi* of Santa Margherita, San Polo, Santa Maria Formosa, and San Leonardo — will be inhabited by the rare human being and a legion of ghosts. There's no lack of ghosts even now; imagine tomorrow, think of the next few years.

I open the paper again this morning, but "as of today" there is nothing: "We will no long carry information on births and deaths." It seems that there's some difficulty in acquiring the statistics from the municipal offices. And so the people diminish and the data disappear. Perhaps it's better, at this point, to have no statistics, so that we can delude ourselves that we are only reduced by half.

A rumble in the canal alongside us signals the passing of the blue motorboat, the *motoscafo blu*. I'm at the newspaper kiosk, with three or four elderly people who are buying the *Gazzettino*. The boat's motor is powerful; its color and form are both strange.

Ah — I find out — it's the motorboat of the dead. "You *called* them," mutter the old people among themselves. "You *called* them and they're coming to You."

But is it empty? It's making better time than most *motoscafi*, speeding happily along. "There must be a lot of 'cargo,'" my companions are sneering, "to deal with this morning."

No longer do we have those beautiful baroque gondolas, silver and black, solemn and slow, adorned with angels and trumpets. "Too slow, disappeared," the old ones say. What a shame; with such accompaniment as that, it was worth imagining being the "cargo," rocked on the waves, here in Venice.

"There are scale models in city hall," the newspaper vendor assures me, "of those funeral boats from the past, with angels and trumpets — like there's a model of the *Bucintoro** at the museum. Soon there'll be a scale model of all of Venice, a beautiful model in colors. With us in it," he laughs, "selling postcards." He gives his small, half-bitter laugh. Sometimes as I pass by, I hear him talking to himself in the cavern of his kiosk: "Hardly any sell, hardly any, what use are newspapers? See the 'slushies' stand over there? The one that's closed in winter? It makes as much in two months of summer as all the newspaper vendors in Venice make in a year." However, if I stop to offer some solidarity, to let him know I'm suffering with him, he huffs like the wild cats in the nearby calle: Back off, friend, this is my territory.

A little farther on I see a solitary being (a Venetian?) on the riva, looking on in total silence at the passage of the *motoscafo blu*. High waves beat in its wake against the banks. They have no time to lose, these "services"; they take off, they make tracks be-

---

*The *Bucintoro*, built by decree of the senate in 1311, was the great, gilded ship of the Doge, head of the Most Serene Republic of Venice. It measured a hundred feet long by twenty-one feet wide and was two stories tall. It was from the *Bucintoro* that the Doge, every year on the anniversary of Christ's Ascension, threw a golden ring into the water to symbolize Venice's marriage to the sea. — TRANS.

hind them. The silent being beside me makes a gesture: "Even the dead demolish the banks."

—❧ 24 ❧—

I haven't gone back up in an airplane yet; for the moment I'm flying in the attic. Roofs, roof tiles, and chimneys unfurl beneath me, assailed by the wind. From the dormer window I can glimpse the mast of a ship moving toward me between the old roof tiles, sporting a tiny flag, which is rippling under the bora. The mast wavers and vibrates. The house, I realize, is vibrating like the ship, at the whim of the waves, in perfect accord. The bora lasts for three days.

On the fourth day the bora dies down and turns into the *levante*.* I decide to go out in the boat — *in sandolo*† — with Alvise, nicknamed Secondo. Why Secondo? I ask. Were there three or four brothers in the family? No, he tells me: In the races, in the *regate*, he always — "ever since I was little" — came in second when there were only two boats competing.

We go out in the boat but stay in the smaller, interior canals; farther out the winds are too insistent. And this, I realize, is yet another function of the bridges: they link up the islands and hold them firm against the wind. Venice defends herself with the aid of these fragile but continuous chains of bridges, all similar yet all diverse; and because of them she is a little more and a little less an island.

"As far as being an island," confirms Secondo, "Venice is never an island-*island*. A hundred and twenty islands-not-islands," according to his double-checked and revised calculations, he assures me. Not exactly the twenty or thirty mentioned in the

---

*The *levante* is a wind from the east, and ranges from a cool, sweet breeze to a cold, gusting wind. Not a seasonal phenomenon, the levante can blow into Venice at any time of the year. — TRANS.

†The *sandolo* is built specifically for the Venetian lagoon. Flat-bottomed, slender, and light, it comes in various elegant forms such as the *puparìn*, nine to ten meters long, and the very light and practical *mascarèta*, which may measure between six and eight meters. — TRANS.

guidebooks. And the bridges: "There are 460, or 480 — it depends on how you count them." The bridges, of course, are extended by innumerable banks, or rive — "thousands, for sure, I'm still counting them" — and prolonged by millions of steep little steps that descend into the canals or lead up into the campielli, large to minuscule stairways between water and earth. "I'll never be able to count *them*," says Secondo. Today the islands we glide by remind me of great rafts of boats hooked up on a river; they hold fast because they're so well tied together, boat to boat to boat.

I read the names of the bridges: Bridge of the Marvels, Bridge of the Tits, Bridge of Fists, Bridge of Courtesy, Bridge of Sighs, Bridge of Butchers, Bridge of Merciful Help. And then there's the Bridge of the Devils, of Paradise, Rubbish, Sepulchres, Miracles, Spirits, the Dead — all linked, one to another.

In the lagoon beyond there are islands and islands without any bridges at all. But the lagoon, once you begin to traverse it (today we're sailing a very small stretch, to the leeward) is neither just sea nor just lake. It is above all another sestiere or quarter of Venice, a liquid quarter. It's a part of her that stretches out to the horizon, similar yet different, fully alive and mysterious; an integral, essential part of the ancient city — the most fluid, the most eternal of all.

At the moment this liquid sestiere is right at low tide, revealing all the intimate, inner channels in the great womb of the water: the old rivers that crossed the lagoon, the most ancient inland waters of Venice. And this fluid space has been forever more or less lived in, or on: inhabited, traversed, abandoned, deserted as fatal, repopulated, built on, destroyed, rebuilt on again. So Venice the Island — we decide, turning back — with all her *other* islands both far and near, is and is not an island. She is earth, she is water . . . she is neither. But she's homeopathic to man — to these poor brief beings passing through her — as far as dimension, space, definition, both as an island and as a human home. Though solitary, she is always with us. And in this she is unlike the classical island, which is "absolute," difficult to land on, impossible to live on. She is never *infera*, infernal or divine, as the classical islands so frequently are. You may come and go, leave the condition of island for the condition of (almost) terrafirma in a few moments. From the meandering stream in the marsh, from the sandbank, all it takes is a few strokes of the oar — precise, chronometrically precise strokes, to be sure, Secondo's *alla valesana** — to bring our little boat from the domain of water to the edge of the shore, to the inland coast. To the domain of earth, sand, stones, and soil: to the continent. Or to the almost-continent, the almost-terrafirma; to the city more or less in emersion.

—◦ 25 ◦—

Sergio, who is a greatly respected professor, confirms my theory that in the course of human history islands accumulate the strangest connotations, ranging from one extreme to the other, from being the Blessed Isles of Happiness to the dread Isles of Death. This is true in a certain sense even here: the moment we move away from the so-called center, invaded by Furies from every country in the world, the island of Venice is no exception, not lacking in its own connotations, which veer from the arcane to the funereal. It's enough to consider San Michele, the cemetery island at the northern tip of the fish-shaped city; or to think of the old graveyard of Mazzorbo, or of certain solitary veins of water wandering through the marshlands, or of the barbaric solitude, in this season, of the island of Torcello. However, their connotations are always still recognizable, never too far from the living, breathing, passing humanity of the moment. And death here is always human, very human. I love the Hebrew cemetery, the most ancient and fascinating of all the cemeteries in all the islands; it is one of the loveliest places on the lagoon. In Hebrew it's called *Betheim,* if I'm not mistaken: The House of Life.

But there's not a single island in the lagoon, you might say, without its passages through and returns from life and death. There are quasi-legendary places and chthonic moments even here, blended of ancient tales and the truth of human history. A

---

*Stroking with crossed oars. — TRANS.

whole archipelago sank beneath the waters of the lagoon not far from Burano, and only a name or two is left to remind us of its existence. Before Rialto, the ancient capital of Venice was Malamocco, which vanished under the waves somewhere between the Lido and the Alberoni. On the edge of the northern marshes, we may search in vain for the great city and bustling port that was once Torcello. Perhaps today Sant'Ariano, more than anyplace else, gives us the feeling of journeying, round-trip, between life and death. So I'll head toward Sant'Ariano, a brief sail *in sandolo* as soon as the wind dies down, with Secondo and Martino.

—ᦢ 26 ᦢ—

We're navigating the northern stretches of the lagoon, steering for Sant'Ariano, skimming waters long closed over ancient islands, drowned and vanished, "turned into water," says Secondo, pointing them out as if he could see them. Beneath us lie the isles of Ammiana, Costanziaca, Terra dei Mani, Terra dei Soleri . . . There is no one in sight, not a single boat, as far as the eye can see. Yet there were once ports here, and churches, monasteries, and houses: human beings. Then came erosions, earthquakes, powerful currents, drownings, tidal waves — here, where today it's so tranquil we're almost becalmed. Some of these lost islands were abandoned suddenly, in the panicky course of a night; others little by little, generation after generation for years, after our ancestors had tried generations before that to save them.

"Maybe each time," says Martino, "they tried it, like us, too late."

A bit of land peeks up out of the water: the tiny island of Santa Cristina. We approach it with difficulty, scraping our bottom on boulders and accumulations of sand. A large, modern house is built on it — incredible, too big, out of tune with its environment — surrounded by beautifully cultivated gardens: a stretch of lagoon saved, in whatever way.

The best-preserved island is Sant'Ariano. We approach it with the help of Mino the fisherman, who knows these shallows, sandbars, and currents well. According to the ancient tales, Sant'Ariano was refuge to exiles, survivors who had fled the barbarian invasions, and was afterward inhabited by their descendants for centuries. A portion of the island sank, no one knows why, about seven centuries ago; now the part that is left lies before us. It's a strange, long, green hill, encircled by a strong wall. We read an inscription in stone that informs us the wall was built by the Venetian senate in the sixteenth century. There are no openings in it, no doors; brown and gray, sinister and still, it rises above the waters, and the plants cascading down from its edge are a vivid green, too intense for this time of year. Within them, for at least five centuries — but perhaps for very much longer — have lain the bones of Venetians; to this higgledy-piggledy pile, says Martino, *"tout venant."* The whole hill is composed of stratified human remains, brought here from the Campielli dei Morti, the tiny neighborhood graveyards scattered throughout Venice up until the nineteenth century. The very island upon which the survivors of the massacres rediscovered life transformed itself over the years into this storehouse of death. Yes, it's death itself that lies here before us; and so far it's not doing a bad job of preserving the island and its peculiar treasure.

The ancient wall with its inscripted stones is pocked and corroded in places; if they restored it soon, it would be no great job. The door to the chapel is also walled up — to keep out the vandals, no doubt. Still, it multiplies the general sense of desolation.

We sail around the island with old Mino, who has brought us here, maneuvering between shallows and cuts in his flat-bottomed boat as light as a breath. Now, however, he doesn't want to come in any closer, doesn't feel up to it; he fears the spirits of the dead, their "influence." In those days, he assures us, they had heads, hands, tibias "bigger than us."

"I've seen them," he insists. "They were gigantic." The water around us is shallow. "They used to walk across it like nothing, with their big, long legs," Mino tells us, "to get to the island."

We just manage, in our fisherman's boots, while he takes off in his little boat for the other side of the channel — to go fishing, he says. So here we are with our yellow and blue boots, on a narrow slope of grass and sand.

Between the grass and the sand, in the silence — only the sound of a distant jet, but it passes — our ancestors await us: skulls surfacing from the soil, human tibias. They seem smaller, not "bigger than us," these slender bones, these poor abandoned skulls. In the meantime certain enormous, gray-green water snakes are slithering through the grasses, appearing and disappearing while raptors hover high in the air; "but they swoop down fast," yells Mino from the boat, "they swoop down in a flash!" And in fact some kind of buzzard suddenly plunges earthward from the heights, lightning-swift, like a missile. He brushes Secondo's head with a wing, plucks up the biggest snake in his beak, and takes off like a shot. The snake dangles in the air and then vanishes slowly into the buzzard's crop.

Other birds are arriving, wheeling in great silent circles, preparing to land on the turf. We think it the better part of valor to recross the channel and explore the little meadow of the Cura, not far away. Under a strange arch and an enormous brick fireplace lie the remains of the old lagoon house we recall as being intact only a few years ago. Although the house is razed, Mino lights a fire under the hearth, which draws in great gusts. He roasts brown sole, pink mullet, gilthead bream.

In the mirror of water around us, perhaps something remains even now of Ammiana, Costanziaca, or the Isle of Hands . . . We ask Mino if he has ever found, while he was fishing, any markers, inscriptions, or worked stones. Yes, every once in a while something gets tangled up in the nets, but usually he just tosses it back in the water. There's still a chip of something here: he thrusts his hand into the hearth and draws it out. With difficulty we make out the corroded inscription: SEMEL, once only. Nothing more. It has a hard sound — once only — and I'm struck by the thought that perhaps it's referring to Venice. Ospreys, or some kind of birds, pass back over us high in the sky, eyeing what's left of our fish. It's late, so we leave it all there, next to the fireplace, and sail away in the boat, hoping for a favorable current.

—✿ 27 ✿—

We make good headway toward Venice, helped by the ebbing tide.

First the *campanili*, the bell towers, loom up on the horizon like the masts of a ship — the great ship of islands, which seems at moments to be moving and at others to be rocking on its moorings. Next, as if out of nowhere, the cupolas appear; or more precisely the cupolas rise, billow, and swell. Then the houses and palazzi, the inhabited city, the windows and bridges and banks — the whole labyrinth swims into view, glinting, this evening, dark gold. But as we draw nearer the marvel, we see — all too well at low tide — just how fragile the miracle is. Great black holes yawn open under the banks, within the foundations, directly under the feet of the walking crowd. How many people are strolling along the Fondamente Nuove, walking and not seeing! Yet from the boat our uneasy glances dart from one black hole to another, from one gaping cavern to the next. Will she hold fast? Or will she sink?

All around us lies the lagoon: green, azure, flecked and speckled with gold, splendid and indifferent, struck through by the rays of the setting sun. Valuable simply by dint of being a lagoon, that rare place of encounter between continent on one side and sea on the other, still it would be no more than lagoon did it not cradle Venice, the greatest treasure of all. But under these conditions, we say to each other as we pass by gap after gap in the foundations, we risk losing it all, Venice *and* the lagoon. And there's worse to come: the moment we disembark our friends inform us that "they" — there's always a "they"; this time it's Agip, the big Italian oil and gas company — want to extract methane from the sea, here of all places, only a few kilometers away. If they do, the risk of the land sinking is tremendous. Venice is divided from the water by a thread as it is; it's the most fragile city in Europe, among the places most at risk in the world. But "they" are insistent. Apparently it's not enough, what's already happened on the coast, on the delta of the Po, in Ravenna. Here, if the land is lowered by a few centimeters, the whole of Venice will be submerged. And then — *addio*, wonder of the world.

All that's going on already is deeply disturbing: exodus, pollution, deteriorations of every kind, holes in the bank of the canals, oil tankers trafficking in the middle of the lagoon, chemical wastes whose dangers we can't even guess at spewing out into the water along the whole shore from Marghera to Venice, toxic fumes unfurling into the sky, newer and deeper excavations in the goddamned channel for the big oil tankers, environmental imbalances of all kinds, *acque alte* ever higher and more frequent year after year, *acque basse* ever lower — all within, or a hand's breadth away from, the most beautiful, delicate city in the world. As if it were the safest and most protected place on the planet; or as if it were the most ignoble, the basest, the most utterly superfluous. But it's *Venice*. And all this, and all that seems to be headed our way in the future, is perhaps the threat that frightens us most, to the depths of our souls, whether we're Venetians or not; perhaps nothing could break our hearts more completely than the possibility of part or all of it sinking, the thought of this fragile miracle drowning, submerged beneath the waters from which it was created.

I think back to the deserted expanse of lagoon we just crossed, once populated with islands now vanished, gone under, lost for all time.

I gather information, make phone calls, protest, write to the newspapers. Martino draws a sign on the earth: the earth, here, on which we are walking. This earth, this land upon which we are planting our feet, was constructed, dragged out of the water spot by spot, shored up by the trunks of trees, filled with entire forests and millions of stones, consolidated for countless generations.

Will ours sink it? So far there is no response. We'll continue to shout as long as there's breath in our bodies.

PART THREE

All a Continuation

Darkness falls early at this time of year, but its arrival is slow, shifting, inconstant; it pools, dissolves, returns, slips away again, sneaks in on the breath of a breeze, falls quiet, blows in on sudden traitorous gusts of wind. Stones and canals are in continual contrast, the compact aggregate of the houses mirrored uncertainly in the waters, now rippling in perpetual motion, now hovering motionless in a dead calm. In Milan the darkness doesn't engage in all these arrivals and departures, movements and stases; or at least, you're not aware of them.

Most of all, I didn't remember the cold and the damp, how they penetrate you, slip under your skin and establish themselves. Or perhaps it's the other way around and we enter the humidity little by little, slowly immersing ourselves right down to the roots till there's no saving us. I've been gone a few years — short or long ones, who knows — and obviously, I've forgotten a lot. Outside Venice, beyond the lagoon, other hours and seasons hold sway, all more or less recognizable, similar to each other: a whole other existence plays itself out, one that has very little to do with ours here. And returning gives me the same sensation, but in reverse: it's another life. Every readaptation has its heart-wrenching moments, its aspects of sorrow and joy, of gradual healing, of loss, and of gain. But which is the *true* place, I wonder, which is the *real* season?

"How long have you been gone?" my nephew asks me.

"Your whole life," I answer.

And maybe mine, too — seven years. I was supposed to go away for seven days, and this is what happened. My nephew laughs. Ever since I've been back he thinks me a little mad. The years you're away, I want to tell him but don't, can seem ten times longer at moments, while at others they seem no more than a breath. There's more to it, too: you leave by yourself, in good humor, with your head on straight (you believe) in one piece; and you come back crazed, in two, in three, or in four. You come back multiplied, and there's something you understand better: that we're all a continuation of each other, and that for this very reason we have to pick up from where we left off. For now, with children and nephews — four at the moment — I start over from the places that they love the most. And I can understand why.

—⟨ 29 ⟩—

Bridge of the Spires, Bridge of the Small Holy Image, Bridge of the Magdalen . . . They have strange names, these places the kids love the best. Maybe, they say, that's why they like them — like Riva delle Zattere, which is exactly the opposite of its name, since there are practically no wooden rafts there at all anymore, only boats, ships, and the water, the immense canal. Stradanova, on the other hand, is waterless, not a canal in sight, always packed with people and with the recurrent madness of people who crowd together all of a sudden to *buy*. Right away I'm no longer sure which are *my* places, the ones I hold dearest within me; now I love *theirs*. Here between Stradanova and San Leonardo the rows of booths and stalls warm the air, heating up sales and hearts. The kids are having a world of fun: CDs, cassettes, fruits, candy, T-shirts, tracksuits, and sandwiches — this is their world. Afterward I take them to the local gym, the Palestra dei Ferrovieri, and have an hour to wander around these parts by myself.

Without the kids, everything seems suddenly closer, truer,

more *real*, or at least more visible and tangible; I can actually come into contact. Children are obstacles in that they require, insist, and demand so much, constantly dragging you over to *their* side. They never let up; and when I'm with them, I lose my forces and a sense of the larger perspective. Now I wander happily among the crowd, which is buying and selling, bargaining, yelling. Even their cries seem louder and clearer without the competing shouts of the kids in my ears. A stage set reveals itself to me, at last, as I enter the scene: Gothic houses, half of them real, half a pretence, a whole continuous theater-world of arches, sculpted stonework, statues, filigreed windows, grandiose palaces, tiny palaces, angels flying off with the pigeons. I never saw them before. And they're all in counterpoint to the booths, the noise, the elbowing through of the crowd, the greetings and cries; to humanity, gay on the whole, good-humored, both sellers and buyers. They're at home in the world, it seems — they're at home in Venice.

Seeing, seeing — learning anew how to see. How long I've been away *without seeing!* This rioterrà, this campo, are like so many other places throughout the city; San Geremia is only one square among many. But Venice is always concentrated, stratified, represented in her entirety in any one of her campi. There's no need to move around very much; it's enough to plant yourself in one spot, since Venice is infinite and micrometric. The carved *vere da pozzo*, or wellheads, I lean against for a moment: Now I'm beginning to see them, how splendid they are. For years I was not yet aware of them, never aware. How many things we see for the first time, returning to a place that we love! Under the vere da pozzo, beneath our ever-restless feet, in the underground of this square full of people, lies the great "machine" that produces sweet water for all the surrounding houses. We're moving over volcanic stones, the masègni, over the mountain of stones it has taken to anchor the Venice-ship. But we're also moving over the strata of sand banked under our feet a thousand or more years ago, thousands of layers of sand beneath the whole city to gather and filter the rain, swollen with water. Here we are, going about our affairs, while the device that allows us to live here lies underneath us, visible only in the lovely wellheads we lean on.

The baroque church, however, is very much aboveground, poised for flight, prepared for any miracle that might come along, with its curved and countercurved walls coming and going, rising and falling between the campo and the sky. At the moment they seem to be winging off, but I call them back. Once inside the church they crowd close, enclosing the other aerial and terrestrial spaces that open and close, widen and wheel above us. In the still chapel to the left lies the body of Santa Lucia, which has been housed and unhoused, lodged and dislodged throughout the centuries, stolen, put back in place, stolen again and returned. This is all quite in line with the flight of the church, its particular gust of madness.

"The Syracusans," explains the old woman inside the church. "It was the Syracusans that stole her."

"Well, but who stole her back from *them?*" I ask rhetorically. "Who stole her from the Syracusans, beautiful Lucia of the eyes, lovely blind Lucia? The Venetians, dear lady, the Venetians."

"The Turks," she retorts.

Who knows? Maybe they stole her once, and then we stole her once, and then they . . . The past is all a miracle, and thus mysterious.

I come back out — or perhaps back "in" — to the campo full of people and the rows of tents, awnings, and stalls under full sail. It's a kind of populated tensile structure, good-natured, affable, endless, communally lived in. In fact, I realize, it's truly a condominial campo, shared with all the foreigners, the *foresti*, cohabiting with half the world, stretched to the limit between remaining itself and changing continents entirely. I hear all possible languages, plus the Venetian dialect. Interestingly, the dialect is almost nonexistent among the booths of glasswork from Murano, predominant among the stalls of fruit and vegetables — especially the *lezione* of east Cannaregio. Hard on its heels comes the song of the Japanese, followed by Slavic variants, huffing and puffing, incomprehensible. Italian is rare.

In the bar it's even more evident. Right away they treat me like another tourist passing through — from the Congo, perhaps — serving me hurriedly, without the minimum of courtesy. So I use the dialect, hoping they'll hear I'm Venetian and treat me better. No way, they treat me even worse. The truth is that Venetians don't spend very much, not like the Americans or the Asians, and it's harder to cheat them — us — the indigenous.

Farther on, beyond the Lista di Spagna, lies the railway station, or LA FERROVIA as the signs on the walls point out vaguely. How many arrivals and departures can one bear in the course of a life? Will I have to leave again? I ask myself with a shudder. Am I there or here? Which ones are my places?

—⟋ 30 ⟍—

I don't know anymore, or I don't know yet, which are my places in Venice; maybe I will later on. But one thing I *do* know for sure after these first days back, spent wandering up and down: At one time my places were everywhere in this city; sudden wild and solitary calli waited for me at every turn, in absolute silence, between the banks and squares full of people. They were in Santa Marta as they were in Castello, in Cannaregio as in Dorsoduro: poor, narrow calli that still, in their brevity and solitude, conveyed a sense of the infinite. A rare voice called out, human or beast. There were innumerable places like this at one time, in which Venice was simply herself, in a state of absolute purity — where there was not one direction aimed at the tourists, not one hotel, not one hidden loudspeaker, not one sign in English. The calle would end in a canal where no motorboats passed, growling and screaming, and the only sound was the lapping of water. Now you might say there's no place in the city untouched by the great touristic machine in one way or another; no way to get there. That strange fascination, those voices are lost. We don't have many others to substitute for them, in Venice or in the world.

—☙ 31 ☚—

But Venice is always up to her tricks and immediately contradicts me. Right in back of the Lista di Spagna and its environs, not far at all from the spots dedicated wholely to tourists, I find them: the *microcalli,* for native Venetians only, even today.

Lined up along them are houses large and small, gardens smaller to tiny. These houses were built four centuries ago *a schiera,** as the architects call it — a horrendous term, to my mind, for these lovely, graceful, personal homes. The gardens are unexpected, magnificent, stately; their trees are enormous. The old ladies' home sits next to a little chapel, which sits next to some taverns, which sit next to the repairs under way in the Saffa,[†] next to other threads of canals, other taverns, new walls and old . . . all the way to San Giobbe (Saint Job — the name is dear to me)[‡] and beyond, way beyond, to destinations unknown. I come upon more large and small gardens, and then see the church, which is both touching and incongruous. Pieced together as it is, it seems to belong partly to Venice, partly to Florence. Its cloister is likewise reduced and piecemeal; I discover worked stones in the rubble. Leaving the church, I stroll around the old power station in this small neighborhood quarter lying along the lagoon and find more of the ancient, work-inspired names: Saoneria for the Soap Makers, Tintoria for the Dyers, Cereria for the Candle Makers.

Certain parts of Venice, like this one, are continuous acts of invention — not exactly planned, but not casual, either — always improbable, duly admired. City of all cities.

I should just lose myself as I wander up and down the calli and bridges. I should quit writing, not make another notation. There's no way I can follow it all, no way to observe it closely enough. I should just look, walk on, respond to each greeting, smile, and retrace my steps. Love her, in other words, nothing more. Only love her.

---

*Row houses. — TRANS.
†A small neighborhood in the sestiere of Cannaregio. — TRANS.
‡A number of place-names in Venice turn Old Testament characters into New Testament saints; there is also, for example, a San Moisè — a Saint Moses. — TRANS.

—◦ 32 ◦—

But here are the boys, already back from the gym. I have barely
enough time to take them home and then rush off again (miles
more by foot) to the same place I just came from, which by now,
however, is entirely altered. My destination is the Palazzo Labia,
headquarters of RAI,* where they're waiting for me to come to
work. Surrounding it are the exact same streets I strolled along
earlier, now gentling into the darkness, half violet shadows, half
blue-black night. Looking up at the windows, I try to follow the
glimmerings shed by the lamps in the booths, the rays of light
spilling out and up from the stalls (*sciabolate*, they used to call
them, slices of light in the darkness) as they play against the
palazzi, the church, and the shop windows of Bottegone al Cav-
allo. The sensation of surreality returns, multiplied: nothing is
real at this hour; the stage is splendid and false, hovering a little
above the earth but also below it, as if it were sinking. It's ready,
set for the play to come — although the truth is that the play has
already started, and the trick is to know what act you find yourself
in. More and more this evening the stage set, with its behind-the-
scene stretches like fading watercolors, is conquering so-called
real life — which continues to go on in its own way, of course, but
more slowly at this hour, enchanted, uncertain. Until finally you
realize: Glimmers of vision ephemeral as breaths, invisible paths
and mysterious crossroads, unvoiced impulses and ecstasies are
passing through this spellbound "reality" on their way to all that is
unknown within and around us. To all that lies beyond, above or
below us; and less than ever do we know where we actually are.

—◦ 33 ◦—

Awaiting me beside the bar, in this peculiar piazza that people
cross only on the diagonal, is a great white backdrop, impermeable

---

*RAI is the abbreviation for Radiotelevisione italiana, the Italian state-owned radio and
television broadcasting system. — TRANS.

by any human diagonals: Palazzo Labia, which I remembered as white, at any rate, but which is pink at the moment — inexplicably, since the evening by now is a uniform gray. Inside are the RAI headquarters, workplace, place of "production," as they call it; in fact, they're expecting me to get down to work in there shortly. But Palazzo Labia is also an enchanted castle, a palace. I'm always somewhat afraid to go into that world of halls and salons and balconies; for one thing, wherever you turn, you are constantly encountering Tiepolo . . . Tiepolo. . . Tiepolo! There are many palazzi like this in Venice, but usually they're more reserved. Often you reach them by way of an extremely narrow calle or some kind of dark passage, and they reveal themselves little by little: first the courtyard with its vera da pozzo, then the Gothic stairwell with its voices . . . But this one starts out right away in full glory, with a powerful row of arches grafted onto exterior and interior courtyards, stairways and great halls, outer balconies and salons . . . How much beauty — and how much money — has passed at one time or another between these four walls! Between these four little islands.

I wonder how my friends manage to get any work done in here. Maybe (I hope) they work just a little, then spend some time following Tiepolo around, admiring the stuccowork, friezes, and marbles. At intervals (I imagine) they run up and down the great stairways or study the vista of Venice from the terrace up there.

I enter at last, and *addio:* I'm sucked into the maze, lost among the halls, balconies, and salons. I find myself face to face with Tiepolo's characters, fairy tales, stories, and myths, with his colors, all on the far side of history, life, the everyday stuff we're made of. Of course, we still need all the rest — in paintings, in dreams, in our imaginations.

My friends have been combing the arcades and galleries looking for me and have now returned to their office to wait for me without much hope. *They're* working, while *I'm* wandering around between false perspectives and dreamed-up architecture, following Cleopatra and the cupids, blocked by the horse Pegasus as he's killing time.

"The program," insist my friends. "The schedule, the copy, the project, the calculations." But how can anyone "calculate" in a place like this, in such a palimpsest with its layers upon ancient layers, traversed by Tiepolo and the centuries? How can anyone "schedule a project" in a city that is, in every particular and in its entirety, purely a work of art? And as far as Tiepolo goes — with those paintings of his, so out-of-the-world, so far above our terrestrial troubles — what planet did *he* live on? Maybe, simply, on Venice.

—❀ 34 ❀—

Opposite the palazzo in the same campo is the *Scuola dei Morti*, the School of the Dead. The Venetian and, I suppose, the foreign dead; Venice has always been a land of exiles. Long ago they used to pray for the dead in this "School," recalling those who had walked on these same stones before us, thinking of them as a continuation leading ever upward until it reached God, *il Buon Dio*. I'm told they not only prayed aloud, but also studied the Offices and Rites of the Dead — the Hopes, the Farewells, the Returns* — with the ever-ready help of the saints. Heaven and earth were all of a piece in those days. Was the world more alive in those centuries we now deem the Dark Ages? Certainly there was less disconnection between life and death than there is today. Everyone had a soul, whether they lived on this side or the other; and the world itself had a soul, as did stones, as did *things*. I don't know if any of their ways of praying or remembering were comparable to the Tibetan Book of the Dead, which comes immediately to mind as I enter the Scuola. I suppose not; although Venice has many ties to the Orient, it has always belonged much more to the West, and anyway, today . . .

"Today nothing's left," snorts someone nearby in the dark.

The Hopes refers both to the hopes of the dead within certain sacred traditions and to the hopes and/or illusions of the living regarding the dead. *The Returns* refers to the appearance of the dead in the dreams of the living. — TRANS.

"There's nothing left in here now," huffs the red-headed guardian, enough of a woman to put the fear of God into anyone.

And it's true. Not only does very little remain in our all-too-worldly life that regards or recalls them, the clandestine ones who came here before us; but during the war a bomb destroyed almost all of the School. It was one of the few bombs that actually fell on Venice, and it fell on the dead. The walls, or a part of the walls, remain. But all traces of the manuscripts, books, paintings, furnishings — maybe even of "them" — were burned by the bombs.

As I leave, a tiny, tiny old woman, lame but very eager, scratches me lightly with long beautiful hands and offers me postcards. The School is closing, she says, but she will never leave her post. The cards are reproductions of the Via Crucis, the Stations of the Cross. "All I have left are these," she says. "No one wants them."

Was this inside, I ask — inside the School, this Via Crucis?

"Yes," she replies. "One Station was here between the windows, one was over there on the side, one in front . . . And I'm still here," she explains, standing between the window and the door.

The true poor today, I know, are these. I buy a few postcards, and then I decide: "Give me all of them."

"No, no," she protests, "not all of them. If I did I'd be left without Stations, without Vie Crucis . . . Someone has to keep them." She grumbles to herself, "Vie Crucis, really, you're never without them, there are always more in your life . . ." She stares at me. "Until the last blow."

She accompanies me to the door, giving a brief, convulsed laugh every so often in the empty dark, and adds another postcard, *gratis*, to my pile, "as a gift," with her beautiful pianist's hand.

Yet another station lies a few steps away from the School of the Dead, the train station, or *la Ferrovia* as they call it here, perhaps to avoid confusion with the Via Crucis. It is swarming with people departing, exhausted from their day trip, looking so tired you feel like giving them a hand; they seem more harried than happy. It's evening; they've seen Venice in a day; now they're leaving, and that much must content them. If I think about the cities not too far away, only a few kilometers from here — the metropoli, the *conurbations* as they call them, continuous networks of urban communities, the infinite termitaria erected on earth — they seem to me, at this moment, to be strange, crazy places, madhouses in comparison to what I see here. Or else the madness is ours. There's no sense in comparing them, really: either Venice is absurd, or the other ones are. But the big cities seem ever-more unbelievable, more implausible the longer you're here; day after day, they diminish in credibility until they cease to exist. We must be the same, seen from their point of view: vanishing among the dark calli, in our . . . what do they call it? Our Middle Ages.

—⌒ 35 ⌒—

The labyrinths of the Bissa and the Mercerie (the Snake and the Hosiers), the Bridge of Heaven and the Ruga Giuffa (Jsfahan), San Provolo and San Lorenzo, La Vigna (the Vine) and Rio delle Vergini (the Shore of the Virgins) . . . I come and go, *andata e ritorno*, as soon as I can and as much as I can, in the illusion of covering it all in the course of a few days, this city I've come home to. Before it disappears, I think in certain moments. On the map it looks possible to cover it all in such a short time; truly, Venice only measures seven kilometers by four. But there are kilometers as long as centuries and others as brief as days, moments, even seconds.

I've gone down into the crypts of San Zaccaria, San Simeone, and San Salvador; I've climbed up the *campanili* of San Giorgio, San Nicolò dei Mendicoli, San Marco, and Torcello.

I've *seen* it and *seen* it and seen it again, as much as I could, with other people and all on my own, from its lowest crypt to its highest spire, from the calli and the rive, from the windows overlooking the tiniest rii, from the water and from the air. I've gone from the *Bàcari* filled with elderly men to the topsy-turvy hangouts of the kids; from the *osterie* steaming with the age-old, provocative perfumes of tendons and nerves, udders and tripe, to the furiously desperate "piano-bars" — where there are no pianos, only loudspeakers cranked up so high that you can't exchange a word, only staccato shouts. I've tracked down, in my random way, places in other centuries where the virgin Ursula dreamed, she who awaits us now in the *Dream* in the Gallerie dell'Accademia. In centuries even more distant, I've walked on the "new" submarine walls of the great Arsenale, among squadrons of silver fish rocketing off through the waters in synchronized flight. In years nearer the present, I've discovered the Liberty style of the Lido and the Gàffaro and the brand-new extensions of stone in the sea, the *pennelli* on the Murazzi and at Pellestrina; then returned to the Middle Ages through Corte del Fontego (the Courtyard of the Old Storehouse), and Corte degli Spiriti (the Courtyard of Spirits). They all coexist within a small, circumscribed area, only a few paces apart. And they're all inhabited, lived in, livable, or at least hold out the possibility, the hope of being so — even for us today, at the start of the new millennium.

In the mingled, endless confusion of signs-realities-apparitions that meet me as I enter and exit the centuries, in the continually mobile maze of waiting voices and imperiled walls, I keep telling myself incredulously, inscribing a hundred times on my heart: even at its most derelict and degraded, this city-that-is-entirely-a-work-of-art is still wholly lived in and livable. The plethora of other ancient cities from Turin to Bari, with their artificially maintained historical centers, are so different from Venice that no comparison is possible. Venice is the strangest of all by far and the most beautiful, the most artificial and natural, the most passed through and trampled, the most visited and unknown. At the same time, it is and always has been animated and ensouled, inhabited by living beings and wandering spirits, by the most diverse strata of humanity and dream. Venice *is* a dream, yet if we can wake ourselves up, she is a city still. Her extraordinary survival is stretched to the breaking point, sinking down into the dangerous waters navigated by our unconscious generation and by the ever-more alien and alienated generation following in our wake.

It's late at night, and I'm trying to express it again: The city in which I've ended up is so different from the one I left a short (or long) time ago, *because* . . . it is continually crossing and re-crossing the boundaries between reality and dream, and we're not up to it, not up to the shifting moment. Or perhaps there are simply too few of us. Certainly the terrible rupture of the modern age with its past plays a part in all this — such a rift in how to feel ourselves, or not feel ourselves, in the world, how to think, act, believe or not believe, build for eternity or for a day, try with a book or a snapshot . . .

I don't know. I'll need more notebooks. Not even a lifetime will be long enough.

—❧ 36 ❧—

The entire city, just as it is, in its great mingling of different centuries, feels completely consistent to me at this moment, profoundly coherent in its logic and various forms of madness. Rare are the tears in this ancient tapestry — it holds its weave. Its structural and constructive elements, its *ways of being*, which either repeat themselves or mutate gently and slowly, always springing from the same roots; its mode of thinking, creativity, and imagination, which are the same today as they have been time out of mind; certain rhythms that return to reveal themselves anew, in physical constructions and the intangible texture of life, as suddenly and surely as if they were elements in a great symphony: because of all these, the tapestry holds its weave. This is reinforced by the island effect, which "closes" and tends to conserve, and by a recurrent choral structure that sends back the same echoes evening after evening and century after century with minimal variations, forever rediscovering and rebecoming itself.

Still, I find that it's no longer possible to explore certain beauties that up until yesterday could be seen by anyone who had eyes to see them with. The lovely tangle of Palazzo Magno, for example, is now closed to passersby like me, ordinary Venetian citizens; it is locked behind a powerful gate, its beautiful external staircase almost invisible. The same fate has fallen on Corte del Tagliapietra, Corte Falcona, Corte del Forno, the passages between San

Geremia and the Grand Canal, and I don't know how many others. Here and there the labyrinth has shrunk and closed in on itself. Luckily for us, Corte Bottera remains open — by the hour, only, however, and "until the sun sets."

Venice is no longer as penetrable as she was, especially in her many — as they say — "minor" places. Attempts at stronger security, fear (of whomever, on whomever's part), indifference and greed, the presence of drugs: all of them tend to direct traffic — our footsteps, that is — outside the courtyards, the campielli, the *insulae*. On the inside, where she's still most herself, Venice can no longer be seen. Always less visible, she may be more livable; we don't know, we know ever less.

I've discovered, too, that in the impressive arsenal of guidebooks scattered around our house, not *one* of them is complete. Each of them is lacking in *something*, missing streets, palazzi, whole neighborhoods or canals, large and small pieces of the puzzle. But of course it's impossible to print a comprehensive guide to an infinite place. Even now, at the end of the millennium, there exists no complete and systematic photographic survey of the city-that-is-a-work-of-art. Certainly it will be a long and arduous task, but it must be done; and I pray, in the new millennium, that this no-longer-postponable project be undertaken by *someone*. At the moment all we can do is to try to keep taking photographs, at least mentally, street by street, imprinting her on our retinas, observing and storing her in our minds as best as we can, aided by the occasional slide and infrequent leaflet.

Days go by, and then weeks. A little each day, I keep telling myself, and I'll get there — I *must* see it all. But months pass, and I grow ever-more uncertain. No matter how much I see or rediscover, there's always more — to see, digest, introject, understand. And then to compare, participate in, listen to: every stone speaks as clearly as a human being. The next few days will not suffice; all the days of my life will not suffice. I shall try to say something, pass something on to my children, to those who come after. But I have the impression that what counts the most is forever slipping out of my grasp. Wasn't the city I saw from the plane little — *very* little? I walk on her stones, look at her, love her, discuss her by myself and with friends. But the more we come to know her, the more she multiplies, the greater she grows, this flower of stone.

I've come a long way; yet I'm always, and only, still on the road — not so much *in* Venice as still moving *toward* her. Thoughts and evenings both come and go, barely leaving a trace, like the water in the canals. The mysterious cores of the labyrinth, and the part in us that pursues them, are ineffable; they cannot be reached. Life is infinite in this swift upsweep of joy, this sudden, happy illusion — that it is true, that life is infinite indeed.

PART FOUR

Memories and Symposiums

—◦ 37 ◦—

This evening I finally come home, to the places I lived as a child. Although I've held them ever present, close in my heart, I've hesitated up until now to go back and see them. I've avoided them, whether consciously or not I don't know.

Calle del Vento, Riva degli Incurabili, Rioterrà dei Pensieri, Rio delle Fornaci, le Zattere all'Umiltà, Corte Balastro.* All of us have our own places of the soul on the face of the earth — here they also skim over the water — ready to reappear and spring to life once again from within us as soon as we close our eyes. Even with our eyes open we can superimpose them vividly and at once on anything at all; the scene never changes.

On the Riva del Vento I encounter my mother, who is no longer anywhere if not in these places. The bank and the wind are the same, and she's just returning from Mass with her old friends who have vanished like her, I know not where. A wave of her hand, that patient look of hers: she's calling to me. All her womenfriends are gathered around her, as happy as if they had come to visit her one more time. Some are neighbors, some come from a little farther away — then as now, I always get them confused.

---

*Calle of the Wind, Riva of the Incurables, Rioterrà of Thoughts, Rio of the Kilns, the Rafts of Humility, Alabaster Court. — TRANS.

Descending the bridge, if I turn around for a moment and stand straight and tall without really looking, I can see my father. It was on a morning like this that he suddenly reappeared, walking across the white bridge onto the Fondamenta del Soccorso. He had just returned from the war; I was waiting for him on the bank. He climbed these same steps and raised his eyes.

He is not the same man, I can see that, but he tries to say something to me; he starts talking to me as if nothing had happened. And yet all the horror of the world has happened on the other side of that bridge. He doesn't want his children to know about that, he doesn't want us to know. I understand.

On the Riva delle Zattere we're still playing each afternoon — me, my sisters and friends, our companions from school — until the great red ball of the sun sets over the water. I've never seen a red like that again. In winter it sets much closer to us, between the ships in the Port; in summer it sinks beyond the cone-shaped profiles of the hills, the pyramids of the Euganei. At a certain point we all stand still to watch it, adults and children alike, winter and summer: the incredible globe. The game stops all of a sudden; the water burns as it closes over the great sphere of fire. On the western horizon lie the countryside and the trees. The great factories of today, the big Marghera of post–World War II, has not yet sprung up; there is only little Marghera, the first industrial zone, and still almost invisible. Even after the sun sets, its light continues to reveal trees and fields among the expanses of water: the vanished landscape of the lagoon.

Today on the pier of Lloyd's of London in the heart of the city, you will find only a fisherman or two, or some more or less romantic couple. The great ships — *Oceania, Vulcania, Conte Rosso, Conte Verde* — that made Venice look so small in comparison no longer land here. Some are resting on the bottom of the sea; the *Conte Grande* burned like a volcano in the lagoon. But we continue to see them here at the *molo*: enormous, splendidly beautiful, bigger by far than all the jetties and banks of Lloyd's of London combined. We see them departing along with our dreams toward the Red Sea, toward India and Australia.

—◦ 38 ◦—

Between India and Australia lies the Fondamenta delle Eremite, or of the Hermits, with its row of small, brightly colored boats almost as swift as the *Vulcania* or *Conte Rosso*, perfectly adapted to us (both grown-ups and children) and to the Venetian canals. All is just as it was along the two banks, the Rive delle Eremite; maybe they're even the selfsame boats. Actually, the boats haven't changed much since then — today there's a space for the motor, maybe some instruments, a crosspiece added or taken away; but they've changed much less than the people. From the wall of Calle della Vida wild vines, white-gray and twisted, rise up naked, crazed by the years. They all face toward the Campiello dei Gatti — of the Cats — given over now to the dogs. Calle dell'Asèo still smells of vinegar: deposits of it, along with wine, spices, and who knows what else, have soaked walls and memories over the centuries.

From there a walk through the trees brings me to Campiello degli Squellini. And those doorbells are still ringing — *squellini! squellini!* — as we called them when we were little; but the earth founders and sinks under its weight of memories. I stand here looking — I'm sure that it's me who's looking — but I feel my face, my eyes and voice change all of a sudden, become what they were long ago. At bottom I'm still the boy that I was, or at least a mixture of yesterday and today. The old campiello with its huge sycamores is still the place we meet with our friends, a place of connections/encounters/clashes/discussions/and growth that I hope will never end. My father, who left us a long time ago, arrives to stand on this brink of stone and wait, with his brief smile, for his friend, who lives on the second floor, to come down. This friend, as happened so often in those days, was also *our* friend — I mean, all of us kids. I can still hear the voices calling each other (even we little ones tried), a chorus of shouts and greetings. Now there are offices there, I've been told. I'm not sure if they're open or closed; there's no one behind the windows. But I still hear an occasional greeting, a call from a friend to a friend; the sycamores are still seeking the light; and the silence, though it comes a little later, is still the same as it was.

I turn back toward Ognissanti to reach the small house on the rio where we lived for so many years, facing the Squeri.* The wall of the house is grafted onto the steps of the bridge, so that you can (whether you're a boy or a cat) enter the house directly from the bridge itself. And it's a splendid bridge, beautifully restored, which has always been called the Bridge of the Dead, Ponte dei Morti. The name hits home now that I, too, have my dead, who no longer live here. But no: suddenly it's not called the Bridge of the Dead anymore; the name has been changed into something more ordinary, Bridge of the Tailors. People didn't want "that writing" anymore; they no longer wanted the dead hanging around their homes.

I meander from there to the Bridge of the Royal Boatyards, the Squeri Reali, commanded by Tramontìn nicknamed il Fischio, the Whistle. He would ditch any work at hand, grumbling and whistling, to save our poor wooden hoop when we lost control and let it fly into the water. The Squeri are silent and motionless now; there is little or no work left. The water lies stagnant at the bend of the canal, without current as if without life. An old, half-destroyed house, wasted by time, with its rotten rafters and breached walls, its toilets and kitchens exposed, is caving in toward the canal. It collapses a little bit more, I am told, every night. This house, which seems to have died of natural causes and is now slowly sliding into complete ruin right in the middle of the small neighborhood, surrounded by surviving and repainted homes, is the most vivid change of all to me after half a century, dating as it does from the time of games, and days, without end. We all played ball inside that house, without speaking a word: it was the Community Home of the Deaf-Mutes, where even the ball itself seemed to make not a sound. Now the walls, day and night, echo with the screams of wild cats.

All the other houses that surround it are so similar, actually so *exactly* like they used to be, that long-vanished faces return to

---

*The Squeri are the boatyards where *gondole* are built and repaired. — TRANS.

peer out the same windows, between the same slatted shutters and uneasy flowers. Someone's walking up there, along the covered roof-terrace that looks like it was designed by Carpaccio, passing in and out between the frescoed columns of wood, disappearing into and reappearing from the same doors, calling out between interstices. These are memories without end and perhaps without a beginning. They are all continuations of other realities, other times beyond time; and because of this, they are much more terrible, wonderful, and vivid than any others. They are mingled with and injected into the stones, as continual as the running of water, as recurrent as the bridges between island and island, prepared to endure long after our last footsteps falter and cease.

They contribute all to the *whole* in a way inconceivable in the great modern cities, which are ever less and less cities, and more and more metropoli or *sottometropoli*, undercities.

Venice, the last real city, holds fast to her ghosts, continuously evoking and "channeling" voices, footsteps, dreams, thoughts, and presences. Perhaps this is the reason that so many detest her as soon as they leave her. For all of Venice — in her most solitary quarters, in her out-of-the-world canals — is first and foremost something unbearable: a powerful conduit for memories.

—⚬ 39 ⚬—

My friends from Milan who are here for the weekend and I try to pinpoint more precisely, as we wander home through my childhood haunts, "what it depends on," this evocative quality of the city, this capacity to channel the past. Which traits of the urban phenomenon we're traversing are the ones that foster it, we ask before it disappears into the dark. Giacomo notes that the modern city is often geometric, or tends to be: geometry stifles phantoms, and traffic, of course, extinguishes them entirely. But here there is neither geometry nor traffic. Architecture maintains its footing by miracle, almost without the aid of walls; while underground, millions of trees are breathing, never rotting, upholding us all. The atmosphere, the shadings of nuance, the water, the constant sense of unreality, the doubling and falsifying, the reflections and mirrors, the labyrinth are all in unbroken relationship with the phantoms, the faces of yesterday — or *di mai*, which in Venetian means both "never" and "always" — down to the most minimal events of their lives.

Besides, sharply defined horizons, the shrill heat of the sun, long, wide panoramas, monuments to patriotic heroes — all these things, too, which conflict so much with the ghosts — are very rare in these parts. In their place we have various fogs, *calìghi*, the ancient lagoonal mists, haze, mutable waters, microscopic perspectives repeated as if in a dream, splendid, senseless friezes, intimately inscribed stones that follow and speak to us, rather than monuments. All these are constituent, intrinsic qualities of the different quarters of Venice, no matter where we may find ourselves. The entire city, because of the way it's made, because of the way it *is*, brings the faces and lives of the dead continually back into memory; and after a while tends to reunite and mingle them, urge them to speech, transform them into each other. At times, I tell my Milanese friends, I seem to see them appear all together, as at the end of so many of Goldoni's plays, to salute the public and their friends. At other times I feel the actors waiting, without a sound or a sign, behind the shutters, behind the curtains, holding their breath. But I know that they're there, and that they can hardly wait to make their entrances, to be recognized and acknowleged before we, the audience, must — *per forza*, say my friends — continue up the road, follow the schedule, try to understand the traffic lights again.

In the meantime actors and audience, all of us on the stage, exchange roles, share our parts, and shuffle the cards as best as we can. "It's a big inter-net," say my friends: a weave within and without us, designed to distance the eager brink ever awaiting us all.

⟿ 40 ⟿

Our friends from Milan have left us and the band of companions dissolves. Everyone's intent on his own path; lonely footsteps resound on the banks on both sides of the canal. There's almost no one out on the streets at eight in the evening. In the surrounding houses someone carefully pulls the shutters — *gli scuri,* the darks — closed with a determined click, definitively blocking any other encounters, excluding all nightmares, closing off with everything and everyone above and below. This is the moment when solitude sweeps into the city, growing and gathering in silence like the tide; the essentially tragic aspect of the islands rises to the surface of the devastated canals. It's the right sort of evening, thick with the kind of humidity that amputates legs and thoughts. Evenings like this belong to no season or hour and are undecided between yesterday and today, winter and spring, day and night. Old stones and eternal miasmas; sudden, luminous glimmers of movement in the darkness of the canals; ghostly reflections between the rare lamps on the banks. These brief, booming echoes descending the bridges are my footsteps.

⟿ 41 ⟿

Today, instead, I walk toward another part of the quarter, accompanied by my friend Martino — toward the Frari, which now houses a canteen for architecture students. It used to be a convent of Catholic Sisters that sheltered a hostel full of young girls. There were a bunch of girls there, each more beautiful than the next; housed by the convent, almost all of them were refugees from Istria or from Dalmatia.

The girl Lucìa, called Lucìa la Longa — Lucìa the Long — was a wading bird from Lussino who came out courting with me. It was incredible how long she was and how red: red of skin, of hair, and of hands — all over, red. In those days she came out with me, if you can imagine it, by consent of the Mère Thérèse.

Since that time I have always loved Istria and Lussino; and also, a little, the Mère Thérèse. Most beloved was she, Lucìa la Longa, in the narrowest calli of Venice, chosen by me with the fondest of care. She was strawberry-blond but encircling her eyes, as clear as the water, was a purple-gray shadow so sweet, so pathetic it broke my heart. I didn't even dare speak to her — until one day when she made me laugh, with her long, skinny legs going *tòc tòc* up and down the bridges, and her dialect from the Veneto of the coast: a little peculiar, wavelike compared to our own, as if it were made of the very stuff of the sea. The shadow around those clear eyes became very sad in the evenings, when we would walk along the deserted beach and she would gaze out from the Murazzi up at the clouds moving toward Istria. Only then did I find out that her father, like all the fathers of all the girls sheltered by Mère Thérèse, was lying at the bottom of a ditch, all of them tied together forever by strands of barbed wire. Some of them — she hoped — had ended up at the bottom of the sea.

Now she lives an ocean away, the girl Lucìa, far far away from Istria and from Venice. Who knows that she won't return someday, with her red hair, her sweet purple shadows, her wading-bird legs? In the meantime I returned alone to her country, not that she knows. In the cemetery there is only a small, faded tombstone; but neither her father's body nor any of the fathers' bodies are buried beneath it. A little beyond the marker lies a sea of frightening clarity and the perfumed Istrian coast. Here in Venice I'm left with the bridges, one after another, still exactly the same except empty: no more *tòc tòc*.

We walk behind the church near the convent, San Giovanni Evangelista. "Closed," Martino assures me, adding, "since then." He has no idea what thundering echoes he sets off inside me. This was the girls' church; and on certain Sundays it was our church, too — I mean, those of us who loved them. At the end of the Mass the girls would sing in the choir. We managed, barely, to hold our breaths, but not the beating of our hearts. Today you have to ring the bell before they'll open the door, then ask them to let you in, and then wait.

"Wait for what?" I ask.

"Wait for the group to get bigger, for the Japanese to arrive . . ."

But I feel *them* waiting, too close beside me: the voices of the choir, the brief contralto of my stilt-bird among all the others. One by one I see their faces again and hear the tones of their voices. Better to go away, walk somewhere else, rediscover some other part of the city, on the other side of the rio — not far away, not very distant, but other. We leave. Without having to speak to each other about it, we leave, Martino and I, as if driven away by the silenced voices, without saying another word.

—◦ 42 ◦—

After just a few paces we're already far, far away. Venice, composed of six sestieri, each of which comprises its own varied quarters, is further divided into *microcittà*, tiny cities or districts — all similar, all completely unique. How many are there and how do they differ? Martino and I count ten, then twelve . . . Starting out from Santa Marta, we pass through l'Angelo Raffaele, then i Carmini, l'Avogaria, Santa Margherita, San Barnaba, and i Frari . . . There's no end to them. It's a continuous aggregate of island-cities, each with its own square, its campo or campiello, its locals engaged on their errands, its rivers of faces and memories, its stores and shops, its church, its old *osteria* or tavern (too often closed these days; whenever it's open, it's a *festa*), its surrounding canal, which defines and limits the island, and its bridges uniting it all to the island beside it.

Sometimes on the far side of a bridge, "any little thing is enough to change it completely," says Martino. When you think about it in terms of *reality*, little or nothing has changed; but your first impression is that it's entirely different, and first impressions are always what count. The lights seem different, as do the canals, the bottlenecks of the calli, the shops, the courtyards and gardens. Often the air, the climate itself, undergoes some large or small transformation. Thus Venice is made up not only

of islands, of quarters, districts, sestieri, minicanals and microci-
ties (there are really no names for all these) but also of *aria di-
versa*: microclimates, distinct enough to recognize as you pass
from one to another. How many are there? At the moment, in
the course of the south-to-north route we've chosen — from the
Zattere to the Fondamente Nuove — we've counted five or six,
but both of us know there are many more. To do it up right we'd
need more time, "more eye and more patience," according to
Martino, "also more nose, that is, more sense of smell." And
then, of course, we'd need to cross the city the other way, east to
west: a longer, more intricate journey, more exposed to the
winds, the presence of the lagoon, the circling of the seasons.
These microclimates have nothing to do with historic sestieri or
quarters, even less with the passage of time or climatic statistics.
They change with a tree, with a crumbling wall, with a breath of
fog, with the bend of a canal.

Yet they correspond almost perfectly to our *memories*; we recognize them immediately — from before the beginning, from forever. Here it's damper, there drier; here the oleanders and
robinias flower early, there later. The ailanthus, called trees of
heaven, burst into orange blossoms in one place and purple in another; I'll never know why. They exchange colors sometimes,
when they're crowded close to each other in the small gardens.

Lucìa the red, who knew them so well, is no longer here, but
they linger on. Perhaps they're immortal; seed after seed they remain. She loved each of them, one by one and uniquely; and in a
way, twisting and thin as they were, she was like them.

—◌ 43 ◌—

Meanwhile my wife and I are trying, slowly but surely, to understand a little bit better the house we've come to live in — with the
help, today, of the two bearded and stuttering architects (the
Venetian stammer, the typical tongue-twisters of the dialect) who
have been "t-t-trying" for months. They t-t-try stubbornly to re-

store the ground-floor study, "villanously" opposed by a surviving remnant of medieval cloisters: three unsuspected Gothic arches, delicate and powerful, incredible. "*Maledetti*," curse the bearded ones. "S-s-so now, we c-c-can't do a thing in here anym-m-more. N-n-nothing," they repeat, "not even m-m-move a brick."

Rolls of blueprints and designs and big boxes of slides are scattered all over the floor, wherever they happen to land. "N-n-not even touch them," laugh the architects now, "we can't even b-b-brush them." Meanwhile they're caressing them: "The arches and c-c-capitals. The Bureau has already c-c-come three times to inspect them." We note that the columns are missing their bases; they've been sunk into the floor, which has later been raised. "At l-l-least half a meter," they both assure me, "since the t-t-time of construction, six or s-s-seven centuries ago." And of course, the city has sunk, "*spro- sprofondata*," and continues to do so. The extraordinary thing is that the arches and capitals are perfect, without a crack, without the slightest sign of decay; they seem to have been made and finished yesterday.

A little farther on, but still on the ground floor, the house is sharply separated from two big rooms that were once the storehouse of an herbalist. HERBS FROM THE MOUNTAINS AND COUNTRYSIDE, FROM THE SEA AND LAGOON, a poster assures us: AN INVENTORY OF HERBS UNIQUE IN THE WORLD. Perhaps; but at the moment it's a disaster, steeped in the suffocating scents of the most conflicting herbs. The walls, stairs, and windows — everything in the two rooms — was carefully covered in concrete about eighty years ago, at the turn of the twentieth century, and now the walls are cracked and flaking, reduced to powder in places, ruined. The contrasting odors of the herbs have soaked into the walls with nauseating results. According to our architects, "C-c-concrete walls don't breathe. A house is like a human be-being, it has to b-b-breathe and move." Which is why it's all so decayed, crumbled, and soaked. Balsamic in some spots — perhaps even then, way back when these were ancient cloisters, the herbalist of the monastery kept his apothecary here. There's still an herbalist in the neighborhood today.

The rest of the ground floor is a carpenter's workshop as enormous as a church. Indeed, maybe it was one. There is only one carpenter, who is continually rushing around and making absolutely everything: shutters, tables, chairs, shelves, gigantic doors four or five times bigger than he is. We greet him but he doesn't respond. He's deaf; no surprise, given the frightening milling bits and fearful, centuries-old saws he's always using in such a fury, both day and night. "They don't come any better than these," he declares, "not even at the Arsenale."

Now we climb up the stairs, steep enough to be scary themselves, as usual in Venice. Between its entrance and hallway, the second floor has wasted half of its available space; we look around incredulously, thinking about modern apartments. However, there is a lovely eighteenth-century painting on the ceiling, split in two by the earthquake of 1976. The kitchen and bathroom both have the same kind of doors with Liberty-style glass panes in pink, yellow, and blue. Passing through the blue door, we find ourselves on a little smoke-gray terrace dating from the sixteenth or seventeenth century. An aged putto, humped and bent by the years and pocked by the rains and the droppings of pigeons, helps hold up the drying laundry with his little arms. The terrace precipitates downward immediately by means of an outside stairway, but the stairway doesn't lead anywhere. At one time it led directly to the elms and black laurels in the garden, but now it has to contend with the unplastered wall. It's difficult to understand why the wall is there at all; or conversely, why the stairway is, or the laurels, be they black or white.

The third floor probably housed the servants' quarters; and this is, as is only right, where we live. The floor is divided in two. We inhabit its southeast end: three overlarge, messily arranged rooms exposed to the full heat of the sun in summer and the biting wind in winter, like the prow of a ship. There are evenings in winter when drafts from the huge windows will lift up pages I'm trying to write on and send them flying around the room. I don't know much about our neighbors in the northwest, or about their rooms or their drafts. I surely haven't figured out yet how they come into and go out of the house; it's possible that they've been there since the times of the Serenissima and have simply never emerged.

Then there are the mansards, the covered roof terraces, the storerooms, the cupboards under the stairs. The whole "s-s-structure" inside, according to our bearded architects, is at least five hundred years old, with a stretch here and there done over in the nineteenth century. A stairway was added but never finished at the beginning of the twentieth century and now hangs suspended in the air halfway to nowhere, waiting for someone who will never arrive. But it's not just a question of the stairs. How this whole heap stands on its legs is a conundrum, a mystery to challenge the modern laws of Statics and Dynamics. The entire house is frightfully tilted (more than thirty centimeters) from the east — where we live — to the west, where our unknown neighbors live. If you let go a glass marble from our part, the east, it will roll very swiftly to where they live, the west. But then if you try again on the terrace, the marble will change direction and roll toward the petrified putto, descend to the garden, and roll back up onto the parapet, then plunge between the trees.

Every single law of Statics, of space/time, and of our perilous human equilibrium, is hereby crushingly refuted. The cracks and creakings in the night, slight yet as continuous as human sighs, are the voices of the lower end adjusting to the upper, or vice versa. Then high tide or low tide arrives, rattles the opposite end, and the house resettles and sinks a litte. The bora does the rest.

—◦ 44 ◦—

At last, in midmorning, I come to *my* campo, which is perhaps the most lovely and human of all the campi in Venice: Santa Margherita. I have to attend a conference, an International Symposium, for quite a few days; and it's located in Santa Margherita, which up until yesterday was one of the poorest places in Venice. The world has changed and yet goes on.

The great campo is filled, above all, with women: at the fish stalls, at the booths selling fruit or hosiery, in the sausage shops and clothes shops, in and out of the butcher's, in the Mini-market and the Mega-mega.* Also in the store of toys the color of cinnamon: mythic Pettenello, where all of us, children and grownups alike, have fallen under the spell of our dreams standing in front of the window of our desires. Farther along, I glimpse women among little bouquets of flowers and big baskets of eggs, going to the hairdresser's, to church, or to the *caffè*. There are seven *caffè* in the campo, two bars, a tavern, four restaurants, a church, and two ex-cinemas — one of which is now the auditorium housing the symposium.

Women's voices, women's words, women's cries, women's faces. They come and go in the great campo, buy, don't buy, talk and shout, greet each other, hug each other, laugh and cry. Their hair is white, black, blond, or red; their faces are beautiful, ugly, young, and old. Their eyes are alight, staring, lost, tender, and spirited; their bodies fat, thin, unsure, ardent, docile, menacing. They walk alone and gather in groups, with or without their children. They wrestle with bulging shopping bags, ramshackle shopping carts, baby carriages with the little ones tucked between bottles and packages. And they're always lying in wait for something or someone, curious and indiscreet, eager to gossip, *cazzafatti*, ready to throw it in your face. Some are kind, some smile, some are simply strange. Seated on the benches under the trees, they tell stories, smoke cigarettes, look around, and wait. When they're alone, they seem to be gazing off at phantoms — not so much those of the past as those of the future.

It's still cold today and the air has a biting edge, but the women don't care; nothing will stop them from talking, exchanging gossip and advice, speaking ill or (rarely) well of people — and all of it's at the top of their voices. What lungs! What energy! The more or less comic dialect — my dialect — is immediately dignified when they speak it, as they talk about food, children, schedules, money, illness, troubles, moods, love, stars

---

*The Mega-mega (big-big) is a new "supermarket" called Mega. The locals call it Mega-mega as a joke, because it's so small. — TRANS.

and constellations, things that will not be addressed, for sure, at the symposium. A recurrent theme is the sharp distinction between good and bad, and the trend is toward repetition and refrain: They repeat the story two or three times, raising their voices with every telling. Or they repeat, at the least, the episode that counts most, the most meaningful "verse," in a rhythmic ritornello like an archaic refrain from the old Puppet Shows. Constant and fundamental subjects, over and over, are sicknesses and *soldi*, money; love doesn't come up much — maybe it's not the hour for it. On one of the two vere da pozzo a young couple is kissing but then, all of a sudden, the girl breaks away and enters the world of the women as if called by them, or by the stars.

Energetic, eager, haughty, irritable, shrewd, spiteful, rarely sweet (almost never), these women are tremendously *alive*. It makes your faith in the future of Venice be reborn, seeing them so full of life. Maybe we'll make it after all, as long as our women are alive.

—◦ 45 ◦—

Men are more random in the great campo at this time of day, like myself. It's not that there aren't any, but that here we seem less corporeal, lighter as it were, than the women. We pass through, slip away, random as always — or almost always — at whatever hour, in the campo or anywhere else.

But here comes a man *not* passing at random: Radar, the neighborhood crazy. Radar must cut across the campo diagonally. His diagonals are sharp and clearly defined, his angles decisive: *zigzag*, first toward the east, then toward the west. He disappears under that portico to complete one diagonal stretch; in a few minutes he'll pop back out.

Campo Santa Margherita is simply the "Campo" around here; there's no need to get more specific. Even for those who don't live in these parts, it is *the* definitive piazza in all of southeast Venice, the great *agorà* of the quarter, the Campo of Campi. Since Piazza

San Marco has become yours, friends — fallen to the Japanese, the Germans, the Russians, and the Americans — this is where you can still find us, the survivors, the leftovers, *fin-de-race*, the last of the Venetians.

The Campo is enormous considering the dimensions of Venice: 180 meters from north to southwest, like Piazza San Marco — I pace them off. But what's more important is how it continues, unlike San Marco, to expand, turning on one side toward the Carmini and on the other toward the Bridge of Fists, slipping down countless calli, portici, and courtyards, entering the shops by one door and sliding out by the other, unfurling alongside the water of the canals and over the canals without water, the filled-in ones, the *morti*. It transcends all geometry, symmetry, and numerical dimension. It's a mistake to try to measure it with numbers, which is true, actually, of every constituent piece of this city.

And it seems even larger because the houses surrounding it are simply houses. No palaces. Houses. Some are beautiful; others are not. They come in all sizes and kinds, from spruced up to crumbling, and are variously resentful, bored, shrewd, humble, arrogant, and, rarely, sweet, just like the women. And like the women they rub shoulders gladly together and speak of their woes, of love and the stars. The great palaces would be completely wrong, out of place here. No, the houses are in tune with the women — except that the houses wear their centuries of age for anyone to see. The most beautiful ones are the oldest, musty and seasoned, between Calle del Sangue, Portico delle Carrozze, and Calle dell'Uva.* They are five to six centuries old, on the average — one is a thousand years old — and they're all still inhabited, lived in as if they were built only yesterday, or today.

Radar is back, still on the diagonal. The last stretch of this particular diagonal is the hardest, because it curves toward Calle dell'Angelo. But Radar travels it as surely as if he could see the zigzag line he must follow drawn on the ground beneath him: his own personal street signs on the volcanic stones of the Campo, ever more deranged by years and the roots of the sycamore trees.

---

*Calle of Blood, Portico of the Carriages, Calle of the Grape. — TRANS.

—◦ 46 ◦—

Radar: a perfectly round head devoid of a single hair; a sturdy
body; blue eyes and a ready smile. He must be about fifty, but age
is as hard to read in the mad as it is in beautiful women. Even his
name is uncertain; a lot of people just call him brother, *fratello*.
Every quarter of the city has a certain number of *fratelli* like him
wandering around — not many, three or four depending on the
neighborhood. Radar comes and goes, always directly toward a
target. To the women, as he passes, he says, *"Ciao, amore."* To the
men: *"Ciao, papà."* To a man whose identity is unsure: "Hello,
uncle" — *"Ciao, zio."* If they're younger, he'll turn around to look
at them and say, in a voice caught between doubt and affection,
"Allò, boys."

Watching him as I wait for the symposium brings to mind one
of his predecessors: an unforgettable *fratello* named Egisto,
known as Do-maggiore. He used to sing out here on summer
nights in front of various *caffè*, always gripping a piece of paper
covered in words and musical notes. Do-maggiore didn't know
how to read; he was almost blind. He would look at the paper and
sing, traveling through a series of off-tune notes until, happily, he
reached the stars or the clouds, which he saw for sure. His
crescendos of false notes were so extraordinary that people
couldn't stop clapping. He died in the midst of his work, keeling
over last year — they tell me — with the heat, with his last paper
in hand. Someone stole it, slipped it into his pocket, but then re-
pented and took it to the parish priest.

But it's time to go into the splendid, recently restored auditorium between the Mini-market and Corte del Fontego. It was the
"Cine-vecio," the old movie house of our youth, when films were
still silent. Before that it was the ex-Evangelical church, and before that the ex-Catholic church of Santa Margherita since the
Middle Ages; ex-who-knows before that. Stratified layers of years,
centuries, visions, and memories, all between these four walls.
And now these are joined by all the equipment of the Millennium, other phantoms wheeling between the arches and altars. I

meet the technicians; this is a symposium of biological engineering. Color transparencies, diagrams, loudspeakers, films, television, CD-ROMS, videocassettes, the Internet . . . They're all here, I see as I look around the old cinema-church-theater shot through with the glaring spots of the TV crews, alongside the old stages and stones, the columns and altars, the ancient frescoes conserved and restored — all of the latter alien, of course, to the conference, opposed to its every word. And yet it's wonderful like this, the auditorium, with its rows of videocams; it lifts my heart to see the ancient place still in use, kept in order, lived in, almost unchanged, apparently — transformed only in substance.

It will change, insist the biologists in their reports, life will change; especially if engineers and biologists work ever more together. That's probable, I say, in fact I don't doubt it. It remains to be seen what kind of life that will be. More slides, diagrams, films, CD-ROMS, and Internet sites follow, since this is the *i/i day*, when "Intel Inside" is hosting communications from all over the world on our subject. We discuss "life," from a technical viewpoint, at length; however, I realize, we never broach *life*, its mystery or meaning.

Until finally we end up talking about life, inside and out, as it happens in Venice, with a couple of Englishmen who love her more than all their research and work and who are presently seeking her — tenaciously, with smiles on their lips — from behind their trembling video cameras. One of them, a Scotsman with the long head of a seagull and his eye plastered to the camera, makes an interesting contribution to our discussion of Venice today: he says that it's *"con-vissuta,"* lived-with-in. Stammering and muddling himself up, as the British always do, he focuses the thought. "Multilayerly," he says in English, a place lived-with-in on many levels, "multimedial in the broadest sense of the word." The wondrous thing about it — explains seagull-head — is that Venice should be "so merrily" lived in by our contemporaries, by beings "more or less human like us" from all ends of the world, and at the same time inhabited in the British sense of being "haunted," frequented by spirits from differing centuries, from yesterday, today, and "even from tomorrow, to judge by what we're seeing in our videos." He stares at me with an air of reproof. "And you people say that Venice is empty," he laughs. "It's the big cities that are empty, the cities that aren't inhabited by anyone anymore, human beings or spirits, whether they belong to yesterday or today — or we aren't able to see them anymore, which comes to the same thing. They don't even enter our minds." It's seems a very apt thought to me, and also very Scottish; I think about the world of the Scots, so regularly teeming with ghosts.

"Here, however," I try to say, "if they exist, we're talking about easygoing ghosts, lagoon ghosts, not like your 'Highlander' specters."

"Oh, no," he retorts. "You have all kinds of ghosts here in Venice! Just look at all your mortal 'Venetian melancholies' . . ."

Or at certain sudden fits of gaiety or madness that take us here at times; or the strange encounters of Carnevale . . .

"Or those dark Venetian tales, so many of them — and we don't forget them up there, you know."

"It's true, we've forgotten a lot of them here," I say. "The result is that we believe more in your ghosts than in our own. It's like we're —" I add, trying to pinpoint it "— exchanging roles."

Two girls from out in the Campo arrive to tell us that a nearby trattoria is expecting us, with roasted fish and white wine. When they hear us discussing the ghosts, they let out a whistle.

"So you really see them?" they ask. "You're crazy, the lot of you, worse than Radar."

───❀ 47 ❀───

The Trani, at the corner of the campo, is half opened, half closed; until a few years ago it sold wines that came out of Puglia, from Trani. The shop has been undergoing transformation, restoration, and repairs for years, they tell me. The part that's already open is now a large, nameless room done up in provincial style and horrendous bad taste, thereby erasing a thousand years of interior architecture, Venetian or not, as if it had never been.

The rest is still a storehouse, fascinating in its inventory, which ranges from old pinball machines to new demijohns.

To the Trani come and go all the shopkeepers of the Campo, to belt down the classic *ombrèta* or to sip on a spritz. All the talk in here used to be of wines, *nostrani* or "homegrown" and *foresti* or "outsider," in an ambience full of smoke, ancient beams, and truth. Now all the talk is of travel agencies — *agenzie, agenzie, agenzie* — and of trips, vacations, the Tropics, surfing, bed-and-breakfasts, after-dinner entertainments, *nèpal*. (Yes: *nèpal*, or *Nèpal* — who knows?) There is a flurry of departures on the part of small-time merchants, the ruling class in these parts, during the "dead" season between November and February.

"At the last minute," explains the milkman happily to his friends. "The last," he repeats, raising his glass, "*salute!*"

A pause ensues. Then a very serious voice inquires from the front, "Standby?"

"Standby, I found a seat."

"Airline?"

"No, charter flight, for Havana."

"And you — where have you been?"

"In Bali, for three weeks." (This is one of the fruit-and-vegetable vendors, whose booth is absolutely tiny.)

"How about San Domingo?"

Other voices chime out: "Mauritius!" "Cuba!" "Seychelles!"

Half the globe emerges from the banter. But what a homogeneous world: charters, hotels, restaurants, dinners, suppers, menus. The Seychelles, perhaps, are islands. But what is this ubiquitous *Nèpal?* It's written IXKJHNpal, or something like that, on the Internet, and seems to mean "superior treatment."

"Superior in what way, exactly?" I ask.

"Superior that in the morning," explains the milkman, "when they bring me my coffee under the palm trees — a beautiful double coffee, very frothy, I have the boy put a fourth of a cup of sugar in it, and then I make him mix it and remix it . . . What coffee, what palm trees, what luxury. Of course, you have to reserve the boy and the palm tree the night before."

Meanwhile the girls from the university are spilling out of the auditorium in squadrons.

"Lovely, lovely," repeats old Annute, seated here in the Trani as she is every day at this hour. For seventy years Annute has sold Friulian slippers, or *papusse*, out there in the Campo from her poor but famous booth. Now she no longer knows what world she finds herself in, between all those Seychelles, Mauritius, and Bali, and these lovely girls in arrival. *"Beate loro,"* she sighs: lucky them. And that's the truth; twenty years old and gorgeous, they are definitely lucky in comparison to the old days of the *papusse*.

"But if you could see them, Annute, in the Seychelles," says the milkman, "the beauties that are wandering around *there!*"

"And in Mauritius!" "In Cuba!" "In San Domingo . . ."

Two girls start playing the old pinball machines, their boyfriends ever ready at the bar. The pinball screens light up to display green palm trees, blue seas, and athletic black women with enormous breasts in full view. One of them is mounted on an alligator, a kind of endless lizard, straddling him with her legs.

"So where is that miraculous place?" stammers one of our own, holding fast to his spritz and eyeing the palms and *la negra*.

"They'll know at the *agenzia*," whistles Annute between what remains of her teeth. "They'll know for sure, maybe there's even a charter flight ready, you never know."

"I'll try them right now," he answers, pulling out his *telefonino*. Immediately everyone else drags out his cellular phone, as well; and they begin to talk, inquire, shout, and protest all at the same time. The dog Bibo (who never stops, who's always forging ahead) halts in his tracks thoughtfully and stares fixedly at the shouting man next to him.

"What's the matter with you!" yells the man.

Someone says from the back, "In the old days only the drunkards used to bawl like this." He laughs with Annute. "But at a certain point they booted them out."

"Did you find the charter?" she asks the milkman. "Good for you. Go on then, go reserve it . . ."

—◦ 48 ◦—

The conference is over, but my good companion Danaka is not about to let me go. He wants to go back out to the Campo — he, too, says *"in Campo"* — to take more photographs. Taking photographs, for him, is the equivalent of seeing, since he can only see through the string of lenses he's always dragging around with him.

Danaka is small, dark, ugly, and immensely likable. An engineer-biologist-professor and veritable well of scientific knowledge, he hails from the "Land of the Snows" in northern Japan. Buddhist? Yes, in his way: a Buddhist with two Canons and a camera called Camera. Stepping daintily, he approaches the old house in Calle del Sangue, inquiring if all the bricks, and the doors, windows, and roof tiles are ancient.

"All, or almost all," I tell him. "There's not a brick here that isn't at least several centuries old. This house has been inhabited almost uninterruptedly since the time it was built. Maybe," I laugh, "by the same people."

He doesn't laugh, but takes a photo with machine number one, the Canon. "Where we live," he explains, "the building materials are continuously replaced and substituted with others, so that a house may be ancient as an *idea*, but not in reality." He repeats: "As an idea, but not really. As for the people, I don't know." He caresses the wall with eyes and hands (photo), climbs a little way up on the external stone staircase, descends the crumbling steps on the other side that lead down into the canal, presses his palms to the walls for a long time (photo).

Sudden, sonorous footsteps come ringing down the tiny calle: a lush, full-bodied, typically Venetian strawberry-blond appears, looking as if she had just stepped out of a canvas by Titian and lugging two enormous shopping bags. She stares at us as if we had just escaped from the madhouse, opens her door, and vanishes inside the house.

"Time embodied in the walls," Danaka resumes, a little less imperturbably now, "hardly exists anymore where we live, whereas here you can actually photograph it" (meaning touch it, feel it, all that the camera stands for) "and it's a time in which there are also these —" he looks at me and hesitates "— these round-bottomed blondes, these resuscitated Madonnas walking around." He caresses the wall once more with the palm of his hand, like a connoisseur (Canon number two, microlens). Meanwhile, *la Tiziana* — the Titian, as we've named her — leans out a window over her door: What are these two looking for under my house? (A quick shot with the Camera.) She looks at us askance and slams shut the window. A minute later she's leaning out another one; then she comes back to the first one; then appears at one farther on. Danaka's right when he says, "This wall is very much alive for its age — surprising." (Camera and both Canons.)

Now everything plunges back into silence. The wall closes in on itself; old, musty and rotting, it emanates secrets and damp, traces of beauty and vague expectation. Also our hopes that — who knows? — *la Tiziana* will come downstairs, open her door, and pass by us again. Good Japanese that he is, Danaka waits, taking it calmly. He shoots another roll of film and notes in the photo list he always has in his pocket: "Photos from number 1,136 to number 1,150: ancient walls in Venice with strawberry-blond reincarnation, shall we say, Titianesque." He actually writes that: "*reincarnazione tizianesca.*"

We wait a little longer while he takes more pictures of the walls, the staircase, the windows. It's as if *la Tiziana* didn't even exist. "And yet she's around here somewhere," he says, "because everything here is an incarnation, a reincarnation, a continual metempsychosis . . . This is the true image of Venice," he assures me, "much more than the great palaces and the churches all draped in marble: what I have here, from number 1,136" — he checks his list — "to number 1,150."

But here she is, our Titian, reincarnation or not, appearing for an instant at one of her windows, redder and more powerful than ever. Clearly enraged, she suddenly turns on the TV at full blast; the old stones echo and boom, the external staircase shudders, and chunks of brick leap out of the walls. *Via! Via!* from Calle del Sangue: This is her message for the two of us. Enough already of these photographs of my windows, go away, get out from under my door!

—❦ 49 ❦—

Although the conference is over, I continue to wander around these parts on my own. I'm sorry not to have Danaka, or someone like him, with me now; it seems I can no longer *see* the great Campo and the tiny calli, certain forgotten canals and practically unknown quarters, the way I saw them with the *foresti.* In their company I encountered, spied on, and brushed against places and atmospheres that changed continuously under their alien gaze, rhythms that repeated, were lost and rediscovered: the curve of canals, the dust of the walls, the banks, the small and large houses, the bridges, the voices on the bridges — whether they belonged to *le Tiziane* or not. And those facades I had neglected — sweet, open, and cordial — fronting the smallest canals and lined up one after the other, symmetrical, compact, asymmetrical, stratified, incredible. How I love our sweet Gothics, which have so little true Gothic about them. They are not to be found in such aggregate anywhere else, but in this city they turn up everywhere, with their double-lancet windows, their friezes, their great front doors, and their eaves worked in white stone as if it were lace. Venice, seemingly so much herself, is in continual transformation; seemingly still, she is actually always in movement. Journeyed to and walked upon, spoken of and lived in; abandoned, shut down, devastated; half vanished in the humid haze, scabby and scaling; painted and repainted, repaired and restored, lived in again, Venice immediately starts peeling and crumbling anew, a shadow of herself between walls and canal banks in motion, moving slowly alongside the waters. Moving toward the last, visible or invisible, canal; perhaps toward the end. She is multiplied under our feet, doubled in the mirrors of the water, expanded in the liquid and then immediately immobilized in the oppressive morning air poised between the levante and the sirocco. My colleagues tell me they're studying Venice on the Internet and seeing these same effects, just a little more mobile on the video screen, a little bluer in the trembling water. When *I* look at these shaky, unsure films, at certain moments I dream my life and in others, among those azure images, my death.

But suddenly at noon, a breath of the true levante, the "white" levante, strikes the city like a dry blow, and she emerges clear and lucid, more luminous than ever, *alive.* Who knows if you can see this, or how you can see this, on the Internet? It all depends on the *règfolo,* the *scontraùra,** the unexpected gusts of wind, and on the light, the angle of the sun, the motion of the water. Naturally, too, it depends on the quality of our eye, more or less attentive, more or less good-humored, fresh or tired, vivid or lethargic, in the perpetual comparison between "before" and "after," life and death. It's all a continuous, arduous, useful-futile attempt to survive, to transcend. Around here, near San Giovanni Evangelista, Venice is splendid not only as architecture "wall by wall" (this from Martino) but also in her relationship between connecting places and adjoining spaces — like a musical whole, like music made stone.

We arrive by the small calli, enter the intimate campo, are suddenly interrupted by an iconostasis (what to call it? a partition of icons?), follow the resumption of the perforated wall and the invitation of the next tiny square, while the mirrorlike marbles, the friezes and sculptures await us around the next bend. Our human footsteps, now swiftly, now slowly, travel a path of harmonic genius as we peruse the ancient pattern pierced into the walls.

A little farther on, Rio Marin, although equally extraordinary, is an entirely different place: houses and water and shops and gardens and canal banks and people on the bridges, in the stores, in the taverns, along the banks, and in boats . . . The milkman's shop is half on the bridge and half on the bank; the *caffè* is half in the calle and half on the water; the tavern has one foot in the city and the other in the country, surrounded by vegetable gardens. A

---

*Both words are Venetian. A *règfolo* is a sudden strong gust of wind, often swirling and always short-lived. A *scontraùra* is at least an eddy, at most a whirlwind. — TRANS.

few paces show you two cities — countless cities — incorporated into one.

It may be true that neither philosophy nor poetry nor metaphysics nor geometry was invented in Venice. There can be no doubt, however, that the city itself was invented, and invented out of nothing: water, sand, horizon. There was nothing else. And within the city the art of living and of representing life were perfected. Theater and painting, a certain kind of architecture and engineering, unique social institutions: All that the city needed was invented for and within her, century after century after century. In those days, I think, no one doubted that it would all be passed on — right up to today, right up to this last generation. It's all here, it's all waiting. It's up to us now.

— 50 —

Bit by bit a basic point is coming clear to me, one that wasn't clear at all the first days I was back: It's not necessary to walk around much; you can do just as well by staying more or less in one place. To be exact, you *do* have to move, but not much; and the most important thing of all is the skill of standing still. You have to be still in order to *see* — to be *able* to see and thus to participate, understand, absorb, and retell the city's tales. Venice is micrometric in scale, and her citizens have ever deemed sweeping vistas and grand panoramas inhuman.

"It's the opposite of Paris," laughs Martino, "which is so excessive and pompous, where everything is *grande-grande*, even when it's not."

Here the most minimal displacement on the part of the beholder changes everything: perspectives, colors, positions, even voices. It requires patient, attentive eyes, capable of registering the details of a microcosm rather than the outlines of a big picture. You have to choose a spot — any spot — stop, stand perfectly still, open your eyes, look around and then look again, and then close your eyes. Furthermore, you must accept all discourse, listen when someone speaks to you about history or tells you the ancient tales, listen with your eyes open or closed (it's all part of the picture), concentrate once more, then loosen your focus. Next you must take a few steps, noting the changing relationships between lines, the profiles of houses, the open mouths of the windows, the colors of water. Take in, a bit at a time, the nuances of the facades, the continual shadings of things. Follow them to "understand" them, in the sense of trying to contain and compare them within yourself. Above all, move very little: one step up or down on the bridge, one pace back or forward on the bank of the canal. The whole of Venice may be rediscovered in this small space; one step farther, and you will stumble upon an entirely different city, echoing the one you just left. Space is scarce but time is infinite — the opposite of the modern world. No speed, no distance; instead, a slow movement through centuries. Will they see all this on the Internet?

"These Parisians, when they come to Venice! They're so nervous, twitchy, quick, in love, out of love, distracted, angry . . . How do they manage to understand anything?" asks Martino as we watch a group of them. The French stand out right away; they appear to be hyperactive, and practically blind to boot. It's true, of course, that none of us has much time, not as much as we'd like; that's the pace of modern life. But at least let's not run, let's not always be rushing around everywhere. Once in a while at least, my friends, let's spend a still moment on the steps of Ponte Lungo or Ponte Storto and watch Venice change. If we're attentive enough, she will change entirely.

Even if we're just doing errands or going to work, we can pay attention sometimes to the rhythms, the motifs, the voices that circle and repeat. Five minutes a week might be enough, as a sort of meditation or a half a prayer (perhaps even a whole one, though I'm not sure we're capable of that anymore). The rhythms of the windows, the arches, the fretwork on the stone ledges, which open themselves and call out to us from every direction; the song of the waters (if not too many motorboats are around to drown it out); the recurrent motifs of human language, the flashes of words given to us like gifts in the streets: Let us cherish them.

There is an angel that shows up here and there in the city for those who are not in too much of a hurry to see him: He stands at Due Pozzi, at the Biri, in Calle degli Spiriti . . . and in how many other places as well I don't know. He is a splendidly beautiful angel of Istrian stone, his wings partly folded. I *think* he's of stone, but you never know; his smile is masculine, ironic, and sweet. In the great gilded arch of the church of the Carmini there is a lady-angel, a little unsure of herself, with small golden breasts. I've never seen lady-angels anywhere else. But the sight of those little gold breasts always moves me to prayer.

—◦ 51 ◦—

I'm rebelling against my own advice as if I hadn't understood it, wandering around all over the place. I'm so strongly attracted by every new twist in the labyrinth, always asking myself where it will take me. Today I meander from Calle del Vento to Corte degli Squellini, from Cannaregio to the Ghetto, from Stradanova to San Pietro di Castello, drawn like a magnet ever inward, ever closer to the inescapable center. But which center is it, and where?

This morning finds me in the Rialto, where years ago I held my first real job. That window of stone above me — how my heart beats to find it again in the midst of the labyrinth! This was the Palazzo del Magistrato alle Acque, the Magistrate of Waters, where we studied and regulated (or rather, diverted) the canals, rivers, lagoon, and all the other waters in Venice and the Veneto. I have never since been so happy to work as I was then. During the day I would study the waters in the city's canals or go out to inspect them between the sea and the lagoon. At night I would dream of rivers: the long, slow, suspended rivers of the Veneto.

From my window of stone in the center of the palazzo, I could look down onto the Market of the Rialto. It was more or less as it is today, only much richer and bigger, noisier, smellier, gayer, and more musical. I lived, worked, and dreamed in the middle of the prodigious sounds and odors of the most wonderful market in the world. How arduous it was for me later, as an exile, to accustom myself to working in the sad ascetic offices, the silent prisons and soundproofed skyscrapers of the great metropoli!

The Ponte di Rialto rises up from the Market, continues and reveals it in ascent, expanding it into the air. The bridge beckons me toward San Marco; but I don't go to San Marco, haven't been there once in all the time I've been back. It is truly estranged from us now, our ancient historical center, ever more alien to Venetians with each passing year. It has been invaded and occupied, sold off to the foreign troops at a loss. A memory assails me, of the last time I happened to come upon it, a few years ago: a circle of hell.

We've abandoned it to them, the tourists, surrendered it up to strangers. Now the newspapers no longer call it the Piazza, but the Area Marciana. San Marco has been desecrated, defiled. Little by little we've removed it, this place of all places, excluded it from the geography of our souls. Foremost among our modern dilemmas, perhaps gravest of all of Venice's dramas, are the millions of tourists — but what, exactly, are *tourists?* — who not only pass through on the fly, seeing little or nothing, but also perceive the places of greatest mystery as a kind of Luna Park, a Disney World, exchanging not one real word with us, its inhabitants. What is worst of all is that these *tourists* wield a terrible power: they bear an image of Venice back out into the rest of the world as a city too-seen, too-visited, too-crowded, too-known to bother with. Venice: been there, done that. On a certain level, not worth the hassle. Old hat.

Yet Venice remains, and is ever more herself, thus ever less recognizable in a world focused more and more on homogeneity, uniformity, and standardization. Most people don't recognize her; they don't see enough, don't understand — they can't. In truth the little city of stone rising out of the sea grows every day as a problem, thickens in mystery, unfolds as a drama-dream-promise-responsibility with ever more urgency. The one thing it's *not* is a "known" and "superfluous" place.

Before long it will all remain to be seen, to be "excavated" from just beneath the surface; but since few have the time or capacity to see and excavate, we shall end up by knowing — and loving — her less all the time. Under the wave, or lava, of millions of tourists we'll have to go searching for *something* among the crowded calli, the secret chasms, the rims, the canals and ravines. We'll have to go look for the city, present in its stones and its waters, yet vanished, invisible.

(I'm writing this down from the top of the Rialto Bridge, under the great arch and the open sky, jostled by squadrons of terrible, pitiful tourists elbowing each other out of the way to catch a glance — "a glance," they repeat — of the Grand Canal. Next to me stands a retarded man with his entire family.)

— 52 —

Yet as it turned out, it was two tourists who overturned my memories of an unbearable, alien San Marco: two amiable Poles lost in the labyrinth between the Fenice and the Rialto, literally lost in the falling dark.

"Prosze-prosze, Markus Platz," they insist. "We've come this far just to see it and now we can't find it." So we go together; it isn't far.

It's between six and seven in the evening, and it's a miracle: The Piazza is empty. There's almost no one all the way from the Bocca di Piazza to the two columns on the shore of the lagoon, and all of it — the Piazza, the church, the columns, the shore — is more elusive than ever. The humid sea air gleams from every marble, stone, and mosaic, and the water is the azure of the sea in the evening, darker in the depths. *This* is something to remember: that if we come at this hour, out of season, San Marco can still be implacably ours, from whichever direction we approach it — prosze or no prosze.

We enter the church by the side door, from the Piazzetta dei Leoncini. The door is just barely ajar and we slip in like thieves. Immediately the golden mosaics of the entrance lower the sky so that it hovers close over our heads, uniting heaven and earth to separate us from the things of this world. Among the elements of our everyday universe, only water is present; humidity sweats and oozes from the stones. The entrance to San Marco is also a sea cavern, a grotto carved from the deeps.

Inside, the church is still the same blue-and-gold cave I remember from childhood. It has not grown smaller, as is usual with places recalled from when we were children, but larger — larger and more profound than it was. Mysterious glances from above flood the space between cupolas with silence. Beneath the Black Virgin, only a few human beings are attending the evening Mass, surrounded by space that verges on the angelic, magnificently solemn yet powerfully gathered, comprehensible even to people like us, random observers. Always with the help, "we hope, we hope," murmur my Poles, of the divine. I would like never to move anymore, to stay where I am forever in the blue-and-gold cave.

Instead I ascend with my friends through the naves while beauty multiplies itself, takes my breath away and fills me with joy. Arches great and small uplift mysterious faces, eyes that return our gaze. Light glints from the sea of mosaics and vaults; other arches and cupolas rise up toward heaven. Space is multiplied, at once measured and infinite, accelerated and rhythmic; but it is, at the same time, definite and precise, fitted perfectly to our human scale: we can hold the whole thing in our hand. Perhaps this interior, these spaces so involved with each other and with us, expanding and repeating as we continue to follow them above, around, and within us . . . perhaps the interior of San Marco is the most beautiful and human church in the world. And yet almost no one has taken time to analyze the fundamental aspects of its architecture — the creation and dominion of spaces, for us and the gods. I wish never to leave this interim place between heaven and earth, happy, exact, reassuring, and magic. But there are schedules even in Paradise: the Mass is over and the Black Virgin veiled. The church closes its doors. Joy is brief, the visit even briefer. We must leave the maternal cavern to resume our descent, down into the labyrinth.

PART FIVE

Labyrinths

"The evening, in Venice. . ." my friends from Milan ask me on the phone, ". . . what do you do in the evening in Venice? With the festivals, the Biennale,* the exhibits, the theater . . . You two must always be out and about."

At certain times, I admit, there's actually too much to do, to go out and see; but these periods are brief and random. The rest of the year there's little or nothing: the movies are a disaster and getting around is hard. Here on the islands, as anywhere else in the evening, we help the kids with their homework, watch television, phone friends. At home, I insist, nothing is very different than it is in Milan, where we, too, were living this time last year — I can hardly believe it. In a little while I'll glance over the paper; the neighbor will come back in with his dog; then my wife and I will doze for a bit in our armchairs in front of the TV. Almost every evening's like this, as it would be anywhere else.

Our friends from Milan feel both disappointed and reassured.

"Everything's all right, then?" asks Carlo, who tends, like all *milanesi*, to summarize things.

"Everything's fine," I tell him.

---

*The Biennale is an international display of avant-garde and contemporary works of art, and is held in the Giardini Pubblici from June through September, only on odd-numbered years. — TRANS.

In truth our reality, I should tell him, is quite different here, uneasy and restive. Even at home among the family, even just glancing over the paper, I find myself holding still every once in a while to listen to . . . I don't really understand what. It's *silence*, my friends, that I feel all around me, within and without me, even as I'm speaking to you: something indescribable suspended in the air and in our hearts, a motionless atmosphere to which I was not, and still am not, accustomed. I hadn't encountered silence for such a long time — nor you either, I imagine. On some evenings it brings me a sense of profound joy, *almost* always. On others, it's agonizing. My wife hates it. The kids don't feel it; they say "it's no problem," for now, for them. If you pay attention, I tell them, you'll feel the water under the house, the tide being part of the silence. "It's no problem." But it's the moment — I'm talking to myself by this time — when the islands will sink, when the trunks of the millions of trees that support them will suddenly feel the weight of the centuries and give way, when the damp will climb up into the walls, crumbling palazzi and houses. Venice won't make it; she's rotting.

Then voices reach us from the calle on the other side of the courtyard, sometimes distorted by the bends of the calle, sometimes bursting into sudden shouts, sometimes mixing all together in shrill, senseless fragments. On rare occasions they blend into a consoling kind of hum, a quiet music; and when they do, I tell myself that Venice might make it after all.

A profound silence settles down over the city again. I recall the tremendous, continuous roar of the traffic surrounding our house in Milan. Here something else slips into the house with the silence: a fear of remaining alone on the island, as the human world is gradually, inexorably, struck dumb. Here that's much clearer and harder than anywhere else I have been.

This silence is followed by, or contains, a moment you can taste in the very air: a kind of menacing dissolution of voices, words, real human communication on the face of the earth. This is true even if someone calls up, kindly, for the latest news — always for the latest news. New fences, I think, ever denser and more difficult, rise up between human beings as the night advances, as life itself passes and grows to a close. By midnight, here in this house on the canal, we're not far from feeling the end of time and the world. And here we are, in the midst of it, in a house like any other, my friends, on the canal of the Carmini in the middle of Venice, even as we converse peacefully, my wife and I, before going to sleep on the waters. It's too late to call Carlo back in Milan in an attempt to inform him of this latest piece of news. Better to step out onto the balcony — a sort of small terrace left over from the Middle Ages, which trembles like the water below it — and lift my eyes to the stars. How many there are out tonight! I can see them hovering white over the profiles of the houses in front of me.

How long it's been since I've seen them together, houses and stars! Tonight they literally recharge me and help me to live. I choose a house and star at random, just to concentrate my gaze and thoughts, and my spirit is immediately seized by the comparison between life and not-life, as you may understand it while staring for a moment at a great light pulsing through the humid sky above the roof of a small house. I make a brief check of the tide beneath the wind, and also of the wind, blowing in with the tide. The silence is so deep that all it takes is this breath, this slight gust, to carry the sound of the sea from the east and into my ears. Then I hear it echoed from the opposite direction, reflected and capsized by some distant wall among the canals.

If I have any energy left, I'll jot down a word or two in my new notebook. It's late, but it would be a shame to lose them entirely: these nights in which absolutely nothing happens, in which there is no late-breaking news in Venice, no news in the islands at all.

—◦ 54 ◦—

"The Scales," as it was known in the Rialto, has closed. It was not an ordinary store, but an ancient shop selling scales and other small mechanical devices, located in the midst of the Rialto

Market. Furthermore, it was all in one, both a shop and an office. My friend Gino the historian assures me that it's always been here, in this exact same spot, along with other small shops of its kind, time out of mind, since the great *Mercato* began — that is to say, since the birth of Venice.

In place of The Scales another mask shop has cropped up. Within a hundred meters you can find four or five others already, crammed with masks small and large. How do they live? There's not one shop left that sells scales. All the scales are in Mestre now, and the office is in Padua. Rialto, for the moment, remains; but it's always more empty — or more full of masks.

Our discussions catch fire again around this issue of masks. All the shops necessary to the indigenous population are closing; and when new shops open, they're senseless, nothing better than decoys for the tourists passing through. These wordy discussions of ours never end. Unfortunately, they often break out into quarrels, arguments, and misunderstandings as soon as we begin to speak of those places in which every brick is a tract of history, a sliver of beauty, a dream in the middle of which real people must live real lives — as soon as we speak about Venice, her troubles and woes. Clashes of opinion arise between friends, associations, colleagues, clans, political parties, confraternities, and congregations over every issue, whether it's important or not. And yet we all love her, Venice, the focus of all our discussions: all that's around and within us, we love. We speak with obstinate fury of a wonder slipping away from us all, no matter what our opinions may be. We are all of us losing her and we are all of us, whether we know it or not, desperate.

It's true that after a while these discussions falter and sag, followed by periods of exhaustion just as extreme. After all, you must work; and then the sirocco lulls you to sleep. But they're always sparked off again, or, as we say here, *si impizzano* — they explode into being once more, faced with the gravity and complexity of our problems and the weight of our affection. Every human activity, that is to say, every technical, architectural, and engineering advance, every science, as well as every experience and sentiment, is integral to the controversy. From the shops closing down to the diminishing modes of transportation, from the hydraulics in the lagoon to the history of the *quartieri*, from urban planning to economic considerations, from geotechnics to architecture, from the restoration of the angels on the bell towers to the sewage in the drains, from the underground cables in the calli to the dioxins in the canals: all of them play their parts. As do stones and souls, memory and oblivion, despair and denial, confusion on every level. Not only every science and creative feeling, but also every ignorance and improvisation, it seems, are desirous of participation in the puzzle, as is their right. It's a rich and concentrated brew in a little, very little space — and always less time, almost no time at all left us in which to solve it.

The truth is that everyone brings his own image of both the real and the interiorized city, her own dream, idea, rejection, comprehension or incomprehension, stupor or reawakening to this tangle of questions, illusions, and interests. Our ancient good humor is diminishing before this multiplication of problems, but imagination doesn't lose its hold. Meanwhile, Venice is "going away," repeat all my friends, "Venice is dying." And I feel just as strongly as they do that it's necessary to talk about it — not to go to war with each other over it, especially in these conditions, but to know about it and come to know each other. Knowledge always leads to the beginning of understanding; and we must understand each other soon now, whether we're friends or not. This is especially crucial when we approach the most controversial aspects of the problem. We must unite the forces that are left us in order to confront the disaster, but how can we do it if we continue to quarrel among ourselves? We need to find a bridge, I say to my companions as we walk out together, like the bridges we encounter everywhere in this city made up of bridges, so that we can begin to talk to each other.

Outside on the wharf, Martino shows us the grebes in the water. Maybe they'll save us, he says: the grebes, the *fisoli*, which are becoming ever-more numerous (there's a squadron of them here now) even in the middle of Bacino San Marco, with its boats and ships always coming and going. Seen from here, the basin is concave, curved, and azure, giving us a sense of the heart of the city, of the nest that we must not lose. The grebes or *fisoli*, whatever you call them, have finally returned and seem to be doing well. We, too, must return, live, settle down in the ancient nest that awaits us.

—⟨ 55 ⟩—

And again, everyone has his own image, his own dream and idea of Venice, which by her nature generates myriad images, real and reflected, of the most disparate sort — from transparence to confusion, from return to rejection to enchantment. She multiplies different comparisons in each of us with regard to other cities and continually creates the strangest of tensions, often opposing, which would be unthinkable anywhere else. Since I've come back I've carried a tremendous tension inside me, a perpetual friction between my impulse to look at things as rationally as possible and an opposite impulse that deals in feelings, gazing into the heart and spirit of things. Today at the Punta della Dogana (a flock of boys fishing from the point at eight in the morning) I feel Venice suddenly fluctuate — drift, even — beneath the powerful assault of the incoming tide, stretch after stretch of the banks catching fire under the wind and a strange, impassive sun, the hard white disk of late February. Then, when the tide swells the canal and both its banks begin to drown, disappearing beneath the waves, the city decides and begins to sing. Her choir consists of the banks and canals, large and small, far and near, all sounding together. The fisher-boys chant an answering refrain, respond to the rive by laughing. Anyone who has experienced these things even once will understand what I mean when I speak of the tension between attempts to understand them and recurrent rejections, between impulses and reactions.

Even when I write, even now as I'm writing these words in my notebook, the conflict between concentration and expansion is unceasing. I'd like to "jot down" a few words very swiftly, rather than "write" them, and I usually start that way, with a simple (hopefully), clear one-line entry. But there's always something else that slips into circulation, coming and going like the water, something that wants to ebb and flow like the tide. Concision is thrown out the window; the discussion must be resumed, expanded, reopened, no end in sight.

It's a difficult city, we know, to write *about*. But it's also a difficult city to write *in*. In the end it's always too present, even in silence. Certain mornings . . . that singing alongside the banks.

—◦ 56 ◦—

Another rare limpid morning. By noon there's a kind of chaotic double exposure of light on the houses, the boats, the taverns, the passersby with their staring, pitiless eyes (who are you, who do you think you are?), the hundreds and thousands of lives brushing by you on the banks of Venice, in the streets of Venice, some of them — calli, rive, windows, people, lives — of superhuman beauty. From the shores of the Giudecca to the Punta della Dogana there is a dance of colored dust motes, of water flowing beneath them and yearning toward them, of tiny, unbelievably luminous wavelets, of marble reflecting and returning its reflections — an incredible rock 'n' roll of slivers of sea-earth-light, all moving in perfect freedom between the old columns of the Dogana. The boys on the bank are no longer fishing; they're running, they're flying. Where is the customs officers' house? Ah, it's tucked away behind here, dozing among the centuries, lying tranquil in the sun, washed clean of its ghosts.

—◦ 57 ◦—

Carnevale, unfortunately.

"We put up with it," explains Martino to Kramer-called-K, who has just now arrived here from Zurich, "because there's not much else happening, there aren't many choices in winter. We Venetians end up feeling abused, but these days of casino are useful to Venice," he insists. "However, believe me, it's a real grind, we work harder than ever, it's not Carnevale for *us*. The hotels fill up again and the whole tourist machine primes itself and rehearses for summer . . ."

What Martino is saying is true, but it's not the whole story. There's also the dwarf, I tell K, who trucks all over Venice during Carnevale wearing an enormous tricorn hat on his head. Day and night, making its way through the crowds *in maschera* and *non in maschera*, the tricorn travels up and down through the largest campi and the poorest courtyards without ever stopping; it bobs along the edge of the banks and flies over the bridges.

"The days of our lives," the dwarf whistles. He finds his friends, marches happily in place for a moment, then continues on his way. There he is, look at him, climbing down from the *traghetto*; he trips and falls. But since he's a dwarf, he pulls himself up off the ground right away, like a child.

"Did you hurt yourself?" ask K, very worriedly.

The dwarf looks at him with cold detachment from under his tricorn: "You better believe I hurt myself, and how!"

"How?" falters Kramer.

The dwarf makes a sweeping gesture to encompass his body from head to toe and says: "Be-ing born." But he laughs immediately, adjusts his powerful tricorn at a tilt, leaps onto the arriving vaporetto, and departs.

So he continues his travels as we continue ours, in these "days of our lives." We will run into him over and over, laughing on the Rialto, at San Martino, in Celestia . . .

Then there's the bank employee who takes his vacation every year at this time. He's known as Pitòn (turkey), which is probably a nickname since it fits him so well, with his great red gullet and beaky nose. He struts up and down as if seeking his place — his right place — in the world, wearing a black cape and *bautta*. Few people recognize him. Now and then some client from the bank does, and sketches a hasty, terrified greeting. At last he situates himself on the riva, throws back his cape, opens his bag, pulls out a great number of tennis balls, all of which are numbered and colored — white, yellow, and red — and commences his act. All year long he has practiced to be a juggler — a *"jongleur,"* he clarifies, *"jongleur"* — and now his moment has come.

And here's Radar again: every morning during Carnevale he meets up with Fulmine at the four telephones in Campo San Barnaba. Fulmine (Lightning) is the resident madman of the adjacent *quartiere,* and is also known as Scirocco, since at times he moves like a bolt of lightning and at others he moves not at all, waiting for others to do so, waiting for life to pass by. All of a sudden these days the two of them are to be found at the public phones, speaking every language known to man. Even if the phone is busy, even if it's broken. Even if it's not there. Three or four Germans arrive, wandering lost in the crowds of Carnevale, wearing masks of Schützen. They don't have correct change, they don't have phone cards, and they're asking for help to telephone home.

"No fear," say our guys, introducing themselves: "Radar and Lightning." They get up, punch in the numbers, convey greetings, speak, pause, and answer. "Everything's fine at home," they tell the Germans.

"Even Grandma?"

"Even Grandma."

And the Germans wander off, their hearts set at rest, to enjoy themselves.

Exactly what they're enjoying is a mystery. There are no great inventions, no hidden machinations, no allegorical floats, no animated cartoons. There are a lot of people wandering around, but not many programs. Not many interventions from on high.

This is the real difference between the carnivals in other places and Carnevale in Venice: here all of us, if we're able, invent it ourselves, piece by piece. It's invented by the dwarf, the bank clerk, Radar, our lightninglike Fulmine, the Schützen-Germans — everyone who gets into the game. Even the cats sliding through the shadows and the crazed dogs that lie down in the middle of the bridges in protest. Even Kramer today, who walks into the office with a beautiful green bowler on his head and a powerful red-and-white trumpet under his raincoat. It's not a wildly original costume, but every once in a while he pulls out the trumpet and blows it when the accountant is talking: a short, shrill sound that astounds our Mestre branch office. (Kramer is looked at askance, anyway, by our Mestre employees. They say he's too *"venezianizzato."*) The third time he does this the accountant gives up.

"I'm going for a drive," he bursts out, "I need a little pickup. Air," he repeats. "Air, air!" And he exits into the traffic of Mestre, into some of the foulest air on the face of the earth.

—⟋ 58 ⟍—

Back in Venice this evening I step out again with Kramer. It's foggy and very few people are out on the streets. In a campo here and there communal loudspeakers are blasting high-volume music, which bounces tunelessly through the gaps of the squares. I catch a glimpse of the dwarf, of Pitòn and Radar among the rare masks emerging from the fog, hovering on the rim of the riva in all their strange beauty as if to converse among themselves. But they never converse; they only walk about and look at each other.

Where is Fulmine-Scirocco? He's too pissed off to come out tonight; he's staying home to protest the ubiquitous cellular *telefonini*, which absolutely infuriate him. If it goes on like this, he explains, he will be constrained to shut himself up in the house. He feels sorry for the Schützens and all the others he's been helping with the public phones lately; but he is never going back out into Carnevale to expose himself to all those damned *drin-drin!* of people's private *telefonini* rocketing through his head — *"in testa, qui in testa,"* he insists.

Instead, we stumble across *il moretto* in the fog. *Il moretto* is that seventeenth-century lamppost in the form of a Moorish boy — life-sized or larger — holding up a lit lamp at the entrances to so many Venetian houses. And now we encounter one here, the loveliest we've ever seen, right next to the fruit stalls. This wooden moretto lights up, *tac!* in the fog, and people stop and gather round it in curiosity. The fruit vendors complain: "Ehi, you, lamppost! Move a little farther away!" and it opens its pedestal to reveal two extremely long legs, cunningly arranged. The lamppost rises and laughs, and the legs go into motion. We recognize, by his smile, an amiable man we've seen around town before.

"But it's Roberto!" cry the kids, recognizing him as well, and bursting into laughter. "Roberto the railwayman!"

He moves on and takes up a stance on the bridge. There's no light on the bridge, so it's a perfect place for a lamppost. The kids all run after him and give him a few playful smacks, still laughing. The lamppost rocks and then settles. "That's enough now!" it says. A thread of merriment winds over the ramshackle bridge, accompanied by just the right touch of melancholy — it's evening, it's foggy, the night's about to end — as places and ages merge.

—◦ 59 ◦—

Once again it's crept up on us slowly without anyone noticing it, this mixture of fog and night. It began swirling in a few hours ago, and now it's muffling voices alongside the canals, slowing down footsteps and sighs. The color of the night this time is dark gray, lightening here and there to gray-white or milk white: *nebbia, nebbietta, foschia, calìgo,** depending on the shores and canals, mirrors and islands. You need to observe, to *follow* the water in the canals at this time of night: a liquid silence in the semidarkness sliding slowly, circulating inexorably between the old walls, the banks, and the houses. It's almost motionless now, reflecting the gleam of the infrequent streetlamps lying more or less perpendicularly across the water, depending on the current. Only certain intersections of the canals ripple briefly into life;

---

*Venetians have many different words to describe varieties and nuances of fog. These are a few of them. — TRANS.

and the liquid condenses in their bends and bottlenecks and underneath the bridges.

"What velocity does the water have here?" asks Kramer.

"A decimeter or so per second," I tell him, since he insists. "It's about to hit its low, when it doesn't move at all."

It's exhausted, as they say, *in stanca*, or becoming-a-painting, *in tela*; very soon it will be temporarily dead, *in morto d'acqua*.

We stroll from the canal of the Giudecca toward San Sebastiano, and then again from the Carmini toward Rio Nuovo and Rio del Gàffaro. There are no tiny rii on this route, only broad canals. CORTE DEGLI SPIRITI we read on the wall between the extremely narrow calle and the bank. All these calli are very narrow in comparison to the adjacent canals, and this one, it seems, has scarcely room for more than its spirits. Better not to go down it this evening; there's the risk that we'll never come out.

We can hear a faint lapping of water, depending on the density of the fog, and a slightly louder slap and plash at the passage (we think) of a boat — elusive, illusory sounds from the mist-enveloped canals. And wherever we turn, it's the same. In fact, we find ourselves back at the Corte degli Spiriti without having realized we were returning, believing we had walked to a whole other part of the city.

K is suddenly struck with a thought. "How many canals are there?"

"A hundred kilometers of them," I tell him, "more or less."

Canals great and small, with slow bends and sudden turnings, rii and *rielli*, phantasmagoric canals and ghostly houses, and we two sliding along like ghosts, attempting to count them. The fog thickens, accumulates, and envelops the world, in the courtyard of the spirits and everywhere else.

"Doesn't anyone ever fall into the water?" asks K.

"No, never."

"Why not? Logically, a certain percentage . . ."

"Logically, yes," I admit. "But a little bit is that sixth sense that we all have around here, and a little bit is because we're in the water already. There's not that much difference between this fog and the water."

"Have they measured it?" Kramer is quantifying everything tonight, so as to save himself from the fog. "I mean, have they measured the density of the fog here in Venice?" He's right, I suppose. "We ought to know it," he insists, "the precise density of the fog."

But by now the world is lost, indistinguishable: shores, people, memories, numbers, spirits. The living are indistinguishable from the living, the dead from the survivors. What's to measure?

Only the cat — do you see him? He sees *you*; God sees you through the cat's slanted eyes. We glimpse friends on the bridge in the swirling mist — is that them? They're locked in an embrace, kissing each other. Maybe she's my old girlfriend; maybe he's the lover of another friend of ours . . . In the all-encompassing fog, the impulses-forms-silences of this incestuous city return, redouble, and multiply. We become, all of us, a continuation of each other, passing from being into being — on the street, on the bank, on the invisible bridge — cats included, fish not excluded. We're not simply sinking, as in every other place in the world, from generation to generation.

Kramer escapes back to Zurich.

—ↄ 60 ↄ—

L'acqua, come noi, pensa se stessa
prima di farsi vortice e rapina

The water, like us, considers itself
Before becoming a whirling and plunder

Montale's syllables, like slow bolts of lightning. Here, too, the water in the canals seems to "consider itself" in these *"momenti di stagna"* or moments of stagnation, as we call them in Venice, at the peak of high tide in the instant before outward ebb, its escape back out the sea. The houses, as well, reflected motionless in the rio, standing upside-down and perfectly still, canal after canal, consider/create an entire upside-down city, a whole city awaiting itself — and awaiting *us*, from deep within the most interrogative of all elements. Venetians, living with water under their houses, understand that the world is (and must be) as topsy-turvy as it is upright; and their strange way of going about things, halfway between indifferent and wary, disjointed and convoluted, reflects the reflected and overturned city. Non-Venetians, of course, find this more difficult to grasp. But there are always exceptions, people who understand it even better than we do; foreigners frequently become more lagoonal and topsy-turvy than locals.

More than along the banks or the calli, I walk between these mute canals: the *forma urbis* is theirs from time out of mind. According to Italian historians, Venice is the youngest of all historic cities still being lived in. Milan, it's true, is much more ancient. But what these scholars don't take into account is the water and the air, the atmosphere. Milan no longer embraces nature or natural history as part of itself. But here the canals and rii, the lost islands and ancient rivers, the sandbanks and muddy bottoms, the flora and fauna, the crabs and the flowers, the voices crying out over the waters, the embankments and boats, the fondamente and vere da pozzo, the ebb and flow of the sea — all this continues to be an integral, lived-in part of the city, under our very houses, *inside* our very houses. Venice's waters are as inhabited as her stones. Her geological underbelly, whether resting on land or on sea, is what we have always walked upon, what we walk upon still, even now. And in fact, this evening . . .

This is what happens at our house this evening. It's Fat Tuesday, *martedì grasso*, so we've invited over all of our friends, filling the house for a change. We've even managed to persuade Kramer to come back. Some are wearing masks and costumes, others not; the resident cat studies the situation, as astounded as we are.

After a while, a masked friend I don't recognize at the moment walks up to the window overlooking the courtyard and notices that the waters are rising, welling up through the stones. The tide has decided to participate in the party, sweeping into the courtyard, gurgling and calling, right down here among the stones and geraniums. *Acqua alta* is rare at this time of year; but here it is anyway, in the dead of winter, in full Carnevale.

"It's been brooding for a few days now," explains Daniela (I see that it's her now, behind the mask), "and tonight, since it's *martedì grasso*, the tide has made up its mind."

I telephone the weather and water information center: *1,35 sul mediomare* is the technical response. Meaning that very shortly half the city will be flooded.

Immediately our friends divide up into three groups:

1. Those who take flight swiftly and at once. It's not pleasant to have to wade home with soaked feet in winter, especially in sewer water. (So: We can kiss this evening good-bye.)

2. Those who decide to stay on until it's subsided — that is, until three in the morning. (So: They'll ruin my night.)

3. Those who hope the forecast is wrong, who remove themselves from the question entirely, who prefer not to think about it, as if it weren't happening — as if the tide didn't exist.

However, every once in a while the Daniela-mask glances restlessly out the window: "It's risen, it's still rising."

In other words, the evening's a bust. Even more so when someone remembers that we're more or less — give or take a month — in the *trentennale*: thirty years ago the *acqua alta* reached an incredible height and lasted two days and two nights. Since then . . .

"Since then it's never really stopped," I say to Kramer. "In a certain sense it continues to rise every day, and life in the city is getting worse all the time."

"But has the tide ever gotten that high again?" he inquires.

"Not quite," I tell him, "but last year San Marco and other low points were submerged forty to fifty times. Our own courtyard, right here, was flooded thirty-nine times in one year. And it can always happen again. They've been working on it, on and off, for the past thirty years — but we're still in the hands of God."

Discussion becomes more and more animated. But in only a few minutes . . . Damn! The water in the courtyard is already so high there's no getting through it; it's lapping at the stairs.

"How can it rise so fast?" asks Kramer, astonished.

"Because now," I have to tell him, "after they excavated those new canals for the oil tankers in the lagoon, the tide has become very swift. It sweeps into the city, the courtyard, the houses much faster than it ever did before. You have to decide right away: stay here or go now!"

"It's even worse when the water's dropping, ebbing back out," our friends inform dear Kramer, "from the lagoon to the sea. It does that much faster than it used to, too, and drags a lot more earth with it. So the houses 'walk,'" they explain, grimacing, caught between unease and hopes of a miracle. "Even this one, where we are right now." We listen to the creaking of the walls as they shudder. "They're moving up and down," say my friends, and they're right; more cracks appear with each high and low tide.

But the moment of enchantment has arrived, down in the courtyard brimming with water. Sewer water no longer, it is (or seems) a limpid gift from the sea. Beneath the full moon laughing at us — after all, she's responsible for all this — I can clearly see from my window the paving stones of the courtyard and the blossoms of the geraniums through the crystalline water. As the minutes tick by, it splashes up stair after stair, lapping at the second floor of the house.

The full moon, a little oblique now, lights up our small, submerged world like a lamp, shedding a milky radiance on the courtyard and stairs. Then Kramer descends into the courtyard, takes off his shoes, and begins to dance. This Swiss, this citizen of Zurich, has gone suddenly crazy and is dancing in the water with the moon. Is it Carnevale, or what? The surrounding houses come to life; people begin looking out their windows. They are watching Kramer, calling out to him, clapping for him from the windows, the steps, the terrace — everything reflected, doubled by water. Cries and compliments drift down to us even from the terrace on the roof, refuge of the young, where rock 'n' roll rumbles in the air among the restless pigeons, on the last night of Carnevale.

—❀ 61 ❀—

March, April . . . The months are passing but I've had no time for anything but work.

"Do people work in Venice?" asks Kramer very seriously on the phone.

Frankly, my friend, people work here just like anywhere else. It's not exactly like Zurich, but that's only because everything's so much more difficult here. Added to the usual Italian disasters are the purely local problems, as you know: *acqua alta, acqua bassa,* fog, lack of transportation, and the city divided in two, three, a hundred between the islands and the terrafirma — offices and stores half over here, half over there, many more over there now than here . . . Naturally, there aren't any cars here and the water taxis cost way too much; there's a real lack of public transportation. In certain sectors, I tell K, you work desperately for months at a time, without schedules, without any letup.

"So then why do you stay there?" asks Kramer. "What's the advantage?"

"I don't really know," I admit. It's hard to tell even him that the advantage is exactly this: this crazy, topsy-turvy world, different, nonsensical. It feels impossible to clarify on the phone like this — the international-cellular — that the only advantage of living here, in this world set adrift, with its sky so blue this evening I could dream my own death and die happy . . . that in a place like this (but there *is* no other place like this) the only advantage (I mutter to myself) is its continual *beauty*. However, even that is inordinate; there's too much of it.

"What's wrong with you?" asks Kramer. "I can't hear you."

But all I tell him is that here, in the evening, whether you're at home or out somewhere else — and if you're not too tired — you can half close your eyes and reconsider your day, find some quiet, read and write in peace.

"At least jot down a few notes in the diary I told you about," I say. "Do you remember? I'm writing this diary at night."

Yes, he recalls it well. But: "When's it coming out?" And in conclusion: "Come back to Zurich as soon as you can." He hangs up.

Then there's the other advantage (we have so few, I'll write this one down in the diary, for Kramer): if you interrupt your work for a moment and go out even just for a little while, you only have to walk about a hundred meters to get to the *osteria* Do Mori. A few paces and you're surrounded by people: it's an adventure!

Of course, this has its upsides and downsides. You may meet a friend or friends, or friends-who-aren't-actually-friends, whom you didn't want to encounter (I've engaged in evasion tactics six times today). Sometimes — rarely — you don't see anyone you know. At other times you run into a whole row of people, one after the other, friends, acquaintances, almost-acquaintances: a prolonged appearance-disappearance-reappearance of faces, each one waiting for you in its own unique way. I can't count the people I've met this evening in the two hundred meters that constitute my trip to Do Mori and back. And they're all so different, as if they had arrived at Do Mori from opposite planets, whereas, in truth, we live only paces away from each other. We exchange a greeting, a word, an allusion, a complaint . . . This evening the adventure, the little adventure of our encounters, the only one that matters in the end — we're still here; maybe we exist — seems to have no end.

Sometimes I go out for a moment because the air is stuffy in my study, among all its papers, and at others just to see, to find out: Who will I meet, who will I run up against? I dive into the river of unknown faces and here and there in the moving waters I find one I recognize. There are some evenings when they all seem to be strangers and others when every face I encounter is a familiar one. The problem is when I barely recognize someone, or think I do — but maybe it's someone else; I go into crisis.

The river is teeming with children, teenagers, old people.

Among the elderly I feel like a youth, and among the youths I feel old. The city is filled with the old and their shadows — so many of them! In other cities you don't see them; they stay at home, or go out in the car if they can. But here they're all around us, the old, those strange beings who are so invisible in modern cities. Wobbly on their legs, poor or well off, upright, crooked, lame, crippled, or halfway mad — they're with us, walking down the street right next to us, brushing against us. I'm so impatient; but my impatience falters in the face of this old woman smiling at me, this old man beside me who wants to talk. Always someone wants to tell his story or hear yours. And there's always someone (more than one) who talks to herself and sometimes provides her own answers. "Where are we, where are we . . . ?" repeats this one, hobbling slowly up the steps of the bridge with the help of his two canes. It's painful. Old people suffer and we suffer to watch them. They're not beautiful, most of them; they're ugly. But at least in Venice they're out here with us, with all the others; if it's not too cold, if they can still walk, if they can move themselves at all, they try to come out and join the human condition. Some of them get to the base of the bridge and stop; the steps are too hard. But at least they can sit down on a bench and dream and watch the pigeons, the people, the kids. At least they can see, watch, and observe, share life a little with everyone else. Watching is very important — this whole city watches itself and everyone else, gossips, chatters, and tells tales.

In fact, there's not much else to do except watch, observe, and exchange a few words — or a thousand. Later, at home, everyone tells and retells what they've heard, what they've seen — most of all, the old people. I saw this, I saw that; he was in a good mood, she was in a bad mood; she told me, he didn't tell me . . . We who are not so old yet don't ever say what we're thinking: that in too brief a time we'll be just like them, the lame and halt of the Gospel, coming to a halt at the base of the bridge.

Coming home from Do Mori after a couple of spritzes, I see it even more clearly: this is what we're in the world for, this is what we're in Venice for — to listen and tell, to tell again, to recount the same old story. And it doesn't matter whether it's true or not, whether the facts are pulled out of shape or not, whether there's a real exchange or not with the other person. This is just what we do in life: circle around within the range of various gazes and different generations, hoping that someone, *someone*, will listen and try to understand us. Then we go back home, our eyes crowded with the most diverse images of the *others*, of *them*; and theirs (probably) crowded with *us*, until none of us knows exactly who we are anymore.

Even this strange little diary written by night, these few lines I jot down when I can, when the evening is over (long over, tonight) is no more than a prolonged kind of *listening*, a fumbling attempt to hear and every so often respond, a kind of beginning-of-the-tale-told-once-again, limited, impatient, fraught with questions, observations, and infrequent answers. It's out of hand, running away with itself, elbowing up and down the calli like the people outside. It won't stick to a line of thought or a theme; it's more like the eyes I encounter and don't encounter in my peregrinations through the labyrinth. In fact, this diary is more driven than voluntary, I realize — full of hope and desperation, like my encounters on certain evenings as I wend my way to Do Mori. When I lived in Milan I tried to do this several times. But after a few evenings I gave up: all that came out was a journal full of traffic lights.

—❍ 62 ❍—

Hidden behind the well-known streets, the calli trampled by everyone and his brother, in the heart of the labyrinth, in the blind bowels of the city, within the dark lattice that takes your breath right away, here they are: Venice's unexpected gardens, her green spaces, her cultivated orchards, her trees. You have to earn them; you have to wind yourself into the innermost turns of the maze — but they're there, patiently waiting for you. I stumble upon one by chance: a great, green, self-sufficient space that incorporates it all — flower and vegetable gardens, wild woods and open meadow, and a bocce game in full swing, all in the hidden heart of the maze. A communal space, at the Angelo Raffaele. And after all these years, as is absolutely right, I find them here: my schoolfellows of old, playing at bocce as tranquil as shadows, as if all of life had not pressed down on their shoulders.

I thought I knew Venice; but it seems I know only the calli and rive that everyone knows, natives and tourists alike. Calli and rive that are and are not part of the labyrinth, that almost always circle the borderlines, signaling (or not signaling) the brink. Yet within them, truly *inside*, between the narrowest of the calli and the humped-together houses, just where we expect a definitive closure to the maze . . . they wheel open, they explode: the *gardens*, the great and small gardens full of flowers and vegetables, and the trees, singular, sparse, or dense as small forests, hedges and bushes, passageways, further labyrinths. And now the clack of the bocce balls sounding between the trees.

I end up strolling around a while with my old companions. Many of them have a garden beside the house, "at least a tree," they say. None of them is rich (they wouldn't be old friends if they were), but that tree feels completely natural to them, even casual, not particularly sought-after. When I think how much a single leaf costs in certain cities . . . We leave the park together, after they've polished the bocce balls one by one, and they tell me about their gardens.

Under his house at the Armeni, says Ernesto, there's a green hummock in his garden-park-meadow, surrounded by robinias, cypresses, and ailanthus.

Beside Ughetto's house there's a courtyard full of grapevines and a tavern with a trellis dripping fruit and leaves.

Behind Marta's house the gardens are so well hidden that in order to see them you have to peer between the houses from a certain distant vantage point on the bridge to locate the tips of two cypress trees, ever trembling in the breeze. After a while, according to Marta, the bridge — and we two on the bridge — begins to oscillate with them.

Paola's house is surrounded by a wild little woods inhabited by the remains of a century-old gazebo, three turtles, two robins, and Mino the cat, who will allow no other cats near him.

We walk down an incredibly narrow calle to Giacomo's house, which has gardens on either side of it between two low walls of yellow, red, and purple bricks. The scaling old stones speak of other, superimposed sets of mazes, now vanished or reduced to a handful of rubble. We can hear the slapping of waves in the nearby canal, although it's hard to tell where it is — in the labyrinth facing us, in the maze of the waters, in the paths of the boats and the waves . . .

In Claudio's garden there are more statues than trees. Frankly, all these statues annoy him. "They're old, they're corroded, they stand there and *look at you*," he tells me. "They're *insistent*. The trees watch you, but not the same way."

There are also — interrupts Nino-the-poet — some of the strangest combinations: gardens suddenly blocked by rows of small houses, bordered on one side by a voluble canal and on the other by a dark, voiceless calle, its black alley waiting. The houses stare at each other, face to face, through their windows over the gardens, their rows of shutters glaring at each other as they have for centuries. In the evening as soon as dark falls the shutters are closed, the hidden spaces behind them whispering like the trees.

Vitale's courtyard, on the other hand, which seems little, actually goes on forever, since it's adjacent to the cloisters of an abandoned monastery, an enormous, empty, devastated place. But Vitale's garden continues "over there." No one is ever inside the monastery except in summer, when a handful of Poles park themselves in its least ruined wing. It was they, the Poles — the neighbors have no doubt on this count at all — who brought the white *fringuelli*, the Alpine snowbirds, back with them from Pomerania. And as far as diarrhea goes, one *fringuello*'s worth three of our pigeons. Now the courtyard, the cloisters, and the roofs of the monastery are snow-white with guano and full of visible and invisible birds: a great wheeling of loons, grebes, herons, and cormorants. Every once in a while furious alley cats appear on the wall next to the playing field, evicted by the cormorants. They're awaited in turn by the dogs barking on the riva, purebreds and mongrels that would like to study the situation more closely, whose chief dream is to join the circus inside the monastery walls.

At San Nicolò, on the other hand, in the vegetable garden next to the church, all there are are monkeys. With their bright pink bottoms, they swing from the fig trees, the grapevines, the garden walls. Every so often one of them tries to clamber up the loose stones of the *campanile*. And here's Fulmine with them — our madman called Lightning and also Scirocco. When he can, he tells me, he serves in church; it's not easy to find altarboys for the Mass. He wishes the monkeys could come to the services. "They have it all," he says, "except they can't speak."

Talking with all these old friends, listening to their stories, I realize that *garden* in Venice means a garden with statues, sculptures, adornments, wellheads, and taverns — and with beasts of all kinds. In the gardens, the courtyards, the orchards, the meadows and campi, trees, human beings, and art always share space with our friends the cats and dogs, the birds and monkeys, as in a painting by Longhi. And the soil is rich, giving birth to powerful trees, although it would seem impossible for such huge trees to spring out of so little earth — "bitter," they say, "because of the sea salt."

Mine (my landlords') is an ex-big-garden, now sliced up into three or four parts and bereft of its former unity and integrity; it's also missing its statues. These great white sculptures vanished in the course of one night; or rather, someone vanished them — but they've disappeared for all time. The sack of Venice has been going on for two hundred years, and it isn't over yet. The statues' pedestals, circular or octagonal, remain, bearing the marks of invisible feet. The statues' shadows also remain — you can see them in the big photographic map of the city recently put out by Marsilio; they were photographed just a few days before their disappearance. The older trees suffer, stripped of their companions, the ghosts they had lived with for centuries. Maybe the younger trees suffer, too, scattered among the vacated pedestals.

"Owners gone, everything sold," says Radar the madman. He seems to be the only one who's noticed their disappearance. None of the others, the "sane" ones, have noticed at all. Someday they'll be found in America, those statues, in some city made out of cardboard and highways in the American desert. Out of their element, stranded in the wrong country for another century or so.

The two Englishmen who have bought the tract of garden in front of us aren't out of their element at all, definitely not stranded. They wander up and down, humming happily to themselves between the empty pedestals, dressed in gondolier's shirts. They're taking the place of the natives, who are vanishing like the old statues.

—◦ 63 ◦—

Spring arrives and everyone hits the streets at the first touch of sun and doesn't go home until late at night: old people, teenagers, children, workers coming and going among piles of rubble and the new fiber-optic excavations that litter the city. There are words in the wind, calls, greetings, and sounds of all kinds — Venice is coming to life. The voices of the first tourists echo from the canals and we can't even pin them down yet, can't tell where they come from. We're out of practice. And, ah — here it is, the first time this year: "*O Sole Mio*" from the gondola tour in Rio Malcanton.* It's the usual singer, looking just a little more tired than last year. Windows are thrown open so that the city can enter the house. Venetian houses, with their many windows, seem made just for this — to let the city in — and vice versa, in a continuous exchange. Soon the mosquitoes will make themselves known.

"The gnats, too?" I ask Martino. "And the midges?"

No, not this year.

"And the water?"

---

*This is an especially absurd in-joke played on the tourists, who recline mouths agape against the plush cushions of the gondola while a singer, usually accompanied by an accordionist, very seriously sings "O Sole Mio," a Neapolitan song. Venice, of course, is rich in its own dialectical songs, but tourists can't recognize them. — TRANS.

The water won't be half bad; it will be less polluted, Martino assures me, than in the past few years. Martino feels these things in his belly, months ahead of time.

Dogs, cats, pigeons, seagulls, flies, ants, blackbirds, and sparrows are all strolling along the canal banks companionably, among the human beings. I can picture the mice, lying in wait within their holes in the banks. Life parades itself in a thousand forms. The cries of the gulls resound from the sky and water (in the streets, they're almost always silent), endlessly repeated, almost exactly alike, like the calls of certain ducks in the country marshes. Herring gulls and what we call in dialect *magoghe* and *cocài*. One lone robin, only one, since robins aren't clever; they're way too beautiful and the cats get them every time. Then there are the grebes, the *fisoli*, at the vaporetto landings, always more of them in and out of the water, even bobbing along in the vaporetto's wake. I've been told there are geckos in San Stae, sunning themselves in the courtyard. The islands are teeming with egrets and *marangoni*, a kind of cormorant that swims unbelievably well, eats prodigiously, and has branched out into the city, making itself at home on the more solitary canal banks.

"Too many," I say.

"Maybe too few," Martino retorts.

"And these," I inquire, "are they wasps or bees?"

"Wasps at this point," he informs me. "The bees will probably be along soon."

Columns of ants march up the marble walls, the stucco, the pipes, into the kitchen and beyond. Gorgeous grasshoppers and clumsy, drunken May beetles are everywhere. Cinches crowd the grass, big, green, and silent. Large and small crabs inhabit even the most peopled fondamente — a good sign. There are eels in the canals, and tiny fish in compact schools: swarms of silver-blue wriggles and flashes beneath the green water. Throngs of mullet, gold-silver, blue-gold, leap in the bend of Rio della Toletta and navigate the canals beneath the Bridge of the Fists, the House of God, and the Banks of the Slavs.

Even the mute dog is out and about. I recognize him: it's Bibo.

He doesn't talk, the kids explain to me, only shakes his head: *Bi* — *Bo*. Then the other way: *Bo* — *Bi*.

Chiribiri the cat flies past, high over the calle, from the eaves on one side to the wall on the other. Radar stops to look at him: "Wish I were a cat." Chiribiri looks back at Radar with sympathetic understanding. But watch out, Radar! Pigeons are relieving themselves from on high, damn them anyway. You must never stop in the street for any reason. Never.

"You have to come to the Richiamo," Martino tells me. I think he's talking about a tavern. "Sure," I say right away. "I'll see you tomorrow."

⟶ 64 ⟵

But it's not a tavern. I'm confusing the Richiamo with the Bacàn. Still, I manage to make it to the Richiamo and meet up with Martino and Martina. Martina is a champion, or championess as they say, of women's rowing, *la voga femminile*. She participates in the *regate*, and every so often she wins them. It's incredible, as small as she is, how much energy she throws off. After twenty minutes of her rowing, starting off from the Fondamente Nuove, we've arrived.

Here it is, the Richiamo: stretches of sand, shoals, sandbanks, and "little woods" made up of holm oaks, tamarisks, and ailanthus rooting around in the water. Nameless up until yesterday, now it's the Richiamo.

This year, evidently, about two hundred thousand aquatic birds have chosen to winter here, more than double the human population of Venice. Pink and white herons, great white egrets in the hundreds, thousands of grebes small and large, ten to twelve thousand teals, and over a thousand cormorants have all found a home here. Even ospreys; and who knows how many naturalists from every territory on earth, to study and observe them. I've never seen so many beasts (the birds, not the naturalists) in the lagoon. They are now considered to be of "international importance," Martino assures me, "according to the Ramsar convention"

— these and all other areas where at least twenty thousand specimens winter. There are ten times that many here, practically in the city. But in Venice, and in the places around Venice, no one cares very much about the Richiamo, sighs Martino. All this beauty, life incorporated in these fascinating forms, these trees, these waters, these wonderful winged ones, these voices of birds far and near, this strange music pursuing us now, only a pace away from the city — no one cares very much about any of it. Yet this music means that our whole environment, including the sea, has improved in the past few years; that it's become less polluted, more limpid, more livable. As soon as we dump a little less filth in it, the sea lends us a hand. *"El mar xe più contento,"* the fishermen say: the sea is happier now. Still, notwithstanding all that we've dumped into it over the years. These are hopeful statistics, to be taken in, to be emphasized right away — but will it last, or not? At the moment it seems so. The lagoon has been preserved over the centuries, the millennia, because we've desired it so; and that's still true today.

We head back toward home, to the Fondamente Nuove. The death of Venice, the slow consumption of Venice: there's no one who doesn't at least mention this when talking about the city. But this new information, this news of the sea's improvement over the past few years, this rushing back home of the birds and the fish, *"el mar più contento,"* is a true gift in extremis from Mother Nature to Venice. We need to acknowledge and record the signs of hope one by one here, they are so precious.

In the bar at the Fondamente Nuove, gangs of kids are playing at video games, dreaming of race-car collisions. Only one seems to be thinking of something else, seeing some secret of his own. I'm on the lookout for more signs of hope; and as we walk back out of the bar, I see them: repairs and restorations, hundreds of restorations, even here on this bank where we're standing, which up until yesterday was riddled with holes. I don't know if there's anyplace else on earth where so many works of restoration are under way; it's impossible even to list them. Some are excellent, others questionable. And while it's true that they never suffice, each one is a step in the right direction, another sign of hope.

Meanwhile, as improbable as it seems, life is returning to the canals, the lagoon, and the sea. We must note this down in our inner diaries, the ones all of us write even if we don't write a word, when we begin to live in Venice once more. And anyone who's putting words down on paper should underline this, and repeat it: Life, in its many forms, is returning to Venice. Hope and the city: We can't afford to lose either of them. We must continue to desire and love them, cost what it may. And it costs a lot to repair so much devastation, wash clean so much pollution, save so much fragility. Yet this city of exodus and abandon, of continual degradation, of medieval impracticality, this city "that is no more," despite all its troubles, remains one of the most livable cities extant in the modern world. Even for us human beings, not just for the winged inhabitants of the Richiamo. Signs of improvement are rare, here and everywhere else, but there are good souls scattered all over the place, even in Venice, and they do what they can. To say this, to know it — it's always a start.

—◦ 65 ◦—

During April and May, as I return home in the evening from work, I see fireflies in the courtyards, in the gardens under the houses. In the countryside — the ex-countryside — where I was born, there haven't been any for years. You must come to Venice, to her ancient gardens, if you want to see Pasolini's fireflies now.

So many things, so many lives long vanished from the countryside of my childhood I find again here — in an environment so different as to be almost its opposite. The ancient walls, which have disappeared in so many cities, are still fully alive here. Moreover, they're loved, "considered" as my aunt Rita used to say, "valued more than the new ones." I glimpse them here and there in tracts between the canals, these walls out of my memory, bearing the scars of their great age, in exile from the lost countryside, perched over the water and inhabited by ghosts. Tonight thick swarms of fireflies hover above the old bricks and the clambering vines unfurling into the first, delicate, wild white roses. I breathe in a strange tangle of scents, a mixture of must and sea salt (that's Venice) and the clean odor of grass (the lost meadows), stung here and there by the perfume of some hidden flower. What were those beautiful, scentless flowers with the violet bulbs on the path to my grandfather's house? Wild peonies? Jerusalem artichokes? I don't know anymore. How we've lost our connection to Earth, her secrets and odors. I only know that the wild peonies, like the birds, have migrated here to the islands. Fireflies and flowers are still in the world — on the Riva dell'Arzere, to be precise.

―⟡ 66 ⟡―

We've traveled to the very edge of the lagoon, first by car, then by foot, then by boat, reaching Valle Averto in midmorning. Ughetto, one of my recently rediscovered school friends, has become the custodian of the "valley" between the lagoon and the mainland, and has brought me here to show me the thermal inversion.

"Only one step more," he explains, "as you approach the water, and you can feel it get colder — or warmer — in comparison to the continent."

That's exactly what he calls it: "the continent." This change in temperature is accompanied by humidity, pressure systems, and fluctuations in wind. If you're on foot you can clearly define, step after step, the curving line — sometimes parallel to the coast, sometimes not — of the thermal inversion. Along this line, shaped sort of like a long S, a wall of wet air rises up from the lagoon, thickening and thinning, expanding and concentrating at various differing points, like a great wave, part sea and part atmosphere, in a slow process of evaporation. At this time of day, says Ughetto, when there's not even the slightest sea breeze or *bava*, we can feel it, follow it point by point beyond the shadow of a doubt, touch the curving border of this moist environment with our hands. A single step backward returns us to the terrestrial weather of the continent, materializing out of the streets, the houses and campi and street signs. A single step forward steeps us in the weather and atmosphere of the lagoon, a purity of distance no matter how near things may be, wrought out of vapors, uncertain spaces, sfumato.

This windless morning is heavy with the sirocco, and the great wall of damp materializes in the air as an infinity of tiny spheres, microscopic globes like infinitesimal soap bubbles. It's more a slow *sfumando,* a fading, shading, and thinning, than a typical sfumato, dissolving and nebulously refracting the rays of a white sun, motionless in its preordained place; the water, too, all rainbow bubbles and tiny, repeated, prolonged, tireless reflections until you don't understand the sense of what you're seeing. In the lagoon the weather "happens" at eleven o'clock every morning, explains Ughetto, who's been watching it for the past forty years. And he's right; every morning at eleven the wind rises, whether it's a breeze or a gale. Here and there, suddenly or little by little, the wall of bubbles, the curving crest of vapors breaks up. Or else it swells, rises, and expands. Bubbles, mist, and vapors: the daily trilogy of weather and water. It depends on the wind, the pressure, the light — and who knows what else that I can't see, and Ughetto knows but doesn't explain: "Feel it, there it is."

A brief breath from the south, and the moist clouds spanning the whole edge of the lagoon, departing from all our real or presumed S-shaped frontiers, move out to fall gently upon Venice. They drop down onto the compact aggregate of houses, the great Fish made up of canals and canal banks, islands and mirrors of water. They permeate the islands and those of us who inhabit them so that we become, not so much human beings, as fish ourselves.

It's the moment in which the cloud overtakes the city from every direction, rising up from the water and descending from the

sky, swirling out in tendrils and fingers of fog, unfurling from
every underground tunnel, climbing up out of the ancient wells,
evaporating from the sewers and drains, stagnating on the canal
banks, invading the calli, winding around the trees in the campi
and flower and vegetable gardens, in Castello, Cannaregio, on
the Lido, wrapping the boats and ships in a shroud, penetrating
both stones and bones. It can last this intensely for days, but
whether it's dense or light, it's always around; there's no escaping
it. My naturalist friends call it a "humid environment." But where
will our little colored boat end up, between these low clouds and
the fog? The humid environment's fine for fish, I grumble to
Ughetto, and for a certain number of pelagic birds; but I don't
know about us, with our rheumatisms and arthritic conditions,
our thoughts and hearts . . .

"No, it's good for us, too," Ughetto corrects me. "If it's damp
you breathe better, and then there's no dust."

"But if it goes on like this for a week or more," I tell him, "we'll
end up transforming into flamingos, marsh ducks, wading birds . . ."

"Sometimes," Ughetto assures me, "we actually turn into fish.
We don't realize it," he laughs, "but it's true, we turn into fish, *in
pesci, in pesci.*"

However, there's no dust — he takes up his theme — and
where there's no dust, there's "no sense of death. It's dust that
makes death."

"Maybe," I say, "but the damp doesn't help."

But the seagulls confirm his hypothesis, a dense flock of them
sweeping over our heads through the gray air. Their flight exudes
a tremendous life force, perfect in and of itself, seemingly unre-
lated to the world we find ourselves in, independent of the water,
the sirocco, the fog and the mist, life and death, and our little boat
skimming the waters beneath them.

But they've sighted us now, the gulls, and they're calling out,
"Who are you? Who are you! Make yourselves known!"

"No," I say, "we're not fish."

At this news they rise up once more, splendid, elegant, and
indifferent.

"And to think," says Ughetto, rowing peacefully *alla valesana,* "there are people who shoot them, those beautiful seagulls, just to have something to shoot."

—◦ 67 ◦—

But it's not just the atmosphere and the weather that change as soon as we're on the lagoon. Clock time changes, too, every single time. We're forced to set our watches and selves to an entirely different rhythm.

You step down from the train. You get out of the car. You take a few paces, climb onto the boat, and it changes. The tick-tock of your watch is different. You can see and feel it right away: the velocity of the vaporetto is more or less a twentieth of the velocity of your car. You can feel it on your skin as soon as you set foot on the boat — that you're not so much traveling across the water as uneasily decelerating, coming to a slow halt. Motion and the measure of motion, the sense and rhythm of time are completely different now. Perhaps time expands; for sure it slows down. Will we live longer this way?

With everything slowed down, our glance becomes sharper and more attentive. We're less insensible, and things become more visible; at last we can see, observe, and feel. Walls and houses slide by. We glimpse someone on the riva and are struck with a desire to reach out and communicate. Little by little the miracle unfurls within us: we see as we feel and feel as we see. Even the sky changes. To be more exact: *this is the sky.*

It's pale blue, pearled and gilded, multiplied by the water it hovers above, according to the day and the hour. And it's azure fog, white wind of the bora, mist swirling into the soul — it depends on us, on what we let in. In the big cities at this time of day the sky is piss-yellow; you don't even know where the city *is. This is the city.*

Does the good Lord change, along with the tick-tock of the clocks?

The world of incommunicable sensations and feelings changes. And we *will* live longer here, one way or another.

—⌐ 68 ⌐—

There's always somone out on the streets; the sound of human footsteps, whether few or many, is ever present. And words are always circling in the air, running down the calli, skimming over the water from one bank to another. Their words, our words.

There are moments, tracts, entire long stretches in which the words floating down the calli and under the portici merge, mingle, and become indistinguishable, turning into a kind of buzzing or hum. At other times and in other places they leap suddenly into the air out of the empty calli, crossing paths, bumping into each other, rebounding from the walls, and then fading away, followed by mysterious echoes. A little farther on they turn back on themselves, mired and sinking in the damp fog or whisked away by sudden gusts of wind. Where I am at the moment (I don't actually know where it is; the name of the place was written on the wall at some point, but has long since worn away), words fly low between the windowsills, leap between the dormers like pigeons in love. I stand and listen to them for a moment from Rita's second-floor window, surrounded by geraniums.

Love affairs, moods, troubles, money, illnesses: although everything under the sun drifts up from the continuous stream of people passing below me, these are the themes that really count.

The husband of a bone-thin blonde has left her, "the pig," so now she suffers, she insists as she passes under the window, "from constipation."

"Do you know Oliver?" asks the old woman with the cane, her tone urgent.

"Yes, he's the mailman."

"No, no, I mean Rita's cat!"

It's almost pure Ionesco except for some local inflection.

A little before the bridge, the words stop making sense. The people stop, too, in a traffic jam of confused sound. At this moment you can tell what the weather's like, what season and hour of day or night it is, just by the tonal quality of the voices.

The most incredible phenomenon is that, whatever the hour, you can hear invisible passersby; it's their words that are visible, that come and go in the air. A bit farther on, it's opposite: visible people, inaudible words. I go downstairs to check it out, confirming definitively, as far as Rita's concerned, that I'm "absolutely mad."

I decide to research a stretch that seems important to me, in this matter of opposing phonetics: the Toletta, which is at once a street and a small neighborhood. Starting off from Campo San Barnaba, from the Casìn dei Nobili, I walk toward the Bridge of the Marvels, le Maravegie.

First of all, Campo San Barnaba is open — phonetically speaking — in five or six directions: the four cardinal points + southwest + the canal. But to leave it you have to duck under the *sottoportico*, where you're bathed in echoes, footsteps, strange boomings, stifled murmurs, mingled words, compressed dialogues, a whole fluid mixture washing between the ancient vaults of the Casìn dei Nobili.

As you exit the portico the street broadens, winding between two little gardens; although they're minispaces, they're large enough to let the bottlenecked words rise and expand. But right away there's the bridge. So now the words expand not only in the air, but also over the water going its own way under the bridge. The sounds slide across the water, are reflected and lost. If you step down into a boat for a moment and press your ear to the water's skin, the words are still there.

After the bridge, you walk along the riva (Fondamenta della Toletta) suspended alongside the rio. The rio is particularly narrow and bordered by banks on each side, so that people on both banks can (and do) talk with the people in the boats. Moored and attached poop to prow, one to the other, glad to be going nowhere, they wait for the time to shimmy by between words. If you speak to them, the boats respond, but above all they reveal, without words, the existential, communal rhythms they share with us, and we with them. From the two facing banks, from one side to the other of the canal, everyone is conversing — from the boats, from the bridge, from the windows and street . . .

Questions and answers tangle, greetings and kisses smack and mingle. Not a single person ducks out of sight. Very few are in any kind of hurry. No one, it seems, has a plan; as soon as they can, they stop and talk. What joy, just to talk.

The canal curves to slide slowly alongside houses and gardens; and the words in the air lose their force, slipping away between branches, winding through the wisteria. But they'll gather again and come back . . . each slightest sound returns to its source, like a bartered word given back.

Now the street enters its most musical stretch. We must stop for a moment, and listen and wait.

—◦ 69 ◦—

In its most musical stretch, the calle widens imperceptibly like an accordion, then immediately folds back in on itself, swerving, turning, and continuing onward four complete times in just a few meters until it reaches Ponte delle Maravegie, the Bridge of the Marvels. And there are as many variations of tone in the air, of timbres, echoes, and vibrations, depending on the varying moods of the conversationalists: in their grievous complaints, comical quips, and sometimes demented asides. Then there's the endless *tic-tic* of shoes against stone . . .

They pass on; they're on the move, words and moods alike, and hard upon their heels come the next ones. Always others, always more. All the words in the world — in a single dialect at the moment — crowd the tiny calle, along with humanity's breath, its sighs and cries, its whimpers and whispers.

Two young girls step swiftly out of a bar — both of them tall and pale with endless black hair and exquisite faces, both of them smiling and laughing. They don't speak, only laugh; it's their way of talking, between themselves and to the rest of the world. But what's behind those beautiful faces? Time, which is following them even now, at this exact moment, right here in the happy calle, dogging their footsteps in silence, as it is ours.

I've just become aware of how often, up until now, I've thought and written "street" — a legacy from Milan. In reality these brief passages between houses change names and structures ten or twelves times in the course of about two hundred meters. "Street"? Hardly. They are *sottoportico, casìn, callelarga, callelunga, callestretta,* or simply *calle*; they are *ponte, fondamenta, salizzada, ramo, piscina, ponticello,* and *riva* . . .

Here it is, the Ponte delle Maravegie: not only one of the most beautiful places I know of, with its houses lowering and rising, constantly changing profile, tilting forward, receding, vanishing altogether — but also a tremendous aerial exchange of voices, familiar and unrecognizable, lost and rediscovered. Meanwhile, gigantic *serliane** open out onto the water and Gothic windows multiply, gracing the facades; small and large gardens reveal themselves, their trees frothing with blossoms.

And that's not all there is to it: the Maravegie is also the stage on which "characters" are exchanged. People wind to a close, come to a halt on the bridge, finish (or seem to finish) their conversations. But it's not a definitive conclusion; more often it's a change in companionship, the discovery of a new conversational partner and the beginning of a new dialogue, here on the bridge. The same kind of exchange is going on in the waters of the canal and on the banks at the foot of the bridge — paths of earth, paths of water, bearing away our words.

I'm walking behind two native Venetians, both very serious, in the middle of the bridge. They're discussing inspiration, talking about the "parallax" or something, and the fifth or sixth dimension . . . It seems about right, on the Bridge of the Marvels. But then they stop abruptly and burst into laughter. Ah, they're making fun of the last Biennale. They laugh helplessly, almost weeping, in

---

*A *serliana* is a three-part window with a broad central arch, supported by two dividing columns. It is named for the architect Sebastiano Serlio, 1475–1554. — TRANS.

great shaking spasms; and a passerby begins to laugh with them, in bursts — from sympathy, maybe, or autocombustion.

And here are two others, locked in an embrace, wound around each other as if they were alone. She's insisting that *she* (someone else, the other woman) is the one who wants to leave him. He's assuring her that it's *he* who wants to leave her, is leaving her. Who knows what we want, on the Ponte delle Maravegie.

All I know is that her lovely insistent voice, the beautiful rough voice so typical of Venetian women, belongs to my next-door neighbor.

—❦ 70 ❦—

Between Sant'Aponal and the Rialto there's a continuous shifting of types of streets and the names that go with them. This is a small quarter of San Polo devoid of canals, but within a short distance I count twenty different sorts of streets: *Calle, calletta, ramo, campo, campiello, salizzada, portico, fondamenta, sottoportico, arco, volto, crosera, riva, ruga, corte, pissina, piscina, pasina* . . . What's a *pasina*? Nobody knows. It's probably the opposite of a *piscina*: it's that bit of the *Piazzetta* that lies between the *portico* and the *riva*. It must have made sense at one time; every name springs from a reason. But what does it mean now? Are there other *pasine* in Venice? Yes, two or three; and they, too, are more in the air than on earth. Or in the water. Is it a joke, an invention? The word feels concrete, though, not like stuff of fantasy. The chipped and worn writing doesn't help, either; if you peer at it closely, it seems to hint at some prefix or completion of the name, and we're left to invent the rest. These names-not-names are part of the ambience of the city-that-is-and-is-not. In the end, everything's a work of imagination.

In this "subquarter," as I call it, there are neither canals nor bridges. But as soon as you leave it, the bridges break out all over the place, go wild in every direction. The Crooked Bridge and the Straight Bridge, the Bridge of Swords, the Bridge of the Pots and

Pans . . . Then there's the Bridge of the Tits and the Bridge of the Melons; the Bridge of Horses, the Bridge of Madonnas, the Bridge of Lambs and the Bridge of Christs, the Bridges of Ducks, Dyers, and Queens.

As usual, the names of the bridges and streets are rendered in Italian or Venetian seemingly at whim, creating a fantastic, non-stop confusion. The most incomprehensible are the names that have tried for the dialect but gotten it wrong. So the sounds that the streets send up, the voices circling and echoing, are more helpful and important than the many names they've been given. Every stretch has its own resonant codas, false notes, warbles, and trills. Here at the Gàffaro, on the big, lazy, lovely canal bordered by breathtakingly beautiful banks, syllables broaden, words settle slowly and wait for you to come along. But what, exactly, is the Gàffaro, what does it mean? According to my friend Bruno, it's the name of an ancient Levantine quarter, probably in Constantinople. And in fact, all kinds of exotic peoples live around here, as you can clearly tell from the writing on the walls: Albanians, Armenians, *Ragusèi*, *Guardiani*, and Turks. For centuries, without any passports.

─⟨ 71 ⟩─

My friends continue to flee from the islands, abandoning Venice, making me desperate. They leave for a bunch of different reasons. I discuss it with Kramer who, on the contrary, has come to stay for a while; he's trying to buy an apartment. They leave because their work has shut down, because their offices, their large and small businesses — whether they worked in the private sector or for the state — have folded. They leave because houses cost way too much and are damp, uncomfortable, impractical, uninhabitable. They leave because transportation is difficult, arduous, slow, having always to span both the streets and the water. They leave because there's no car by the house and no cheap taxis ply the canals; because stores are closing every day, so that it's always more of a challenge to find bread, fruit, or vegetables somewhere near home. No supermarkets have sprung up in exchange. Thus Venice is subject to the highest peaks of inflation in the whole country. The so-called touristic monoculture jacks up prices on a daily basis and puts the weaker segments of society out of business. We are steadily diminishing in numbers and also in money. What's worse, we're losing our best and brightest, our young people, our up-and-coming minds. The minds that remain here, I say to Kramer, after a certain passage of time, deteriorate. (There has been research on this; there are statistics.) Some of them, after a while, go mad.

"Do they realize it?" asks Kramer, worried but not too worried, as if what I'm telling him is excessive, when in reality I'm understating the case. Or as if Venice had a special star that would save her and hers from everything.

"Of course we realize it," I retort, "but there's not much we can do about it. We live between plunder and colonization — even by you, looking to find a house for a few days a year, and leaving it empty, closed, locked up tight the rest of the time, days or years . . ."

Even when they build big new offices here on the island so that people will stay— as was the case with Enel, which we're passing right now — it doesn't effect much of a change. The employees can't find homes here: houses cost too much and are old-to-ancient, too big or too small, more or less in bad shape, forever in need of repair and restoration. So the workers move to Mestre, on terrafirma. That's how much it helped to build the Enel offices here; now everyone has to commute.

We run into our friend Lina, who shows us the two apartments from which she's been evicted in the past three or four years. Time rolls on, and the apartments — "Do you see them?" — are still empty, exactly the way she left them. The last straw was that up until yesterday the piazzetta she lived in, her own campiello (when it was still inhabited), was called Campiello dei Morti — Little Field of the Dead (one of the many to bear that name) — and, she says, "they were all alive then."

It's true that she could sue the landlords who kicked her out and are now holding the house empty; she might even win her suit. But it's costly. And so she's gone off to live in Spinea. It's a lot cheaper there, she says, "but it's not Venice." There are thousands of reluctant exiles like her, more every year, who look back and wail: "It's not Venice." In the Campiello dei Morti the old survivors speak all the time of the "castoffs" who have been forced to leave, who have been thrown out of the campo, out of the city.

"Soon we'll go, too," says old Gaetano, "but not to Spinea, to that other place." He gestures vaguely at the clouds overhead and gives me a half smile.

Although Venice is emptying, real estate agencies (I'm looking at one right now) are proliferating. I spent years of my childhood, I tell Kramer, in this *quartiere*, in the poor streets filled with people and swarming with kids — how well I remember them all — and now it's almost completely empty. However, the once-poor calle (we read on the real estate brochures in the window) has "character." I'm assailed by a fear that the silence I love so much at night is nothing more than a sign of the growing void. A silence with "character."

—◦ 72 ◦—

"But the modern world. . . ." begins Kramer.

"The modern world," I have to tell him, "at least up until this point, has been based above all on big industry and automobiles. It has been, and still is, *against* Venice by definition."

I say "up until this point" because it's entirely possible that in the near future new technologies that don't require a lot of space, endless highways, and concentrations of factories may find a way to make their homes here.

Kramer and I are on our way to the Maritime Station, to the Scali della Scomenzera and the Tronchetto — great empty spaces of water and earth. A crowded vaporetto rumbles by the naked, deserted wharves of the Port.

"The peripheries," remarks Kramer. "In any other city they'd be built back up already. Just think of the docks in London."

"But London's not anything like this," I say. "London digests everything: any constructive intrusion, whether it's ugly or lovely. Venice suffers from poor digestion."

Kramer laughs. "But if Venice is going to save itself," he insists, "it will save itself here, on the edges." He gazes at me interrogatively as we step onto the next vaporetto, which will leave us off at the Tronchetto.

I have to admit that he's right. I, too, think that it's time to put these kilometers of empty, abandoned docks to good use. We bat the idea back and forth for a while. A new kind of cohabitation needs to be attempted, between what remains of the Port and what could be made into a new, modern quarter. New houses, interspersed between marine industries.

"It could be splendid," says Kramer, enthused. "Probably even the railway station could hook up in these empty spaces with some kind of parking lot for arriving cars. Maybe a new kind of Venice could be born here."

The idea alone makes us sick, as we both admit right away. The very thought of a new version of Venice invading, crossbreeding with the ancient miracle, makes our hairs stand on end. Even though we're on the peripheries, to introduce modern construction into a city like this . . . We'd run the risk of altering profiles and labyrinths, of ravaging the whole integral sense of the city-that-is-a-work-of-art. We'd imperil, maybe even destroy, both the reality and sensibility of measurements, rhythms, footsteps, encounters, thoughts, dreams, and perspectives umbilically linked to Venice — goddess, being, or monster — and to our own selves as we maneuver through the labyrinth. Who knows if the novel inventions we dream of will be able to coexist with the ancient realities as embodied in her? We have few examples to inspire us among modern cities. Perhaps people can only build suburbs now, not real cities.

Still, we must try. Venice is dying as she is. And here on her edges are the spaces we could use to augment her possible houses, and thus, hopefully, her population. We have the chance to do something really new. Absolutely new, as conservators (as we are) — as we must be . . .

"Or else," according to Kramer, "we'll have to try half and half, do you think? Since places like Venice have always held off the new until they could mix them smoothly into the old?"

As we talk, we walk, until without realizing it (it doesn't take long) we've circled back into the labyrinth calling to us, into the little calli between the canals.

And here we find them! in the tiny canal drained for repairs: the ancient tree trunks we've so often hoped we could see. These are the trunks that were driven into the mud to support, first, the earth on the water, and second, the houses. Millions of tree trunks; and we, who live by their grace, had never seen them before.

"Yes, they're still here," says the shipyard surveyor with a sweep of his hand, "keeping the faith, doing the work they started so long ago. All of Venice, over the centuries, has been built and re-built upon them, the same exact trees."

"The *same* ones? Always the *same* ones?" asks Kramer, incredulous.

"Of course," the surveyor explains. "When they had to rebuild, or when they made modifications to houses or palaces, or when they had collapsed through old age or earthquakes, or when wealth required additions, or when fire devoured them or the tides overtook them . . . everything new was still built on the ancient trunks. Venice has gone through her many changes, but they never change; they are now and forever the same trees, and they are immortal. They never die, only petrify. They never die," he insists, "no matter what happens above them."

So now we know, and say to each other, astonished, that this is part of the same labyrinth made of water and earth (and now we know) of eternal, subterranean forests. We dream of doing something new, but the labyrinth commands us. Innovation will be hard. Perhaps the edges have been left empty for us, for what we wish to attempt, if we have enough courage and imagination. With or without submarine trees, with or without constituent ele-

ments, we don't know. We know very little of Venice and even less
of her peripheral places. Probably there are expanses beneath us
filled with submerged trees — and also tracts without them, composed only of sand, earth, and water as in the most ancient of
times when they had to construct the very ground on which to
place their feet. Over this foundation, little by little, they raised
the most difficult and delicate city in the world.

"And maybe that's why," says Kramer, aptly as usual, "it makes
us afraid — because all of us, here inside —" he makes a gesture,
here inside "— carry around our own piece of the labyrinth. From
way back when, damn it all, from way back when, here inside."

He says, "we" and "way back when" as if he were truly Venetian
— as all of us must be, at least in some small part. And he's right:
it makes us afraid because it all *depends on us* — on all of us, on
what we have "here inside."

We've only begun to glimpse it, the labyrinth.

PART SIX

The Ghetto

—❀ 73 ❀—

Only a few steps farther bring us to our ancient Ghetto, and to a
different Venice altogether.* Or are we mistaken? Is this still the
same city — here among these calli, a little grayer and lonelier
than the ones we've just come from, in an atmosphere that feels
closer, more still, more all-enveloping?

---

*The word *ghetto*, or *ghèto*, actually originated in Venice and at first simply meant
"foundry." One particular foundry was located on a Venetian island later used to segregate the city's considerable Jewish population. By 1394 Jews in Venice were already
required to wear a circular yellow patch on their clothes "as large as a bread roll"; a
century later the mandatory distinction had become a yellow beret. This was waived
for physicians (who, for the most part, were Jews); travelers en route; during
Carnevale, when all class and religious distinctions were thrown to the wind; and for
the first three days after arrival in a new town or city. General prejudice grew so strong
that in 1569 a body of judges in Mantova decreed that any Jew who had sexual con-
gress with a Christian woman would be subject to the removal of both testicles. Despite all of this, Jewish communities flourished, especially in Venice. Highly cultured
and possessed of great business acumen (many were moneylenders, since this occupation was forbidden to Christians), Venetian Jews became so prosperous and powerful
that the Republic's authorities decided to segregate them on the island that had
housed the foundry, or *ghèto*. Its four gates were locked every night except, of course,
for physicians, who were granted the privilege of healing their Christian clients.
Venice, however, was not the main culprit, being exceeded by the Holy Roman
Church: In 1555 Pope Paul IV, in his *Cum nimis absurdum*, decreed that all Jews
should be isolated in locked communities, forbidden to accumulate more than a spec-
ified number of possessions, and required to wear the distinctive yellow signature of
their faith. They were also forbidden to sell anything not already used. However,
Venice, never a friend to the Papal State, applied hardly any of these strictures and its
Jews continued to prosper. But segregation *was* enforced nightly; thus Venice has the
unhappy distinction of having named the first ghetto. — TRANS.

A dark portico departs unexpectedly from the crowded riva in Cannaregio, a corridor of walls without cardinal points, which leads us to the most defined/undefined space in all of Venice: the great *campo-conchiglia*, the shell-shaped piazza that lies in the heart of the Ghetto. Flowing behind Martino and me are our equal and contrasting shadows; when we speak to each other, our voices are low and uncertain.

The small cupolas of the synagogues are barely visible above us between the silent roofs, restless and shifting as in any Venetian architectural profile. The linchpin of the campo-conchiglia, as of the whole island, is the gravitational center of canals that here as always, everywhere in the city, circle and surround the space they delineate — joining, uniting, closing, or separating them — depending on human decisions.

The work in progress on Rio della Macina reveals the ancient, mud-slathered poles that support these modest houses from deep under the water: the same tree trunks that uphold the palaces, distant or near, the places invested with wealth and with power. The few people we see here, on either side of the destroyed "guardian" gates, on either side of the bridge spanning the rio, are no different from anyone else: they have the same gait and glance, speak the same dialect, reflect the same recurrent solitude of the islands. The first tender leaves are unfurling on the trees; the old bricks and vere da pozzo are steaming dry in the sun; and the Istrian stone is a dazzling white after the rain shower. The exact same thing is happening all over Venice, in every one of her campi.

Our "home Ghetto" or *Ghetto nostrano*, the very ghetto of ghettos that signified, for centuries, a separation between human beings in the heart of a wealthy and powerful city, has now come to resemble its ancient mother-stepmother, just as Venice has come to resemble her segregated child. This melding together is the opposite of what is happening in so many other ghettos in the world, be they old, new, or as recent as yesterday's news. Here the urban framework, the setting that makes us fall silent — all we can do is listen, think, and most of all, *feel* — transports us, takes hold of us by its bridges, calli, and portici, which are almost identical, stretch after stretch, to so many other expanses of water-stone-earth, ones we've rediscovered, ones we've just come from, actually, to get to the Ghetto. Venice has a tremendous capacity for assimilation and repetition, reflection and response, between island and island. But here mergence surpasses itself, creating two coexistent, reciprocal worlds: the Ghetto and the City, at once similar and unique.

Old and new divisions speak from every stone: Venice is evermore separate from the rest of the world, while the Ghetto, up until recently, was separate from the rest of Venice even as it nestled within her. This, then, is a double Venice, a city within a city. It seems to the two of us here, as elsewhere in the city, that it takes hardly any time at all to cross a campo, duck under a portico, stroll down four little streets and two bridges — yet in truth there is no end to it: present reality and all that lies beyond it are constantly transforming, changing places. If Venice tends to the *oltre*, the beyond — a perpetual *oltre*, from her watery past to her problematic future — the Ghetto-within-Venice takes this to the second power.

"Our *Ghetto di casa*," murmurs Martino, "is homeopathic to us, like all of Venice." He looks at me under his lashes. "Even more so."

It seems to me that he's summarized our first impressions very succinctly. We stop and dawdle like two little boys on the steps of the Ponte Nuovo, whose two hundred centuries or so are more than apparent.

But the moment he says "like all of Venice," we realize that he's wrong. The houses around us are too narrow and high for the usual proportions of Venice. Their facades are pierced with rows of tiny windows, not much more than a repetition of little holes. Each window seems to be crowded with human faces, packed all together as in no other place in the city. The domes of the synagogues reach desperately for some small ray of light from above.

The *bimah* insinuate themselves between the compacted flanks of the houses in an attempt to finally look out over the water. This place, which had seemed so similar to so many others around it, now transforms in both shape and significance, showing us its search for space and air, the hopelessness of its life.

The campo-conchiglia resounds, to our inner ears, with echoes that turn into cries, resonances revealing the betrayal of faith, atrocious sufferings alleviated only by the rare ray of hope. Venice always seems to set limits, visible or invisible, within her fluid walls, to even the most terrible of tragedies; but this has gone beyond them and cannot be contained.

Only the innermost weft of the city remains as if waiting, patiently dormant, for events to flow through the weave of time, its successive strata receptive to every variation of of fate, humbly willing to preserve within themselves memories and the echoes of anguish. This aggregate structure — made up of centuries, voices, the interpenetrant scales of the Fish — offers up at each step we take a unique and unspeakable history, expanding through all of its strata. Lumps of lime and clots of whitewash combine with memory to become the burls of a communal tragedy we attempt to approach, in the hope that by suffering together we will never again be so deeply and terribly divided.

In the brief space and minimal time we've spent here today, sorrowful echoes, uncertainties, memories, and gleams of hope have wavered time after time between similar and diverse, observable and elusive. Although the two of us are walking among the sharp corners of the ancient stones and chipped bridges, in reality we seem to be *waiting*, unable to compose our thoughts in the slightest, only brushing against a great accumulation of gathered and repeated sensations. As we head toward home, Martino remarks that the expression *Ghetto di casa*, frequently used around here, is a contradiction in terms but also an acute interpenetration of opposites that moves our hearts. Until at last, on both sides of the razed remains of the "guardian" gates, Venice's luminous light brings us back from our scaled layers of imagination to this great sweetness in the air, diffused and limitless. We pass under the ancient "cries" of the stones toward the crowded canal banks, toward home — yet it is as if we were always, we two, in the solitary Ghetto that we love so much.

As soon and as often as we can we return, today or tomorrow, morning or evening, even if we can't linger for long. We go in and out through a little garden and big nursing home, skirting elementary and middle schools, ancient shops, magnificent synagogues and precious archives, bare funeral chambers, and venerable museums. Martino's sense of it being "homeopathic" follows our every footstep and makes more sense all the time. Perhaps it feels like the right definition precisely because it's so uncertain, semantically speaking; the Ghetto feels intensely homeopathic to us because of our own internalized suffering, which we share with everything we're seeing around us. We feel this small space, this tiny city-within-the-city ever more profoundly in our own depths and islands, which counts so much more than what we see or think we see through our eyes.

Bit by bit the *Ghetto di casa* puts me in crisis concerning my journal, this diary-tale that is no more than a continuous attempt to bring some sort of unity to what I'm observing. But here in the Ghetto I perceive ever more clearly that there are places in the world where the act of seeing is less prevalent and less important than in others, where dominion is held by voices, memories, interior resonances — where, rather than looking, you must listen and feel.

Between its presences and its absences, the Ghetto is the place *par excellence* in which we confusedly feel so much more than the apparent can account for — where we *are*, even without observing, speaking, or writing. In it the infinite voices of spirits are always coming and going, indifferent to these ephemeral sheets of paper, winding like wisps of wind through the stolid walls. Thus the walls become, more than anywhere else, a communal countenance of the collective, channeling the close and distant echoes of all the voices ghosting up out of the past.

In the dark portici, in the shell-shaped square surrounded by synagogues, in the brief splashes of light where we've stopped for a moment, in the whole tiny city of speaking walls, we two who had at first come "just to see" are continually at risk of contact with the unobservable — with the invisible.

Or perhaps the level and tone of the observable lift between these poor houses, so that it's harder for us to follow it; we need to raise the quality of our glance, our register, our very breath. So we sum it up for each other, in slightly more secure voices: It's a place with a powerful soul of its own. It is at once composed of profound distances and repeated recognitions and, despite its utterly unique aspects, also shares something of the soul informing the imperiled marbles and restless canals of the poorest and loveliest sectors in Venice lying outside it. That is, if Venice still has a soul, which we're not too sure about. If she doesn't, we say (maybe she's lost it or maybe it's in transformation), then this is the one we need to seek out, understand, and adopt as far as it's possible for us to do so: *this* soul, this violated soul of the Ghetto. We must never abandon our search for the breath that continues to animate the world between heaven and earth, despite all the ghettos — the voice ever calling to us, urging us to become human beings.

By now we love them more than ever — these high, dramatic houses, these ancient synagogues, these magical spaces, these dark and narrow portici — just as we've come to love all of Venice more, wrapped around her old Ghetto.

We feel ourselves at home here at the moment, in this most moving, most heartbreaking campo-conchiglia; even more than in any of the other shell-shaped squares that leap immediately to mind, unfurling mysteriously here and there from the mouths of narrow calli all over Venice.

One that springs inevitably to mind — a campo not far away, yet which seems to me at this moment to belong to another world — is Campo San Polo in the Rialto, with its splendid conchlike curve. But it feels almost *too* beautiful for the vulnerable heart and eye, thus distancing itself from us a little in these years straddling the millennia. It lacks a certain resonance; that is to say, in San Polo you can't hear the substratum, that dim, continual sound that may or may not be the water, the sea. We hold within us, as well, the shell shapes of San Giacomo dall'Orio, Sant'Angelo, San Michele in Isola, and Piazzetta San Marco . . . But none of them are as definitive as this one. Everywhere in the city, of course, it's the water that determines the spaces we hold in our mind, the curves of the houses, the bends of the palazzi, the shape of the shells. But no other wheeling of water and stone continues to speak, to express itself, like this in the Ghetto. Here sorrow and flight, fear and suffering have steeped the stones' very fibers for centuries, culminating in the extremities of our generation, the terrible years of war, genocide, extermination. All this is still perceptible here; you can touch it with the palms of your hands. Grief is embedded in each tract of wall; suffering exudes from each curve awaiting our comprehension, rendering these stones not only unique, but sacred. The whole of the Ghetto is sacred and resonant, urging the inner self to awesome and awful reflections. Scenes and events, though we take them in through our eyes, are not about the scenario, the theater of life. Instead they tend to deliver to us the essence of all that has happened — the things that have befallen this world, the lives of others, the life of the self.

In confirmation, here are the interior passageways, the paths of reunion and flight, the secret stairways between one house and another, as if they were one. Our friend Leo is up there waiting for us: Leo the rediscovered, known as Leòn when we all went to school together. We hadn't seen him since we were children together; yet here he is now, smiling at us from within his two little rooms. One of them is spilling over with books, the other with old and new computers, mountains of cassettes and CD-ROMs, fixed screens and laptops, antiquated recordings, everything from Hebrew and Israeli folksongs to the most extreme rock 'n' roll. Even his old violin is hanging there on the wall. I recognize it with a strange sense of guilt, the young boy Leòn's little violin, which he played to amuse us.

Leo, too, is moved. He shows us the walled-up doors and the secret doors, the preserved and demolished passageways, the long, silent, stairwells. He seems the incarnation of an old Orthodox rabbi, stepped out of centuries of tradition, sorrowful and joyful at once.

"There are others all over Venice," he says, "secret tunnels of every sort. Everywhere," he repeats, "all over the city." He speaks lightly, introducing a vein of humor into his words so that we won't be too overwhelmed by these homes full of sad, unexpected surprises. The Ghetto, he assures us, is not the only place in Venice "with these ways of escape, these theaters and means of disappearance."

But this was not theater, dear Leo-Leòn; this was no staged scenario (we know, we feel so deeply, so dreadfully in our hearts); in no other place in Venice was this drama played out. No other human beings have needed, from time out of mind, paths of escape so urgent they opened up out of the family kitchen; no other human group has had to choose, for so many centuries, to wall themselves up alive or vanish from the face of the earth. Even in Venice. Even in Venice.

We manage to carve out a space and sit down at last, in the midst of the strange pile of computers and other modern *diavolerie* that seems to be both the means and end of Leo's days. It's a tangled nest of this and that, past, present, and future, opening to and withdrawing from the outside world, a kind of silent, labyrinthine stairway. Emotional events chase each other across our old friend's face like clouds against the sky: encounter, acquaintance, knowledge, colloquy, escape, and return, all embodied in his eyes and smile.

As we take our leave he accompanies us to the stairs behind the cupolas of the synagogues. The wall drops off sheer below us to the solitary, enclosing canal.

"We'll see you soon, Leo, we'll expect you at the park for bocce with Ugo, Paolo, and Enrichetto . . ."

He promises that he'll come. We all act as if we had last seen each other only yesterday evening, when in truth half a lifetime has passed, and with it an epoch of hell.

Martino and I wend our way home at our own peculiar pace, walking through San Geremia, San Zaccaria, and San Moisè. Hebrew saints of the Christian calendar — who knows if the latest papal decrees have decided to recognize them or not? Rome has never influenced Venice too greatly. Here in the city great churches are dedicated to them, whole zones and neighborhoods are named for them. They manage to be prophets and judges of Israel and household saints without any visible conflict. There are a lot of them, too: we count ten or so just from San Giobbe to San Daniele, democratically scattered throughout rich quarters and poor. This is pretty much an anomaly as far as Christian, especially Catholic, cities go: it would be difficult to find even one in Milan, say, or in Rome. But here the Old Testament prophets and judges cohabit happily with San Marco, San Martino, and San Francesco, rubbing sanctified shoulders together on all the islands — aided, of course, by a certain number of angels of uncertain origin. It is probably this kind of encounter, this sort of spiritual mingling, that leaves the most profound traces in the track of the centuries, in the desperate attempt over time to render humanity human. This evening we two find ourselves in one of these places devoted to a double-equivocal saint; and though we're just a few paces from home, we stop, feeling/hearing something that emanates from the echoes of the Ghetto's campo-conchiglia. We are seized by a need: need of a memory, need of a prayer. Even we, who no longer know how to pray.

Homeopathic: Venice and her Ghetto. Naturally it's subject to whim; there's a different Venice, a different Ghetto, and thus a different Ghetto-within-Venice for each of us. It all unfolds in so little space, but time . . . We can stretch time in the moments stolen from the fury and din of our daily lives. We can stop every once in a while for our individual Stations of the Cross, trying to tap in to and maybe even decipher some cry in the silence among the tender green trees, the waiting canals, the portici steeped in the dark. The resonances carved like secret passages in the labyrinths of our hearts need no more time. To the degree that we're sure what we feel, they live within us; nor will they abandon us. Notwithstanding our limits, they are ready to be passed along.[*]

---

[*]By the mid–seventeenth century, more than 5,000 Jews lived in the Venetian Ghetto. Now, of the approximately 600 Jews left in Venice, only five families live in the Ghetto and only two synagogues still hold Sabbath services. Nevertheless, the Ghetto is home to a Jewish library and various kosher food shops and bakeries. There is also a Holocaust Memorial and a Jewish Museum — the Museo Ebraico — but the sad truth is that the Ghetto today is more a conduit of history and memories than a contemporary Jewish community. — TRANS.

PART SEVEN

Summer's End

The resumption of work, after August's vacation, is always hard in September. During summer we put off innumerable tasks, saying we'll tackle them in the fall: and now we have to do them. September becomes the briefest and most breathless of months.

It's also the most dreamed-of and looked-forward-to month by workers in Venice; but it's never actually *reached*, never lived in the way we had wished it. We're prickly and restless, waiting for something more to happen, something transcending our daily troubles and woes. We're waiting for the friends we have no time to meet with, when it's just the right season for getting together; for those who left at the end of summer, whom we won't see again; and for these beautiful evenings with their siren calls to come out, out, onto the endless lagoon of autumn, when we know we have to refuse. The entire city is signaling summer's end, splendid sunsets setting fire to the sky as if to illumine the end of the world. All that awaits us on the other side of this time of transition begins to reveal itself in the course of these magnificent evenings in brief, urgent pulses like alarm bells, while we're stuck at work in the ascetic room we call the Projects Office. Such precious hours, these fleeting days of September, with their luminous golden light encircling us and our projects — their waters, banks, and drifting sunsets attempting, it seems, to prolong some ineffable piece of our own existence — but they pass, they all drift away. The places we glimpse are the places attached to our pasts, profoundly transformed by the span of our lives, intervening. How we wish, now more than ever, that they would not vanish forever, without us!

But there's nothing to be done about it: September is rolling to a close, and I haven't been able to find a moment in which to meet with my friends, even briefly. It's the loveliest month of the year, yet I haven't found time or nabbed even a minute to jot down a line in this journal of mine.

—❧ 75 ❧—

However, there's always October. In the office, though, we've managed to lay out a year's worth of work, while outside the gorgeous October evenings await us like newfound lovers.

In fact, these may be the most beautiful evenings of the entire year, always briefer and more filled with yearning, the last of all before fall overtakes us, before the sudden change of the so-called legal hour — daylight saving time — disrupts our lives. Now the light is still lingering, spinning itself out just for us, whose workday seemed endless. We step out of the office and it's like tumbling into the sea — a sudden, total immersion in the last rays of the sun, which now seem to gather and strengthen on the *molo*, the bridges, the infinity of banks and canals. Walking back home through these ephemeral evenings begins to feel like a real return.

There's a moment (does it change every night?) when the street-lamps come on, most unfortunately, ruining the finale. But they're not as disturbing at this time of year as they will be later, since the sky is still clear. Some evenings the air is a pale green, limpid and green as in the verses of certain Persian poets, while others it's red, orange, and azure, splashed with the indescribable flickers of light emanating from the water and the potent damp breath of October. It's the hour of enchantment in this most enchanted of cities. I return from the office to the house, striding exuberantly up to the familiar, familial courtyard, the kitchen upstairs announcing itself by the bright light spilling out of its windows. I've walked these same streets a thousand times, a hundred thousand times. This is the living geography of my childhood, youth, and adulthood; an ongoing map of a history like so many others (although it feels unique); a shaky chronicle from which we are — I am — ever eager to delete the silly, senseless, ridiculous aspects; a drama with its moments of anguish, sudden departures, and the tentative groping of fragile new roots. In fact this return home from the office becomes a route leading backward in time, a remembering of things, an anxious and tender investigation of places well known but never seen enough. For the moment I'm barely brushing against them, both places and images, rediscovering and ear-marking them, so to speak, setting them aside for when I have more time to explore them. But they're there — that's what counts — they've returned, they exist, in every stone and breath of wind, in every glance of every human being I encounter.

The city wends her own independent way on evenings like this one, flowing slowly upward from the earth and water toward other, inconceivable lagoons, lights, and clouds. She'll wait around for us for a while; but we're always having to stop, go into some shop, take care of some human errand; and then she continues on, flowing through paths of her own creation. We're too slow, we don't know how to follow, our dreams are too meager. We always have schedules to live up to, ours or other people's, even in these evenings of October. But *she* rises upward, in this beginning of autumn, in this prelude without end, toward hours far beyond our ken. *She* is not concerned with daylight saving time, but only with the eternal, which even now is readying new routes for us to travel.

The sensation, on evenings like this one, that the city is going her own way but calling us to follow her is at once multiplied and rendered more subtle, in place after place, by the *beauty* pursuing us. The entire trip home from the office, from any office to any home here, is informed with such an intensity of beauty that we wish it would let up sometimes, not keep following us wherever we go; we push it away, seek to leave it behind with every step . . . And yet it's just this tenuous, unyielding beauty that transforms the brief stretch of street into a path winding through the eternal; or at least holds out the illusion, the hope that it continues on- ward beyond any we've walked in this world. There is something about it that leads us to believe in an experience more intense than any we remember or rationally expect — one we can just barely intuit, between campi lilting in a different kind of motion, visible and invisible bridges, and fleeting canals. Yet it's one that so many other beings, passing through the world with us at this selfsame moment, are also trying to intuit, to grasp as best as they can — to love, alongside us. And in this openhanded beauty grazing us quietly, patiently brushing against us, nothing is showy or unknowable, nothing is excessive or grandiose, so that it may approach us more closely.

The men and women of this generation are coming and going along the canal banks, seeming ever smaller and more fragile with the gradual advent of night. In our human lives an intimate tie binds our footsteps to the things around us, which we hope, perhaps illu- sorily, will lead each of us — this evening, tomorrow — to happier hours than those of yesterday. All of us, be the sentiment superficial or deep, feel the possibility — the necessity — of interpenetration with places like this, if we're capable of feeling at all. Our lives are so brief. The places, too, may be temporary, but maybe not; maybe they'll last to continue on, among the many human beings who will come after us. Nothing at all ends when we do.

All of a sudden the streetlamps sabotage the fading natural light — Venice's ugly modern lamps, worst among them those awful neon tubes at the vaporetto stops all up and down the Grand Canal; they're frightful. Farther on toward home the last of the lampposts continue this unhappy series of crude, new, glaring lights, from the Punta della Dogana and along the whole length of the Zattere right up to the Accademia and beyond, in the most magic places. The streetlamps play an important role in Venice; they're an integral part of the atmosphere, the sfumato, the con- trast of shadow and light. They should be soft, subtle, enveloping — the contrary of crude. They should wrap gently around the soul, not beat on the stones.

Soon, sometime this week, darkness will drop as suddenly as a curtain the moment we leave the office. The "legal hour," right; daylight saving time. We'll step out under the new superwatts that are supposed to be helping us home and wait for the vaporetto under the damnable neon tubes, dreaming of lingering evenings of light that are lost in the past.

—◦ 76 ◦—

I'm much more taken with the little seas — I realize in these last days at the end of the summer — than with the great oceans. The oceans are too much for me. At first sight, at first breath, they fill me with enthusiasm; the first long waves and endless horizons move me. For a time my enthusiasm continues. After a while I lose contact; in the end I find I'm bored by the ocean.

I like to keep the coasts in sight, not too far away from the boat or the ship, the islands with their trees and houses within arm's reach. I like the little sea without end that starts in the city beside someone's garden in the quotidian quarters. Here by us the ocean starts at the Zattere, the Giudecca, the Gallerie dell'Accademia and continues through the rive of Castello, swirling into the Arsenale and Forte di Sant'Andrea . . . The mirror turns, widens, and expands at just the right moment, leaving you to invent for yourself not only the distant reaches of the lagoon, but also the most unknown and mysterious seas. I've already seen the known oceans; it's enough for me now to imagine them.

Today the lagoon is all a series of great luminous mirrors, the last of the year, scattered with tiny islands carved out of the light. The air is so clear that the islands stand out in sharp relief against the horizon, one after the other, revealing their every detail point by point. We're moving slowly, Martino and I, almost minimally, in our drifty old boat, our *deriva*; but they, the islands, glide forward to meet us more swiftly than usual in the clarity of this air, revealing their holm oaks and saltwort, raising up hedges of tamarisk burned by the summer sun. On their shores we see pink and white herons, men at work, ancient solitary basilicas, and patches of wilderness as pristine as in the first days of creation.

We feel we've gone back, in our little boat, to those days; and instead we're constrained, willy-nilly, to throw together the poetic and the quotidian: little houses, embankments, shacks perched on poles, boats getting ready to cast off. Both the signs of man and the ancient basilicas, which seem no more than the markers of time, slide away together over the water under the breath of the breeze. On certain stretches of the banks the fishermen turn around, some of them, and give us a wave or shout out a greeting — even now, at the end of the second millennium. Human presence matters to me; even here on the sea I continue to seek it, as I seek out the seagulls, the egrets and grebes, and the fish, be they tiny or huge. Life in and on the water is not so different from human life on the land. For the great depths and marine monsters, the gods of the deep or the distant, I care not at all.

The wall of the cemetery slides by, with our dead and their crumbs of memory; we circle the Forte between our ancestors and their faded tombstones. Those poor dead ones crossed, like us, these mirrors of water, truth or illusion; they breathed in the same air, even purer than it is now. They, too, reveled in the long, luminous days and suffered from the same winds, tides, tempests, and troubles of every sort.

This, *this* is the sea for us, Martino and me: an almost-sea, an under-sea, with the Venice-ship drifting away uncertainly into the distance, turning into spirit — but never wholly invisible, appearing and disappearing in the first fogs of autumn. After each disappearance we wait uneasily for her return.

—͡ 77 ͡—

In these last, lovely days, I decide to take the *motonave* to the Lido. The *motonave* is the "motorship"; up until now I've been traveling over on the public *motoscafi*, the "motorboats," which are always crowded with people and ride very low on the water.

They're too closed; sometimes I feel like I'm suffocating. According to my friend Giulia, the *motoscafi* are dangerous, "as closed as coffins," especially in rough weather. And she's right: years ago there was a real disaster. But Giulia is young and beautiful, and the wind is kind to her upthrust breasts, which always seem to be *smiling*; and if there aren't too many passengers we can sit together outside, on the tiny poop deck, and feel ourselves to be very much in the water. During these days of soft sea, the boat seems to adhere to the barely moving liquid beneath it, and its course is as light as a bed set afloat or a gently rolling cradle, rocking its peaceful way across the lagoon.

The *motonave*, on the other hand, rides high on the water, which today is greener than ever, except for occasional pale blue swirls and powerful dark blue daubs. From the basin of San Marco to the island of the Lido the ship traverses our own home sea, steering a course through the very heart of the city. It's a quarter of an hour of joy, a splendid movie unfurling on the lagoon. What a shame that Giulia's not here, with her smiling breasts. The openness of the sky and water feel immense as you emerge straight out of the labyrinth; but it's all navigable, all recognizable — not a big sea, not an ocean. It's also a trip that doesn't cost much for all that it offers. Some elderly people — and some young ones, for that matter — make the journey both ways two or three times before nightfall. Flowing by under your eyes are mirrors of water unknown until now, or not known well enough although practically under your house. Both nearby and farther away, the islands entice and intrigue you; pale bell towers slant up against the horizon, and behind them swells the gentle line of the hills. This *motonave* is almost a real ship (five hundred tons, perhaps?), and the water it navigates shares the characteristics of a lagoon with the deep flavor of the sea: our open lagoon, our *mare di casa*. Meanwhile, Venice is sliding away along her own shores, her great, rich, most beautiful parts alternating with her poorest, shabbiest, most beautiful parts, continuously doubling and mingling, opening and closing. Even from this vantage point she changes within a few minutes, in a few meters over the water, just as she does when you're walking through her on foot. Venice: micrometric and inordinate, immeasurable. Even from a ship.

This short trip gives you a feel for what it must have been like, departing from Venice, bound for the open sea. Her shores have undergone many changes, of course, since the most ancient of days; but the sense remains of a slow farewell, house after house, window after window. You feel you're absorbing the beauty about to vanish, vanishing, already vanished, one facade after another, one profile after another, in order to bear it away with you, to hold it close and never forget it, even when you're long gone. For soon we'll all be long gone. Before I go I'd like to get to know that house better, the one with the big windows carved out with such whimsy, as if just to open the walls; or that Gothic facade, so rhythmic, so impeccable with its little geometric windows, which is maybe an imitation but beautiful just the same. Or this other one gliding by where one of my sweethearts, Stefania, used to live and be always up on the roof-terrace — who knows what terrace she's standing on now? Maybe she's just down in the garden. She was a peaceful sort and had a weakness for peonies.

The two "bridges" of the *motonave* await us. From the first and lowest, if you gaze into the water rolling away from the side of the ship, you can clearly see — you can almost touch — the continually changing colors, the direction and bends of the currents. For a moment you can even forget the problems that come with this water: pollution, poisons, toxic disasters — all caused by us, passengers in this world, in this city. If you climb to the second bridge (there might be a third one up on the prow) you can see from on high the distant islands file by and, closer up, the white clouds; islands and clouds are exchanged again and again, mirrored, doubled, reflected. There are few people on the bridge of the prow at this hour, each one keeping a proper distance from the others and watching intently as the coast, the shores, and the islands slide by. Even the commuters who make this trip every day keep their vigil. One of them takes a deep breath of good air, breathing in with it the infinite landscapes he's seen in his brief journey by ship, and tucking them away inside to carry off with him.

But here we are already, in the second part of our outward-bound trip, crossing a stretch of lagoon that's widening all the time. A light azure has overtaken the green, becoming a clear rich blue as we move forward, with here and there a stain of color deep as ink. The lagoon extends itself, reaching out to the north and south; and the houses abandon you suddenly, leaving you only a memory of their spaces and pasts, smiles and dimensions, people and peonies, and now . . .

Now, within a few instants, this space of water and sky seems to pass over some border and cross beyond time. It no longer has any reference to time as it's measured in cities or houses, by people's smiles or tears. It's just time, undistilled and unbroken; it's just space in its purest form: a tract of lagoon and of sea that exists in the realm of the infinite. At this moment I wish I could melt into the great river of water, whose very breath has transformed into something colder, more open, into something warmer and ampler. Among the coasts disappearing into the distance and the green islands rising up and falling away, isolated bell towers turn into clouds. And now a brief game between the finite and infinite begins, in this stretch in which the lagoon expands, elongating simultaneously toward the north and the south as if following some meridian of its own, its barely definable horizons tilting toward the eternal, its winds gusting, its mouth turned to the sea.

Such magic can't hold; all too soon the world reassumes its recognizable, measurable aspects. Yet in its wake there's a sudden silence on board as the ship glides through the water for a while without the *ron-ron* of its motor. The middle-aged woman who's just finished work and is standing beside me loses herself for a moment in the noonday sun, letting the wind wash against her and forgetting her household and whatever troubles await her. It only lasts for a moment — the infinite, in Venice, is brief. And there she is, behind us: Venice, our Venice. How hard it is for us to separate from her, to pass from one island to another; as if we had been together always, we and the city, as if we had been born together and grown up together, and now we're voyaging away among the islands forever.

We are about to arrive at the Lido: the island, or the idea of island, that divides the lagoon from the sea, immersing itself now more in one, now more in the other. Among the houses and trees coming forward to meet us, there's one house I'd love to know better: a strange Moorish affair, with cupolas and pergolas and aerial passageways that may be waiting for me — or at least I feel it's waiting for me each time I arrive at the Lido. Here there are bicycles, buses, even a few cars, the *viale*, broad streets and gardens. At this time of year, when not many people are around, its island character asserts itself more strongly day after day. The Lido is even more of an island than Venice, especially now with the fascination of a sea-lashed winter looming closer and closer. But summer will follow; already we begin to dream of it opening out over the sea.

Our return back toward Venice is an entirely different journey. It gives you an idea of how it must have been, in the past, to sail into the city of magic — built on it, inhabited by it. It's a very different experience than arriving by train or by car; only arrival by airplane is at all comparable. But there's not enough participation in a plane; you always have to wonder whether the city you're about to land in is this one or some other one instead. The means of transportation is divisive.

But this way, we approach her while listening to the benevolent vibrations of a familiar motor and standing on the deck of a familiar ship, little by little participating in the return of every light, every shore, every house and window. We see it all with our own eyes, no screen between us: Venice coming to meet us as we arrive across the waters of the lagoon, by means that are still very human. And *her* eyes, the city's eyes, are so responsive that they return our every glance: lights and reflections greet us from every window; the journey becomes ever more an encounter, until at last the ship turns slowly between San Giorgio and San Marco, between one window and another, the better to let us see into her heart and touch the center of the miracle that endures.

The ship makes its silent headway along the riva and deposits us, with a sense of sweetness, right in front of San Marco. For a moment I find it difficult to step away from it — *Eraclea*. Before Venice was born, Eraclea was the first capital in the lagoon, an island long vanished beneath her green waters. I won't forget her, this *Eraclea*. Fourteen minutes, outward-bound; fifteen minutes returning. Too little. Now the sea-city, as always immersed and emergent, captivating, winds away into her own labyrinths beyond the golden cupolas, gilded this evening by the last rays of the sun. Or by reflections from who knows where? Perhaps from her "sister" Marghera, the one we saw from the plane: hangars, oil tanks, cranes, loading docks, power plants . . .

— 78 —

Streets, squares, and canal banks are all more crowded than usual, as if everyone wanted to take advantage of the last evenings of light. Statistics tell us that in the last three or four days of October there are more tourists than ever. There are no data on how many Venetians are out on the streets, but they seem to have doubled since yesterday. No one wants to lose the light, the city, the day slipping away.

In the long, packed calli — even if I walk very swiftly, even if I run, or try to — there's no salvation. I duck into a detour or two in the parallel calle but am soon drowned once again by the human river, by words, syllables, tones, modulations. Every day, even today.

"But today I'm not talking," a man walking next to me keeps on insisting. "Not saying a word." However, he continues to speak, trotting along by my side, airing his views on everything from weather to politics, until finally I'm forced to turn and look at him.

You study them and they study you. Not too overtly, just up to a certain point — the sudden point of arrival, which is different for everyone. It's a microcosm reflecting the larger walk of life, in which someone walking next to you may suddenly vanish, and you may never see them again except in your heart.

It's not a *listòn* or a *struscio*, this crowded calle,* but an essential, daily route used by people going to work, going shopping, walking to school or back home . . . so many of them . . . tall, short, lame, lovely, ugly, young, old . . . Actually, it *is* really a *struscio*, a sort of continuous *struscio*, a rapid but always slyly observant promenade. Noticing our neighbors or the people in the street is second nature here, even when we're in a hurry, even when we have things we have to do, at whatever hour of day or night. It's never intrusive — Venetians don't stare — but it's enough. Judgments are formed.

Here's a sudden apparition in the crowd: a long row of Polish women of all ages walking single file, each of them holding a life-belt firmly in her hand so as not to get lost — God forbid they should get lost — as they head toward the Sanctuary of the Salute beneath the angels in the eaves and the Gothic windows, the impassive cats like ancient bronzes, the pigeons ready to let fly at the first raincoats they see.

Standing at the foot of the bridge, I notice the prevalence of women today, climbing up the steps. The less visible their faces, the more leg they show — it's human nature — in whatever season. Even if the ensemble is not so great: strange big bottles of legs in continual motion are ascending the bridge as I watch, large pink columns topped by the tiniest skirts, hiked up as high as they can get them. At certain times of year they make more of an impression, but at others they're putting themselves out for nothing; it's a waste of energy and effort. Passing naturally and unselfconsciously between their ranks, climbing straight up the bridge, is the most beautiful woman–human being I have ever seen.

The most beautiful for me, that is, in this moment. It's individual and inexplicable, what calls out to each of us. Rarely is someone the most beautiful of all in everyone else's eyes. In fact, a thin young man suddenly pushes his way through the crowd and springs up the steps at a run toward her (she has her back to him),

*A *listòn* is a promenade, given up to strolling and people-watching. The most notable is Il Listòn adjacent to the Procuratie in Piazza San Marco. A *struscio* is a Sunday promenade, deriving from the verb *strusciare*, to rub together. — TRANS.

and catches up with her, laughing out loud for joy. But she's
someone else; he's made a mistake. And so she vanishes, or it's as if
she had vanished: he descends the steps indifferently; he never followed her, never saw anyone. A few paces more and they all disappear as if they had never been, as if nothing had happened at all on
the Ponte delle Maravegie. Perhaps something passed by that for a
moment took on the strange form of a woman; and now something
remains that has taken on the strange shape of a city. How many
times the episodes and encounters of my life have vanished or
reappeared in random gray, ordinary places in which both human
beings and objects have seemed all out of place, therefore unrecognizable — and I've felt despair. Here, now, they all assume their
right, inalienable places, in this city that is, at the moment, awash
in a pale rose light; they're as recognizable as it behooves them to
be, sweet with just the right sweetness. With this beauty of theirs
hovering on the interrogatory, poised on the threshold, no more. If
it went any farther we'd be lost in the dream, or perhaps in the reality. It's the moment when looking — which is everything, almost
everything in Venice — is no longer enough, when you have to tilt
your ear toward the sounds.

And here comes the tinkling that you expected.

—❍ 79 ❍—

She arrives and flies up the bridge, descends, turns around, and
climbs back again. It's the young dwarf who's so *simpatica*, dripping with silver and gold-colored dangles, ringing and tinkling
wherever she goes. I've seen her around here quite often, draped
in her charms and necklaces, her many different pendants, her
chiming little bells. And now she's flying up the bridge, with her
restless smile and tremendous, low bottom, her ample, mobile
hips; she, too, it's clear, wants a role in this play. But now, on the
other side, she comes to a halt, sits down on a bench at the vaporetto stop, and opens a book. A book, I'm telling you, in Italy!
Not a magazine, not an illustrated paper! Does this mean that her

role at the moment is more spiritual, more inward, indeed more literary than she's led us to suspect, displaying her charms and dangles up on the bridge?

But no. There's the man who takes care of the four trees in front of the Accademia — young, handsome, sturdy, with a face that's perhaps somewhat stolid. She gazes at him hungrily from her bench; she's quit reading. Her eyes flash, tearing him away from the colossal German, somewhere between forty and fifty and dressed all in blue from her head to her feet, who's walking up to him, looking as if she could eat him, damn her. Aside from everything else, this enormous German woman is so badly dressed: a ridiculous little blue hat, a three-quarter-length blue jacket, blue shoes, electric blue eyes straight out of the northern skies. Frankly, she's frightening. Trotting beside her is her girlfriend from southern Italy, who's fat, dark, and greasy with blank black eyes. They approach the gardener together and begin to talk to him.

But now a new variation on the program arrives, blocking my view: a long row of English school-choir girls. They're still very young, but already they have the lost eyes and enormous chin that come only from England — an incredible file of huge chins and jutting jaws, sprinkled with tender freckles. Their legs, like haunches of ham, are bare to the wind, but the smile between those eyes is always eager.

As far as smiles go, though, I know a little band of Anglo-Danish women, all of them between the ages of twenty-five and thirty, with eyes that recharge themselves regularly — with sympathy, kindness, joy, and surprise — at every step they take. They are the greatest women-with-smiling-eyes I have ever had the privilege to know. They arrive every year between springtime and summer as the swallows used to do and happily make the rounds of the churches and museums for a few days, as if they enjoyed the most intimate ties with the ancient artists — each one has her favorite. They demonstrate the highest degree of culture, rare sensitivity, and a great love of art. Then they disappear. Who knows where they are now, in these first days of autumn? Oh, I had forgotten: they're with the last available gondoliers.

And the Venetian women, *le venexiane?* We rarely speak of them among ourselves, we friends. We speak (sometimes) of the Danish or Germans we've met; or of the Japanese, the Americans, the Sicilians . . . Maybe it's because there are so few of our own left to us now; or maybe, I don't know, it's because it's like talking about ourselves. This evening after work, however, walking the beach of the Lido, already wild and gray with the oncoming winter, we do — we speak of our own. The beach cabins are shut up and locked, and the first wintry gusts, the cold *bave*, blow through the air.

—◦ 80 ◦—

"There are three or four types of them, *le venexiane*," Venetian women, according to my friends Alvise and Gianni, one of whom is younger and one of whom is older than me. Alvise is a painter and Gianni, although he works at the Generali, is taking courses in creative writing. "The ancient ethnic groups," they assure me, "are still recognizable if you pay a little attention."

I'm paying attention. This is what they teach me:

1. *"Tipo levantine"* — Levantine. These woman have dark or olive-skinned faces, but everywhere else they're a smooth, delicate white. Black hair: smooth beneath the sirocco, flying every which way with the bora, always *tormentati* (the hair, never the women). Huge golden-brown eyes, or else golden-green, or something between nut-brown and bronze — with or without their knowledge, the eyes of a medium, of a fortune-teller. Slight and small-boned, yet sturdy in the hips . . . and those eyes without end. More persuasive than docile in manners and character, with their "winning ways." Ready enough with the men, when they *want* to be. Tenacity to burn, often obstinate. Indifferent at times; yet at others, clinging and vibrant with passion (this from Gianni).

"The picture I'm getting," I say to my teachers, "is the iron fist in the velvet glove."

"Right! But with a great, natural sense of humor, always ready to do something crazy."

"They exude an appeal," explains Alvise the artist, "that is truly sensual. It's more than sexuality," he clarifies further, "its's *complete attraction*, emanating from every pore, every glance, every word they speak in that hoarse, tuneful, lilting voice. It's hard to describe, hard to capture."

Add to that the fact that they speak *"soft"* — never trampling their syllables like their southern cousins — and never moving their hands. They move only what counts the most, in or out of their clothes. Naturally, they know all this, but they appear (with just the right touch of Venetian nonchalance) not to know it, and to care even less.

"And then they appear," says Gianni, in the grip of a poetic-creative moment, "in their composite nature: something between human and who knows? prehuman, marine."

(At this point all three of us gaze out to sea. The beach is deserted; not even a dog in sight.)

"A local variation," I hazard, "of the Mediterranean type?"

"Probably." But they're on a roll: sometimes these women are focused (they say) and at other times scattered; but they're always fairly spontaneous, improvisational, ready for the *comico*, the *maschera*, the *scena*.

"Faced with any question that counts," say both my friends very seriously, "they have a distinct tendency to debunk . . . whatever: the subject, you, what you're saying, your relationship, everything."

End of subject, for the moment. A brief, relaxed silence; sighs all around. It's cold on the beach.

2. "Blondes in general, *tipo cadorine* and such."* Tall, slender, wiry, with a kind of *démodé* distinction all their own — not a bad change from Type One. Sensitive, even spiritual — in Italy! It's hard to say if they're more intelligent or more spiritual. Or more hysterical. The ones we've known have been constantly anguished and ambivalent, with a tendency to fall into states of ecstasy (over sunsets, lagoon, islands, and such). But those colors of

---

*From the Cadore region of the Veneto. — TRANS.

theirs that you never forget! Blond, strawberry-blond, straw-blond; even lemon, canary, and orange. Splendid clear skin — pale blue and rose, like a tender evening sky in the foothills of the Alps.

"They'll follow you all of your life, these ones — good luck!"

3. "Intermediates," somewhere between Type One and Type Two. But it's important to make the distinction between the Slavic blondes and the black-haired beauties from Friuli. Both are solid and generous, big, wonderful women. Only sometimes they're kind of like *wardrobes:* It's hard to embrace them — *they* embrace *you.* They have a certain way of opening and throwing back their legs like wings . . . If you've ever been with one, you'll never forget her again.

"But watch out! Once they've got you, they turn the key in the lock," warns Alvise, not laughing, "and you won't ever come out again."

Now they laugh.

"The truth is that they hold, they enclose in themselves — how can I say it — so many beings," tries Gianni, in another creative leap, "so many *persons,* even though they don't seem to." He explains: "Friends, lovers, companions — everything: they can become anything, even that comfortable presence-beside-you that's natural at times in a manfriend — if he's a true friend (which is rare)."

A pause ensues. We understand that Gianni, in his own way — not because of the creative writing courses — will become a writer.

4. *"Tipo marrone-italiota,"* according to Alvise: the brown-Italiote type. "Our own ethnic group," he says, looking at me, "yours and mine — there's no need to say anything else." At this point we could mix them all up and start over again. Whatever.

There's no doubt — I admit to myself, going home, watching the islands and the women on the boat — that Venice has always filtered men and women, as America does now, from a great number of reservoirs: from the Levant, from the North, from the Germans, Hungarians, Croatians, Istrians, Dalmatians, Friulians, from the Greeks, the Hebrews and Arabs . . . What mixtures are whipped up in this richest and maddest of cities! And who knows what it will be like from here on in, in the near future?

Alvise and I, for the moment, are most attracted by the representatives of Types Two and Three. However, for some time — we mull this over with Gianni — it seems like there are more Types One and Four around; whether there are just more of them, or they're more on the scene, or what, we don't know. The truth is, we're attracted by all of them; we hardly know where to turn.

Maybe Venice has always been what she is — strange, feminine, changeable, surprising, utterly beautiful — because of all those streams of women, those galaxies, those constellations, those beings wrought out of stardust. (It's night by now; could it be affecting my thoughts?)

As a final result we know nothing, neither of Venice, nor of women, nor of the world.

—◦ 81 ◦—

The constellations, or galaxies, go on, but here at the Caffè Rionale they're a whole other thing. It's late at night and still hot, so all the tables are out in the campo or rioterrà, crowded with groups of young girls — gangs of young girls, in this city without even a discotheque. In the houses and apartments upstairs the windows are shuttered and dark; it's already way too late for the people behind them. We look around: all we see are the opposites of Type One, Two, Three, and Four . . . or at least nothing recognizable among all this green, purple, yellow, red, and blue hair. We must have invented "our" types, then; or maybe they're extinct. We feel lost, can't seem to manage to talk to each other.

"Once upon a time," I falter, finally, "there were more blondes, real blondes, weren't there? Or am I wrong?"

"What blondes?" retorts Gianni. "There were more women with black or chestnut-colored hair — I mean, *real* black and chestnut . . . *Everything* was more real." He's a little older than I am.

So: Eyes change, hair changes, everything changes in the course of a few years; while we continue to consider the women each of us knows (or thinks he knows) and sees (or thinks he sees) as the only real ones. The others seem like poor imitations. Or maybe it's simply that "ours" are the individual human beings whom each of us, by the grace of God, has brushed against once in a lifetime.

And for them, for the women — we wonder, eyeing all these different faces around us — who knows how it is or how it will be. At bottom, maybe *way* down at bottom, not much different. All we know for sure is that among the young these days everything changes very swiftly, perhaps from one hour to the next. There's a big turnover, a lot of shuffling of partners, swapping and switching. There's a lot more experience-that-isn't-experience; everyone goes with everyone else; no grace of God. The new "Slavs" are the vague and powerful Americans, or the Australians you see wherever you look, whole squadrons of them. Once we would have said they were enticingly "provocative" — today they just make us laugh, except for their bouts of ingenuous imagination, which are more likely to make us cry. For the Australian women who come here everything rides the wave of a precise and prefabricated symbolic fantasy, which leads them immediately to encounter the symbols and marry the allegories of Venice: gondoliers, waiters, nobles, and so forth.

In my opinion, however, as far as I've been able to touch on the subject (not enough, never enough), no one can compare to the English. It must be the story of the double island: they come down from theirs — populated, perhaps, by very few males — and are, how shall I put it? ready and willing. Can it be that only the most eager and lusty of women from Britain make it this far? They come here and find the Venice-island, the place of their dreams: Carnevale, boats, sea, beauty, classical characters, Romantics, postmoderns . . . Who will ever write the infinite story, which continues generation after generation, of the *inglesine* on the lagoon? Even today the journey to Venice, the islands, the Lido, becomes for these British women a voyage beyond the confines of the common, transcending the ordinary human world and sailing wildly into the mythic. (This, too, I've experienced firsthand — "on my own skin," as we say; it wasn't easy.) It's a little like that for us in the British Isles, as well, in the Shetlands and Hebrides. It's as if there were a dark nucleus crying out from island to island, subconscious, and language were no barrier at all.

But how many there are — or seem to be! All these women brushing by you, only a breath or a touch away: in the *caffè*, in the calli, in the dark, solitary *sottoportici*, on the bridges and canal banks, on the little outside staircases of the houses, on the huge inner stairwells of the palazzi . . . All the different voices, languages, and scents wafting around you envelop you in fantasies. These clouds of perfumes-voices-signals become very concentrated when women walk alongside or pass by you in the longest and narrowest calli (San Barnaba and Santa Maria Formosa, for instance). They wheel, return, and then vanish like smoke between the canals and the campi. And you: you either swiften or slow down your pace, or duck down a side street, depending on whether you want to follow them or just save yourself; but it's no use, they're imprinted on your retina (or on something) — salvation is not a possibility. Is it the way they're dressed, or does it take no more than a particular color, some little nothing? All of the above, I guess, depending on the time, the place, the occasion. In the great observatories of Campo Santo Stefano, the Rialto, and Stradanova, you can mistake one face or one dress with another; but on the small, nameless bridge it is *she* who comes toward you: the unknown woman you will never see again, who has nonetheless entered and become part of you forever. Radiant marvels in blossom, dressed in gossamer and set afire by each smallest gleam of the sun: beauty lighting up beauty. Later on in life all this may fade; but not always, it isn't a given. I think it's this way everywhere, more or less. But we may *see* it more here, since we continue to find them beside us, our wonderful women. They keep walking with us, brushing lightly against us, touching us, spilling their scents on the air, spying on us and each other. They *want* to be looked at, listened to, noticed, observed, remembered. Venetian calli are brief, briefer still the aparition we call life. And *le venex-iane*, oh my God, are ever-more rare.

It's the hour when *they* arrive, in small groups, two or three at a time, as furtive as shadows: the Senegalese, the Moroccans, the I-don't-know-whos. They spread their white sheets on the gray stones of the calle, beneath the feet of the ladies, the *signore*, passing by. At the moment their sheets strike me as pallets, poor little beds. Lovingly and carefully, caressing and polishing them, they set out their wares: necklaces, belts, pocketbooks, purses, cigarette lighters, lipsticks, charms, chinaware, little games for the *signore*. And the *signore* are more than glad to stop, talk, barter, and buy. They laugh; they're in rare good humor. The black men are young and strong, tall, courteous, and gentle. Only the best of them make it this far on the long journey north. Venice has always welcomed and assimilated different peoples, from sources both near and far: here we are in the Calle delle Razze, the Street of Races. And of course there's the ancient Calle degli Albanesi, the Albanians, on the Riva degli Schiavoni, the Slavs, the Bridge of the Croatians and the Bridge of the Turks . . . We have no fear here in Venice — just the contrary — of new infiltrations. There's always the occasional instance of antipathy, an infrequent brawl or misunderstanding. But we, I suspect, have more need of them than they of us. They await us among their wares, and they smile.

─◦ 82 ◦─

"The *signora* from Milan," Celeste the newspaper vendor announces to me this morning, with subsequent confirmation from the proprietor of the bar, the florist, and the fruit-and-vegetable man. She's the first to arrive in our campo, at this close of the season; soon the others will come join her. The season is brief, and the *signore milanesi* are immediately conspicuous in the local stores. Elegant and discreet, they are — no doubt about it — "distinguished." They speak (almost always) as if everyone else, whether they're present or not, were their subordinates. How they remind me of my evenings in Milan! Yet here, as at home, they always conduct themselves with grace and elegance, with class — yes, that's the word — with unimpeachable *class*. My almost-next-door neighbor has, furthermore, the fascinating and unbearable lightness of the rich; discreetly rich, of course. She's intelligent, lovely, and refined — there's the other word: *refined*. Even in the colonies, in Venice.

Almost all of the *signore milanesi* have "a hole": a second home in the right places or what they consider to be the right places, and these holes of theirs are, naturally, "just precious." We're talking about a mansard among the roofs, a pied-à-terre in an old palazzo . . . They make conscientious rounds of the exhibits, flit back and forth between their "holes," and look (discreetly) for gentlemen friends, perhaps for one particular gentleman friend. I have to wonder what they know about our perpetual problems as islanders or the infinite troubles assailing Venice, and whether it matters to them at all. There are sociologists who insist that statistics on the "permanent" or "indigenous" population, which continues to decline, must be "integrated" with those of the nonresidents who own secondary homes here — in other words, with the *signore milanesi*. Perhaps; but the nonresidents are just passing through, if not actual fly-by-nights, and they participate little or not at all in the real life of the city. My neighbor the *signora milanese* disappears very quickly from the local calli, the campo, the *caffè* under the house — either because she's found a lover or because she's gone back to Milan.

But at the moment she's ringing me up on the phone: "Shall we go out to eat at Remigio's this evening?" she inquires. "It's so darling. Or at Montin's; it's so romantic."

Lonely nights are hard in Venice, especially during this season. So as soon as she finds someone, *addio*, we won't see her around. This is the time — my younger friends assure me — to go back to the English. Even if they "don't have much class"; even if they're "sluttish," downright "indecent," according to the lovely ladies from Milan.

The truth is that English women in Venice, ugly or beautiful, slender or fat, are always *ben disposte* — in whatever hour or season, in whatever place and with whatever partner; they're impartial in polite company. Outsiders may not believe it. Venetians may fear to say it. But it's what they tell each other and it's what they believe. A minute after getting together, they're ready for anything, all the more so since they hardly have any clothes on to begin with, whether it's hot or cold. They want to go out in the boats and learn to row *alla venexiana.* They learn swiftly how to row with one oar, two oars, even *alla valesana.* The next thing you know they're smiling up at you from the bottom of the boat, stark naked, so pink and white you want to eat them alive. Up until recently we thought that they came here to harvest lovers before being stranded in the northern winter, with probably not much to offer in the way of consolation. But now that we know more of what's going on in Britain — and they're not (or they *are*) fooling around — we're not sure exactly what the attraction is. Except, of course, that they're both of them islands, *islands,* a fact not easily understood in Milan.

I think it was Erasmus who said that madness originated on islands. I concur with him but would like to go one step farther and suggest that women — I mean, these *women-women,* are born from the islands as well. There's no doubt that they're rejuvenated, invigorated, incited, and aroused here. Some islands are more provocative, of course, and others less; Venice certainly doesn't hold herself back, and *Britannia rules the waves.*

The last of Britain's best are still on the Lido, having grown either slimmer or fatter during their stay, playing in the wind and the sea. Some of them go about topless, on this small beach in Venice where everyone knows everyone else and where, at this point in the season, all the locals are wrapped up in shawls, wearing pullover sweaters and woolen berets. Still the English-women, stunning or homely, pale or roasted, leap in the water like dolphins, no matter how cold it is. They challenge the jellyfish, scoff at the undertow, and play on the beach with a tiny red ball they found somewhere at random. Now their attraction is a hundredfold what it was in the summer for the few males left —

but with goose bumps (us, not them), the shudder that runs through the dream.

Then they vanish, all at once and together, on some damp purple night. A short, sharp, falsetto cry (so characteristic I'd recognize it among thousands) and they're gone. It's as if they had never been here at all. All that remains is the tiny red ball on the empty sands of the Lido.

—◦ 83 ◦—

Returning from the Lido over the Ponte del Rimedio, I run into my almost-next-door neighbor, the lady from Milan. Signora Lidia, according to Celeste the newspaper vendor. She's with her friends, all of them looking very distinguished — as does she — all of them wearing short, stylishly cut winter jackets in leather or beige. The whole group's basic, much-reiterated question (repeated even more often, it seems to me, than it used to be) is: "What's to *see?* Is there anything to *see* here in Venice?" By which they mean openings, exhibits, festivals, *novità*.

They are genteelly annoyed — just enough; a few refined nostrils flare — when I say, ingenuously, that there's *Venice* to see. Venice herself, at whom nobody's looking — forget the exhibits.

They admit that yes, certainly, Venice is worth seeing (they know how to live, the *signore milanesi*). "But the city, dear friend, will still be here next time," they cry. "And meanwhile, we might *miss* something!" Then, with that swift, inexorable glance: "And it's so difficult, so closed here in Venice! The society's closed, the palazzi are closed, the families are closed, the churches are closed. Only Celeste and her newspaper stand are open all the time."

I have to keep myself from retorting that in Milan . . . the first months, the first years I was in Milan — oh, how closed I found that city to be! A closed society, its families difficult to get to know, its churches I'm not sure about. Only the Society of the Quartet in Milan was open at all hours. However, it cost an arm and a leg to get into; and then when I did I'd be so tired from work that I'd drop off to sleep in an armchair — or a hard-backed chair, depending on the room and the night. And they, after only three days here . . .

I make an attempt to explain, to touch somewhat on the life of everyday Venice — which is always visible, I assure them — and infinite; all you have to do is walk around. Perhaps with a little more patience, with a slightly less swift and unforgiving eye . . . I'd like to tell them something about the invisible Venice, as well; but it's best not to be too insistent, subordinate that I am, in the face of their fascinating, insupportable lightness of being, their aura of wealthy travelers just passing through. They exhibit the precisely right touch, of course, during their brief sojourn, as on every other occasion: the touch of the ready, attentive, gracious mistress of the manor.

Proof to the contrary. Within a very few days . . . They're not like me; they've managed to get around everywhere and know everything: from the elegant stores in the *centro* to the little shops in the campo, from the insides of palazzi to the ancient, carved vere da pozzo in the abandoned campielli. They've learned all about the parishes, cliques, and political parties, the Women's Center, the antiquarian, the humane societies for cats, dogs, and seagoing birds — even the associations for human beings, old people in difficulty, handicapped children. Money helps, of course, but it's also a matter of character, temperament — an eagerness to always be *doing*, a reluctance to ever slow down. Milan is Milan, even in Venice.

"It never ends," they explain to me this evening, after I encounter them, to my astonishment, in the Bar of the Frari. No, Venice never ends, I find out, within the world of streets they've discovered, most of them different from my streets; everyone has his or her own version of Venice. Maybe the *signore*'s days, perhaps even their lives never end, either; their energy is so vast and unrelenting.

"No, Venice never ends and it's hard to understand why, as small as it is," Signora Lidia tells me. "What a disaster," she adds, "my hair in this humidity."

I find her very *venezianizzata,* between the humidity and the infinite; the truth is, she's already cut to the core of the problem. Bit by bit, I feel sure, they'll all become more Venetian than the Venetians. But meanwhile they inquire, with severity: "You write? You work?" And they admonish me: "Work, dear friend, work, don't ever stop." Even now, at the end of the season, they press me to forge ahead swiftly (in Venice!), to work diligently on this species of diary "and everything else," whatever in the world that may be.

— 84 —

I go to visit Rico, still called Richetto as he was when we were in school together; I was in elementary while he was in middle school. Now he's old and ill, growing older and sicker all the time, but with the same fine, thin face he had as a boy. He's a great deal more interesting now, though; there's been all of life in between. And the city, as well: he hardly ever goes out anymore, but from where he's sitting in his poor little room, "*sento tutto,*" he tells me, he hears everything. He puts a finger in front of his nose and the other hand to his ear. "Ss," he says: Be quiet, listen.

And he's right, you can hear a continual humming, the buzz from the calle downstairs with its people passing and talking. In the courtyard children are playing and every so often shouting, in waves of sound; Richetto watches over them, keeps an eye on them until their mothers come home. The two oldest boys, he says, come up to get him every once in a while and carry him downstairs. But the most extraordinary thing is that right here under our feet . . . Right here beneath us is the *sottoportico.* Richetto creaks up very slowly to show me the flat, movable tile, like a trapdoor, in the floor.

"Lift up," he tells me.

I lift up. There right beneath us is the front door; you can see who's ringing the doorbell and talk to them, you can see and hear all the people walking up and down in the street. Someone stops right away, raises his eyes, and calls out a greeting.

"You can hear everything," says Richetto happily, "from every direction — even the pigeons and cats up on the roof."

The walls of the house merge with the walls of the calle in the *sottoportico*, the "portico" being this little room in which we sit talking intermittently, between long silences. The boys give one last shout and disappear. Even the seagulls and pigeons have fallen silent and the walls — of the city, of our lives — are suddenly still. We cock our ears to the stillness. At a certain point . . .

"At a certain point," says Richetto, "everything stops, the walls and the sounds. Except for over here," he amends, waving vaguely. "I've never understood where those incessant boomings come from, that kind of muffled thunder, day and night . . ."

I look down and see an internal courtyard like a gray funnel, chipped and flaking between its disintegrating walls. Maybe those walls never stop moving. "Day and night?" I ask. "I don't hear anything."

"It could be my ears," he says.

"Or mine."

From the north-facing window there's a clear view of the Church of the Frari looming high above the city, its stained-glass cathedral windows Richetto's last piece of work.

"Go see them," he urges me. "Then you can tell me how they're doing. If you have trouble getting in, talk to Bìbole," he says, and repeats, "Bìbole. Meanwhile," he whistles, "if I find Vittorino, I'll have him carry me down to I Nomboli."

I set straight off on my errand, although between *sottoportici* and calli it's hard to get out of the house.

And there they are, the stained-glass stories of the angels and saints, restored by Richetto, high up in the Gothic windows. What faces, characters, visions, and hopes must have merged in my friend as he worked! The rubble of scattered dreams and prayers, the lost riches . . . Who makes windows like these anymore? I can imagine Richetto up there for months, for years, among the angels in restoration. In contrast, the panes he never got to belly out under the sudden touch of the wind heralding winter. Standing twenty meters away, I can still feel the gusts. An old woman interrupts her prayers for a moment to pull her head scarf more snugly around her neck.

"We still need Richetto," says the priest, suddenly looming behind me, enormous and incredibly tall: Don Annibale, known as Bìbole.

A girl comes in and swiftly approaches the gate closing off the small chapel. She tosses in a branch of those tiny roses that blossom two or three times in the gardens best-protected by the houses around them, the roses that flower last in the fall.

"It's Monteverdi's chapel," she explains. "He's buried in there." She gestures as if she could see him.

There is nothing written on the stone except MONTEVERDI. I had noticed, at other times, a rose or some sort of plant on his tomb. And as if Monteverdi had understood, the gate swings ajar. The girl enters and arranges her roses; she prays for a moment, "for Monteverdi," she says, looking at me, "and for us all."

I go back to find Richetto and tell him about my visit to his windows, cutting toward i Nomboli, thinking he might already be there. But between portici and *sottoportici*, somehow I lose my way. Then I hear a heavy step behind me: Bìbole. It's the right street after all, he tells me — there's Richetto, just arriving with Vittorino.

"I thought I'd drop by to see him," says the priest.

I look at the name of the street, written on the wall: CALLE AMOR DEI AMICI, the Calle of Love Between Friends.

—◦ 85 ◦—

How to set a book — a novel, a story — in Venice? It's difficult; Venice takes too much for herself. The background, too powerful and too often used, soon becomes a dangerous protagonist with whom you must wrestle. As a character or setting she's been worn out, used up, falsified, hated, exalted, and deformed by so many writings and films, so many postcards, so many great painters, small painters, painters of no worth at all, old and modern oleographic "art," television programs, publicity shots, Internet specials, popular imaginings, and phantoms false and true — what's to be done with her? Worse, she's been squashed down, ridiculed, shattered in pieces by her collision with the so-called modern world. Yet she remains strong: once she appears between the lines, logs onto the computer, there's no getting her out again — Venice is there to stay.

Let us imagine that the protagonist of our tale walks out of the house one morning into whatever Via Vittorio Emanuele or Piazza Garibaldi; he walks out the same way and finds (more or less) the same street, whether he's in Milan or Turin or anyplace else. In fact we, the readers, recognize at least somewhat both the protagonist and his trip; we're out on the streets of our city in pretty much the same way — we recognize ourselves in him.

But in Venice our character doesn't walk out "the same way," and he finds a street (*if* he finds a street) that is completely different — to the point that it's not *even* a street, and for a while you you can't tell *what* it is. It's like no other street in no other place in the world. Or if it shares any similarity at all with any other spot on earth, it still ends up always being a little more *over there* or a little more *over here* — on the other side of the air or the water, not where you expected to find it. In the water with its roots in the air, upside-down, incomprehensible. In truth it is like nothing except for itself and its reflection — we can't recognize it.

So the "setting" — that touch of background needed to shore up any tale — becomes the entire environment, spreads out across the whole page. The ambience is so unique that it overrides (whether you're aware of it or not) both you who are writing and your characters, waiting for faces. It swindles everyone at least a little, raises the tone or renders it banal, generalizes or localizes things, and distracts from the players, tending to substitute itself in their place and dominate the whole story. The human protagonists are ready to speak, but fall silent; or else they talk too much when we wish they'd say nothing. You *have* to deal with her, that's the curse of Venice; and naturally, once you start dealing with one Venice, there's always another one lying in wait to pounce on you

— and always at the risk of endangering the picture in general (or at least this is your legitimate fear). You try to circle around and outflank her, look in from outside, maintain your perspective, avoid the magnetic, infernal field, escape the attraction of the maze always pulling you in, farther and farther in, remove the living beauty seeking you out. You try to stay on the peripheries, on the distant islands, in the lagoon, on the coast, or in indefinable, invented locations . . . And then you don't penetrate her at all, not even a little — it's just not enough. (Perhaps you can circle around her to some degree; I tried this approach in my book *The Last Islands*. But it was hard to keep her at bay; always in the background Venice was calling and shining.)

The outer and inner walls, the stage or cliché, the visual or visionary stretches, the superficial or profound events between which your fictitional shadows must move, are always both too particular and too strong. At other times they're too weak, simply because the old city, alone of her kind in the powerful, uniform world, is *too* different. And she's always — though it's hard for me to keep having to say this — always and perpetually too beautiful and at the same time unknown, unrecognized in her beauty. It would take a great artist to be up to rendering the smallest stretch of the scene. (Visconti in his film *Senso* or *Morte a Venezia* comes to mind.)

So I, our hypothetical writer, change the backdrop and city of my burgeoning book. I go back to Milan. Both of us, my character and I, are glad to escape; everything is relatively easier here. My character is definitely happier: he had been asking himself for some time whether, when he walked out of his house into this world of canals and canal banks — without cars, without traffic lights, without recognizable reference points — he was still a human being.

Perhaps it's possible to be in Venice and "write" about Venice in some other way, branching out into other worlds: music, painting, cinema, photography . . . whatever, as long as it doesn't demand the precision of words. To try to express her in prose, in the written word, is the most difficult task of all, I believe, and the risk of failure is very high. For Italians, above all, it's almost impossible to write about Venice when she's right between their feet — or in their souls. It may be different for foreigners, even the ones who have come here to stay.

The French, certainly, take it to heart; with them there's no middle ground: they're either *Pour Venise* or *Contre Venise*. This old caryatid moves them more than I would have thought possible, one way or the other. When my latest book on Venice, which I thought was a new thing under the sun, came out in translation in France, I discovered it planted in the bookstore windows along with ten or so other treatises on the city, one more beautiful than the other, except for those that were awful. Those unforgettable French window displays were a systematic encyclopedia, pro and con Venice, that was always open for reference.

English and American contemporaries, on the other hand, tend to wrestle with the specific problems of these four small islands even more than we do: conservation, aesthetics, restorations, money, the Fenice, the Arsenale, depopulation, environmental impact, the petroleum in the Adriatic, the sinking of Venice.

The Germans talk about isolation and distance, of culture and absence of culture in a place that is, by now, almost *solely* culture, true or false — therefore more false than true: an aggregate of locales that have become almost purely mental visions.

Do strangers, the ones who come from farthest away, feel and understand certain aspects of this better than we do? The Americans or Japanese, the Chinese or Indians, Russians or Scandinavians? It would seem that they do. And the Germans, in their poetry? They are probably incomparable in their interweaving of philosophy and poetry, even when the theme (Venice) seems obvious at first glance, a subject for common prose and "journalism" by this time.

What's truly hard, yet inevitable, is to try to understand anything while you're living here, *"tra un ponte e una calle,"* as the people in the Campo keep saying to me, smiling and attempting to explain for the hundredth time the history of the *quartiere.* It's difficult to describe it while keeping it at bay when it's all around you, right outside the window, inside the house. And trying to write a diary "from the inside," as the English would say, is almost impossible; there *is* no "inside" or "outside" — you have been wholly enveloped in Venice, penetrated down to the bone. And whatever you wanted to hold close, you lose right away; and what you never thought to find, you rediscover. But one thing is sure: you won't find the linchpin, not even the thread. I had something very different in mind myself when I first decided to write a "Venetian diary"; but the diary itself has taken over — that is, *she,* the city, commands my pen. Her unique beauty and ambience even now, as we approach a new millennium, exert at every moment an irresistible force of attraction that once belonged to nature.

And nature, whether we like it or not, is disappearing. Venice remains.

PART EIGHT

The Necessary City

It's been *acqua alta* every day for three weeks. Lugubrious sirens sound in the dead of night, calling at intervals from atop the buoys, crying out warnings from bell towers across the city.

Here in the courtyard under our house there are 110 to 120 centimeters of water in the early hours of the morning, and sometimes 130 or more. And that's at midtide. But even before high tide sweeps in a certain number of key points in the city are impassable. How many? I've never managed to figure that out. The points and levels change day by day, according to the wind, the zone, the distances involved, the watersheds. However, there are a lot of them. It depends on the moon, the winds, and the *sesse*, the varying oscillations in the lagoon, the storms, and how far a particular point is from the new canals dug into the lagoon. Each time — I explain to my usual band of children, nephews, and nieces — there's the slightest disturbance in the Adriatic, we get *acqua alta* in Venice. Now, I say — because when I was your age that wasn't true. Reduction and lowering of the soil, both on the surface and deep in the foundations, excavations in the lagoon for the tankers, thawing ice at the poles: it's all grist for the mill, I say to the kids, who don't know, who haven't lived through the years of the changes.

When I was a child, we spoke only (or almost only) of the Moon: it was she who was responsible for our *acqua alta*. Of course, the

wind, oscillations in the Adriatic, and the *sesse* in the lagoon all
came into play; but above all it was she, the Moon, who ruled us.

We were much taken by references to the movements of the
heavens; we spoke in astronomical-meteorological terms: "the
storms with the moon." The Moon enchanted us; we stood still to
gaze at her through the clouds. Everything that was happening
down here — the submerged streets, the canals swollen with water,
the boats stranded on the banks — depended on that white sphere
in the sky, on her relationship (who knew?) with the infinite.

Now the moon is second in line, and we're not sure anymore
how much the infinite counts. Now we know all too well that we
ourselves are the cause of so many *acque alte* — we human beings,
my generation. First of all, we extracted too much water from the
subsoil and the soil sank; for a city balanced on a thread of water as
if on a tightrope, that means drowning. Then there are the canals
we dug in the lagoon, precisely when the greenhouse effect was first
taking place in the sky: deep and straight, these new canals bring
seawater rushing into the lagoon at frightening speeds. The sponge
effect of the old natural canals, which were shallow and curved, has
diminished or disappeared, so that the high waters are ever more
frequent and violent. The city rots and its people go into exile. This
is not at all what we wanted, but we've acted as if it were.

"But right here where we live," ask the kids, "here in the courtyard, how many times a year was there *acqua alta* when you were
little?"

"Once," I reply, "every couple of years."

Now it's at least five or six times a year. And this year: thirty
times.

—◦ 87 ◦—

Every morning for the past thirty days, as I've walked from my
home to the station, where I must go to work, I've encountered at
least three impassable points, sometimes as many as four or five.
All it takes is for the water to rise above eighty centimeters at

midtide, which is frequent these days — "normal," say the kids, who enjoy it. They think it's fun.

But to get where I have to go every morning, it's a matter of high boots and swearing, rushing and ending up late, crowds of frustrated workers, detours around the calli invaded by water under the beating rain. Tonight the warning sirens didn't sound, so this morning we all left the house "certain to make it." And instead we found ourselves blocked by high water in all of the usual places. More than usual, actually, since when the sirens go off someone or other sets up the *passerelle*, the planks we all cross like catwalks over the water; but today, since the sirens were silent, no *passerelle*. So we Venetians — balked on this side of the lake of high water, which has welled up under our feet within a few minutes — and those coming into the city from terrafirma, balked on the opposite side, are one in our vehement cursing, our most vivid and senseless *mòccoli* uniting us over the waters.

All it takes is a few centimeters of water in the calle or riva to block us for hours. It would help, at certain points, to raise the pavement, or "walking surface," as the engineers call it, just a fraction; then we could get through. Every once in a while this partial solution is heralded in the papers as if the idea were new; but I remember them talking about it thirty years ago. It would be costly, for sure, but not as expensive as it will be to reverse the long-range damage caused by the tides. What little is left of the city is blocked every time, "brought to its knees," as the newspapers say. By dint of being brought to its knees so often, one day it may not rise again. The trouble is that these are the tides that bother people the most: these high tides, these sudden, brief lakes that invade us so stubbornly and repeatedly. In consequence, no one pays much attention to the medium-high tides, which will prove most fatal to the life of the city in the long run. Circling around in search of dry passage, cursing our way down all the possible calli, we no longer know where to turn.

Tonight the kids and I watch a wonderful documentary on TV about Alexandria in Egypt (sometimes the TV is useful). The greatest library of antiquity, the most bustling port in the ancient world, Caesar's immense ships, the legacies of Anthony and Cleopatra: they're all at the bottom of the sea, mired in the mud and the sand. While we watch the program, the rain is beating down hard on the canals outside. At a certain point the sirens go off: *alta marea*. A few minutes later the courtyard in front of the house is submerged, and a surreal silence falls on the city. Why did Alexandria end up under the water? Tremors, earthquakes, landslides: natural causes.

"And here?" ask the kids, as the courtyard fills with the violent shout of the sea.

"There have been natural disasters like those here," I say, "a few centuries ago. Remember Malamocco, vanished, swallowed up by the sea, or any of the islands that sank down into the lagoon and were lost. There are natural causes even here . . . But if it happened to Venice now, it would be mostly by *human* causes — in other words, it would be our fault. And the thing is, we know it, we all know very well that even Venice can die. Whereas maybe back then, in Alexandria, they didn't know it."

Or maybe, I think, we believe that Venice is somehow strangely unique. Maybe she *won't* die. At times, when she "rises" out of the waters, dirty and wet, her houses cracked and her foundations devoured, at least she rises — we all say to each other — some way or another. Look, we say, she's still here, perhaps she's immortal. Maybe she's capable even of this.

"She's capable of anything," I say to the kids, "as long as we give her a hand."

—⌐ 88 ⌐—

And here they are again, damn it! the sirens sounding off for *acqua alta*. It's only seven in the morning; they're starting early. It's time for me to go to work and the tide's coming in, high, low, who knows? but will I get there in time? And the kids, can they make it to school . . . I bet I'll be late . . . Moments of haste and anguish for everyone in the family.

But suddenly this morning I realize that they've been going off for a few days in a row regularly at seven o'clock. Which is strange: high tide sweeps into the city half an hour later each day. Nonetheless, I duck out the entrance, pull the little ones' boots on, throw my own over my shoulder, and rush out.

I pass the Vini Piavi, a tavern close by the house, glance in, and screech to a halt. Inside I see Fulmine, also known as Scirocco, and a group of his friends.

"Come on!" shout his companions. "Start up, it's time!"

Fulmine climbs up onto the step next to the counter. A silence prevails. And then he begins: a low ululation that rises higher and higher, becoming ever louder and ever more urgent with every second that passes. He howls as if he were seeing the water rush in, wave after wave, cresting up from the sea to swell inexorably between the counter and tables. And he's perfect, reproducing precisely even the mechanical clicks of the Sirena dei Frari, the most powerful voice calling out against the fury of the lagoon. He's tremendous, lugubrious, ascending from one successive tone to the next, ever higher, and following them with the far-off echoes of the sirens at the Arsenale, the Giudecca, and Murano.

And the first alarms of the sirens are followed by second and third urgent warnings (marea molto alta!). All of Fulmine's friends stand up to belt out a solemn chorus, a prodigious crescendo of sirens and echoes, down to the final, piercing wail before silence falls.

Everyone in the neighborhood springs into automatic acceler-ated action: some run away; others bellow out for their children; a couple of maniacs launch bunches of boots from the fourth or fifth floor to land on who-knows-whose head. In reality, as everyone realizes before very long, the water in the canal is tran-quil this morning; there's no wind, and it's gray out but sunny and unseasonably mild. People react. They're astonished, worried, maddened, enraged . . . Then they see the humor in it and play along with the game. Then they forget about it.

The Vini Piave with its Human Siren at seven o'clock in the morning *is* the quarter, is all of us. Inside or out, true tide or not, it turns into a local joke. Then, little by little, it fades into a memory, a work of imagination held together by the voices of friends, an event as phantasmagoric as the whole city.

—❧ 89 ❧—

"This is exactly why we're here, to lend a hand," the two men from Emilia-Romagna assure me courteously as we're standing together at the Vecchio Paradiso.

"Really," I say shortly, paying little attention. I'm suffering from a moment of incredulity, of downright discourtesy, in the wake of the past days when all of Venice has been shipwrecked under the flood. This evening, too, we've been held up here at the Paradiso by a sudden incoming tide unheralded by the sirens.

"We heard," they try again, "what you were saying here a few nights ago: that it's hard to write in Venice, that Venice takes too much and there's nothing left for the writer."

I'm not in a good mood this evening, but I'm stuck here by *acqua alta,* and so I admit, "Certainly, it's difficult to write in Venice."

The two men smile at me broadly in confirmation. "But that's true for so many other kinds of work, too," they say. "It's hard to get anything done here and that's no joke." They gaze genially at Martino and me, these two engineers *emiliani* with a pair of degrees under each of their belts; they're *simpatici,* very open and direct, unlike us Venetians. Martino made their acquaintance at the Rowing Club. They've come to Venice in "midcareer" after having held jobs across half the globe, somewhat like me.

"And now?" I ask.

"Now we don't know *where* we are anymore, except here at the Vecchio Paradiso with *acqua alta.* At any rate, the Rowing Club closes in November, so we'll be seeing each other here sometimes in the evening . . . We'll be able to exchange a word or two."

I understand that tonight — with the high water as an accomplice — they are especially eager to talk, to unburden themselves to us. Well, actually, so am I; my mood's changing.

"Five years in Venice," I say, "to do what?"

"Oh, there's no end of things to be done here," they reply, as if excusing themselves for being here, "right here in Venice, in the water, on the earth, everywhere."

"Is it better here," the question comes to my mind, "or in Turin, in Milan?" Would I had never asked.

"First of all," they begin, "it was hard to catch on, to figure things out in a place like this." They look around: rotting tables, minimal light, the right touch of odor-de-toilet, water lapping at the door — and here we are in Paradise. "Harder than in any other place, and we've seen a lot of them. Difficult to fit in with the people, the human *acqua-terra*." They laugh. "One moment everyone's too closed, much more closed than in Genoa — and then in the next they're incredibly open, *too* open, as if this were an island in the Caribbean. But it's understandable," they immediately admit. "The island is small and isolated, and people defend themselves as best they can, by closing down or opening up according to their fears, their moods, the phases of the moon."

Given that we have nothing to respond to this, they go on, talking in tandem, tripping over each other's words; I'm not ever quite sure which one is speaking.

"Out on the street, the Venetian eye —" they burst into laughter again "— scopes you out at a distance. Then they have to decide whether to greet you or not, what face to put on, whom to speak ill or well of. We've noticed that among themselves, Venetians don't open their mouths until they've spent a moment studying each other, sizing each other up. Imagine how it felt to us, coming from outside — for a long time, we didn't realize what was going on."

"Do you think it depends on the way the city is built?" I ask. "The way it's structured around its campielli and things of that sort?"

"That's part of it, for sure," they admit. "Within this sort of structure there's no saving yourself. But that's not the whole story. There are Hertzian waves in the air here, dear friend, emanations that rise, radiations invisible to the foreigner, weaving between the

windows of every campiello. And then, inside the houses, the walls
. . . It's as if the walls were perforated, with an ear always pressed to
them to hear everything that goes on. Venice, damn her!"

Period, exclamation mark, silence. It's time to drink on it.

"But how about in the office, how about your work?" asks
Martino.

—◌ 90 ◌—

"In our work . . . When we first arrived here, we thought it was superfluous — Venice, you understand — in the modern world.
Beautiful, moving, strange, laughable, whatever . . . but superfluous. Then little by little — and angrily, angrily — we had to
acknowledge the existence of total-difference right outside the
door, of a place that, without seeming to, puts up a resistance to
the whole rest of the world. And so it resists our profession, too,
our work, modern technology. We've never experienced anything
like it, not even in Africa. Right away you're up against a dilemma:
You can either try to understand this sort of world apart, with its
characteristics, misfortunes, necessities, rejections, and rhythms
— do you think 'rhythms' is the right word? — and even with its
own kind of modernity, there's that, too . . . Or else you're better
off renouncing it entirely, getting out as soon as you can. Not even
in Africa.

"But if we stayed on," they continue (as the water keeps rising;
it's the right evening for long conversations), "there were strange
things to confront, things we had to learn to deal with, more unthinkable each day that passes in the modern world."

"What things?"

They look at each other with a certain amount of embarrass-
ment.

"It's hard even to talk about things like this," they say, "hard
even to list them: slowness, indifference, nonchalance, fragility,
asymmetry, age, compromise, torpor, beauty, and insecurity all
mixed together. And this beauty everywhere, bound and unbound,

on earth, in the water . . . There's no saving yourself. In other words, there's a great number of problems, all of them different — and none of them things that we tackled at the Polytechnic or even the Cantiere . . ."

They consult with each other. "We've seen a lot, but here there's a concentration of real and presumptive problems, and it's hard to understand how they all came together, hard to figure out what's really happening. Certainly, it seems to us that what we have to offer — and even we have *something* to offer — that all that we have available to us is simply not enough. Nothing is *ever* enough here."

The water outside has reached its apex, even licking at the Vecchio Paradiso, which is on very high ground, a little island between the waves. There's nothing left to do aside from talking, except to see if we can find something to eat in here and wait for the water to subside before we go our separate ways. And yes, there is something to eat — not exactly *bolognese* dishes, but these two feel like honorary Venetians by now anyway.

"The point, however . . ." they begin, as we wait for our risotto in squid ink . . .

"The point is that after a while you begin to understand," picks up one of them, as if he hadn't had a chance to open his mouth yet, "that the global *baracca*, the planetary junkyard as they're beginning to call it even in Emilia, that is, the society in which all of us live now no matter what continent we're on, tends to throw out exactly those few things we were talking about: fragility, slowness, compromise, beauty of water and earth . . . all the things you find everywhere here in Venice. The global *baracca* represses those things, it detests them, it makes fun of them, and so it multiplies our diffidence and antipathy, our hatred of this different order of things and ideas."

"And naturally of the few places," breaks in the other, "where this different order still survives, or is trying to survive."

The risotto in squid ink's not bad. But what a strange combination: white and black, rice and ink.

"Whether to stay and understand it or to leave and forget about

it — how many times we've mulled it over! Some of our friends
and colleagues left right away. But we're going to go find them,
we'll try again to convince them to come back. Because there's
something new here," they say, staring at us intently, "or almost
new, which they couldn't evaluate since they went away so soon.
And that is, that a city like this ends up creating, little by little and
very subtly, new individuals, new aliens in the modern world, a different kind of human being, even new specialists/nonspecialists
among ourselves, the architects and engineers . . . Maybe this
would interest even them, the ones who left. Without any special
courses or diplomas or postgraduate degrees, new beings are taking
shape by themselves, strange mixtures . . ."

"What do you mean?" I ask.

"Well, just look at us," they reply, no longer laughing. "We've
had to spend much more time *learning* here than applying what
we already knew. There's so much to learn, or to unlearn, or feel
— is 'feel' the word I want? — a ton of things: about stones and
water, spaces and absences of space, atmospheres and distances,
the urban phenomenon being the same thing as the lagoonal
phenomenon. And you have to take everything in all at once: an-
tiquities and innovations, movable sluices and fixed environ-
ments, foundations and mosaics, electronics and nuances, voices
on the street and Internet in the house, rice and squid ink in Paradise . . . It takes courage, a lot of courage to stay here — to work
here, dear writer."

I stare at them in astonishment, but:

"You become someone else," they conclude. "She *makes* you
become someone else, this damned, double-damned city, nonsensical, half dead, and maybe . . . maybe, even though we didn't
believe it up until yesterday, maybe *necessary*, *essential*, since she
turns you back into who you were before —" they grapple for the
right words "— before you set out to make money, to work like a
dog every day, to believe that there's only one way of being in the
world. In other words, dear friend, she makes us rebecome, so to
speak, ourselves."

Silence. The moment's not easy and the tide won't quit. Now

the wind picks up in gusts and a flood of rain begins pouring down: water from heaven and earth. But what's this floating toward us? A sandolo, and then another . . . A small fleet of little boats, the lightest boats in the world, gliding over the canals and drowned banks to save us. And in these little boats sliding above and below the storm-tossed waters, are Paolo-the-astronomer, Sara-the-engineer, Giacomo-the-philosopher, Flavio-the-botanist, Sergio-the-professor, Gino-the-historian, Giulia-of-the-laughing-breasts, Nino-the-poet, Ughetto, Enrichetto, Kramer, Marta, Paola, Celeste-the-newspaper-vendor . . . and even those inimitable two, Radar with his accordion and Fulmine-Scirocco with his red whistle: the friends whom we've known, who have accompanied us this far on our journey.

"We found you by the 'green numbers' we carry around in our heads," laugh Radar and Fulmine, "those numbers that you think are rubbish, just something we made up. While you . . . you'll damned sure never manage to nab us if we're lost! In spite of all your *authorized* cellular *phones.*"

Kramer, the practical man: "We brought you boots and raincoats."

And now here comes the waterproof, submarine, surreal *micro-micro* of Lidia-from-Milan.

"But let's stay here!" cries everyone. "We'll wait for it to pass."

And so, for the moment, there is music and song, a chorus among the old tables of the Vecchio Paradiso. At least until Paradise closes down, and always in the event that we don't end up singing under the water.

—❍ 91 ❍—

This evening the scene and all of the characters change. The difference is signaled by the front door beside me: the sharp clap of its knocker resounds in the silence like the closing stroke of the day, of the place, of the brief passage between evening and night. It's nine o'clock and the great square — Campo Santo Stefano —

is empty. It's true that it's November and the autumn evening is damp and gray; but this "piazza" (which is what I'm calling the campo at the moment, for my friends from Milan) is smack dab in the center of the city, between three important intersections, three or four well-traveled "arteries," and two canals.

"It's the exact gravitational center," according to my friends, whom I've just left surrounded by guidebooks and maps — *milanesi* seem to go to bed very early — the gravitational center of Venice. Empty.

I stand for a moment to gaze at the "piazza" in the half dark: It's grandiose, elegant, refined, and disquieting. Gothic and sixteenth-century palaces, medieval and Renaissance palaces stand motionless beside others dating as far back as the six and seven hundreds, one more beautiful than the next. The nineteenth-century palazzo has a garden opening up to the south, with a huge, magnificent staircase in the glassed-in background, so that even at night your glance can pass through the walls and lose itself there. There is almost no concession anywhere to the twentieth century; I try to imagine how it would fit in here. But it's almost impossible to visualize in such a "high" and coherent synthesis of images and centuries. It's almost too beautiful, Campo Santo Stefano, its only elongation lying to the south from the garden, at once open and mysterious, balanced to the east by the Piazzetta del Conservatorio. It's almost like some sort of golden model, something approaching the perfect — inasmuch as Venice values perfection, precision of measurements, classical models. And it's empty, at nine at night.

Three human shadows flit through the great rectangle toward its intersection with the calli to its north. A small group — four women — crosses from one side to the other without uttering a word and heads for the Accademia Bridge to the south. It's time to converse with the statues, a moment of silence in heaven and earth. The rare footstep echoes faintly from someplace else, not from here. I wander around by myself , moving slowly among the stones and the centuries, between time past and (perhaps) time to come. You can't be too sure of one or the other, while the present . . .

The present — this synthesis of the brief eternity in which we happen to live — is entirely lacking in the urban masterpiece, by this time sealed and untouchable. Stones, voices, institutions, visions, experiences, prayers, music, methods and materials of construction, certainties on the earth, hopes in the heavens: for centuries they all worked together in perfect combination in this ancient city. And here's the result: this emotion, this miracle in the evening at the close of the millennium. Today's mark is missing. It's almost as if we didn't exist, or as if the present, which is the only real time we have, didn't exist. Echoing uneasily in the air is the sound of one set of footsteps, my own, crossing the stones. A single light, some small details, a syllable from the current years of our lives here and there is our only representation. Not even a vestige that counts.

But here comes the fog, rolling in on short waves, rising up from the stretch of canal to the east and unfurling across the piazza in loose tendrils, condensing again against the half-hidden canal to the west. The empty stage becomes a funereal backdrop.

I know it will still be like this, with a shadow or so more or less, even later tonight: at ten, at eleven, at midnight . . . as if no one ever passed through here. Everything's already past.

—⌀ 92 ⌀—

But I'm wrong. An underground or submarine hissing is making its way toward the campo, not sound but the echo of sound. If I pay close attention, I can feel its approach: it's the tide, the inevitable *acqua alta*, washing onto the stage at its predestined hour, playing its part in the space/time that awaits it. Driven by the bruised and half-hidden moon, suspended obliquely halfway up in the sky — remote-controlled, it seems, from here, from the world of statues. The tide is not very high, but it's enough to put water and earth on the same deceptive level, forcing a continuity on the elements. And over the water come floating two boys and a girl carrying a guitar.

They tie up their boat with great care at the intuited, invisible edge of the canal. Then they wade across the stage to settle down on the steps of the monument in the middle. They glance up at the statue, a stiff old man with his books, and they laugh. Before they begin to sing they announce, in English: "*Dangerous.*"

Maybe it's Michael Jackson, this song that they're playing — I don't know, I'm not sure. They have the hoarse, husky voices of people who come and go in the damp between islands. Dangerous. The strange thing is that, although an occasional person goes by, nobody stops. They glance up and quickly move on, as if this were not the place, the hour, the year to stop and sing. In any of the other nearby campi — Santa Margherita, for instance, or San Giacomo, or Santa Maria Formosa — crowds of people would stop to listen and join in on the chorus. What a strange destiny for Campo Santo Stefano, the "gravitational center" of Venice; perhaps it's precisely the utter self-confidence of its beauty that draws you in but then distances you, being both tremendously attractive and at the same time repellent, as it would be in a human being. In order to conserve its refined perfection in the course of this century, this place without a present seems to have renounced the life of continuous relationship unfolding at the market, in the shops, in the taverns, in choruses of any kind, rock or reggae, dangerous or not. People go shopping in the nearby calli, not here in the campo. There's no dearth of *caffè* large and small, so it is a meeting place of sorts, but encounters here are momentary, reunions without roots. Yet the campo and its environs are extraordinarily articulated, attractive in a hundred different ways, with all of the perspectives, corners, arrival points, passageways, stopping-off places, and paths of escape you could possibly ask for. But for all its potential it's never managed to become or remain an *agorà*, a place to hang out in, a place in which to live at whatever hour of the day or night. We may meet each other here, but it's only to show we exist, we're still around. Then, one shadow much like another, we slip away. Campo Santo Stefano remains, in self-contemplation.

At this late hour of the night, now that the three singers have fallen silent and still under the statue, I have to make an effort to move, to detach myself. It's as if I had to overcome a magical circle blocking me in every direction. It's blocking us all: those three, me looking at them, the waiting boat, the motionless monument. Finally I tear myself away and make my escape. I'll come back; I'll try again. But for now I dodge around the corner, disappear without even waving, like an intruder. Like a thief.

—⌒ 93 ⌒—

And in fact I return to the spot, just as thieves do. I leave home a little earlier than usual in the morning so that I can cross through the campo on my way to the office. The memory, the "dream" of the evening before superimposed itself inextricably on my first sensations this morning, like a damp fog still unfurling out of the night.

I try to extricate something. This splendid place lives, indifferent to day or night, in its own "elsewhere" — wherever that may be, in its rectangle of beauty — much more than in reality, or "life," in the realm of empty appearance more than in the realm of the real, the tangible and solid. Even if people talk to each other, call out a greeting, go into a *caffè* as they're doing this morning, they maintain a certain detachment, something between arrogance and fear, toward those of us passing through quickly — because we must, because we have a schedule to meet. This great rectangle of stone and marble could be a symbol of the whole city these days; if I think about it any more deeply, I'll fall into despair. An emblematic place verging on the inhuman, the beautiful campo is always grazed by the shadows and cold, by detachment even when it echoes with voices, even when it's finally struck full by the sun. Beyond or beneath the long or brief meetings, the warm or casual encounters, lies the sense of an experience that has been exhausted, or is being exhausted even now, as we live it.

Of course, these are the gray days of November; but it's always more or less like this. The task of this campo in the middle of the city is to reveal and transmit this thought: Perhaps in this world we can no longer live, ever, in a place whose too-extreme beauty shuts it off from life as the average human being — for instance, those of us now rushing off to work — understands it, sees it, loves it, and suffers it. The common humanity of life inexorably slips away from the sense of place, and all of us together can do little or nothing about it. It's reached the point where now I don't know, none of us knows any longer which road, which calle to take — there are two, three, four possible choices but "they're all the same," as they say here — to get to the office, to work, or to ourselves. We're seized by a desire to stop dead in our tracks at the crossroads and not take another step more. Some things help: a voice calling from the *caffè* even for us, a quick wave, a greeting. And we have our schedules, colleagues who expect us; we have the time clock, waiting for us to punch in.

—◦ 94 ◦—

This evening the fog has vanished and the sky awaits the wind, which is already blowing in fresh, chilly gusts up and down the calli. Once again I'm headed toward Santo Stefano, returning home after an overlong day of work, both in and outside Venice. Outside on terrafirma in the traffic, among the factories, in the shipyard, in the chaos — both the tasks and the day seemed endless.

But now the great campo opens up between the dark calli and so, of course, I stop for a moment. Thank God it's still here in the heart of the labyrinth and also, by this time, in mine. I'm awash in sensations colliding head-on with those of last night, of this morning, of always . . .

Having just returned from terrafirma, I find that a campo like Santo Stefano, and with it all of Venice, is the precise embodiment of its — the continent's — opposite; it affords me a sharp, clear vision, a rare confrontation between "here" in the old city and "there" outside. By its beauty alone this place charges us, as we gaze at it, with a certain responsibility and offers us a cognitive and critically discerning lens, very rare to come by, through which to perceive the current state of the world. For reasons inverse to those of Venice, the other cities we've been in, cities we know and love, are drowning at this very moment beneath the weight of their own contrary but equally fatal problems. They are becoming unlivable, between the chaos of traffic, the grand waste of the use-and-toss culture, and securities more apparent than real. They are foundering in a seemingly unstoppable process of pollution, a growing disfigurement, and a way of life that has become mechanical, to say the least, suffering from the increasing difficulty of human connection, the drama of solitude and alienation. The very idea of a little more tranquillity, meditation, or inner contemplation is so rare in these places as to have practically vanished. It's enough to think back on the streets I've just been down today, only a few minutes away from Venice by car — always fewer minutes away — where no one sees anything surrounding him, neither the people next to him nor the city itself — only the traffic lights, if he sees even them. Some tract here and there in the city, some solitary spot seems more resistant, saving a bit of what it once was; others much less. But they're all imperiled — the word *dangerous* comes back to haunt me. Meanwhile the unrecognizable countryside has become, at its best, "the environment"; it's not *campagna*, not countryside anymore. This is the defaced, polluted, haphazardly built-on and lived-in "environment," violated and violent, disastrous, where we search in vain for what remains of our roots. Certain suburban stews of city and country, certain peripheries, seem to me to reveal in their essence the catastrophe that is the history of the modern world.

It's not a matter of making an absolute choice between the tiny world of Venice and the ever-increasing metropolitan suburbs, between this dark maze of calli and the countryside stripped of its trees and sprouting ever more streets. Instead, we must attempt to make the extreme effort needed to unite what we can of these contrasting urban and human experiences, these two ways of being in the world. And we must also make the effort to integrate within ourselves, as best we can, these opposing forces, in order to bring about our common aspiration toward horizons both more beautiful and more rational; to fulfill our potential for human equilibrium; and to renew habitability and humanity in our aggregates of cement or stone, in nature and in the world. Caught between infinite uncertainties, still we feel within us the task we might undertake; but we're also under the impression that everything is slipping away from us as never before, that everything's rushing by way too fast, not flowing naturally like a river. Yet we have to hold out our nets for a few strong values, fish them back out at all costs from the river — even if they're held in low esteem, considered worthless, like so much of Venice.

Walking through Santo Stefano and its environs, as I must do every day now to get to work, crisscrossing the center of the city, which in these gray days of November is devoid of a single tourist; and more, losing my way in certain splendid, desolate quarters, I'm struck once again by the thought that perhaps Venice, as she is today, is becoming truly uninhabitable for this generation. Perhaps we must change a few things — add, modify, choose; accept some modernity even here so that we don't end up drifting across an empty stage. But this thought is swiftly followed by yet another, by a certainty, actually: that there are also some fundamental things we can *export* from here — perhaps *only* from here. They're difficult to express, since they're neither measurable nor definable nor (or only partly) material: a sense of the continuity and fluidity of time, of time that does not end with us but continues after we're gone, for the others, the people we love; a concept of what constitutes a city, so that its growth is not limited to a recurrent technological hell; and a sudden, tender breath whispering to us of a less convulsive existence, of the necessity to slow down. A certain renewal of relations between yesterday and today, between fathers and sons, mothers and daughters; the possibility of reconciliation between the world in which we journey for the span of a few years and the one that continues on, living in things and in beings; a concordance between art and technology, between spirit and stones, without which we will all surely be lost. For these reasons, I believe Venice to be essential to the world, to be the *necessary city.*

For sometimes, in its most abandoned calli, it happens that we are opened to perceive the "imperceptible" without even desiring it and when we least expect it: the presence of something beyond us that yet comprises us all, in the past and future as well as the now. This occurs during certain moments elsewhere considered "lost time," in those infrequent fringes free of appointments or schedules, which seem to most of us both unobtainable and senseless. It is the advent of a living presence, a "beyond" beyond definition, that nevertheless knocks clearly on the human heart in the most unforeseen hours, here in the ancient city.

As long, that is, as the beyond has not become (as it has, for all of us, a little) no more than the video running nonstop, computer science and data processing, television, Internet, and all the other infernal deceits that inhabit the realm of the apparent and castrate the imagination. In the meantime real sorrows and recurrent dangers loom over us all, whether we're in the old calli, the towns or the suburbs or cities, menacing everyone alive in the world. So we *can't* refuse to connect with each other, especially today when it's so much easier to do so than ever before; we *can't* hold back from exchanging our thoughts and our "consolations" (as my grandmother and grandfather used to say); we *must* find the courage to share our words, whatever we have to say or write, or want to write, no matter what miseries engulf us, no matter where we find ourselves scrabbling to hang on to life. At this point we urgently need to carve out a new kind of conscience, a new way of knowing ourselves, both personally, as individuals, and together, in community. There can be no one who doesn't feel this in some way, no one on the face of the earth. We must do something different, since we are, every one of us, waiting for a new kind of hope — we'll never renounce it — for a little more joy than we've known so far to grace the hours of our days. Because that's what we live for, in Venice or anywhere else.

—❂ 95 ❂—

In the midst of these thoughts, I am given the gift of a great surprise — in the very same place, in the same great square that's been haunting me so these past days. I happen upon it at three o'clock in the afternoon: Campo Santo Stefano, only last night so empty and still, is now filled with babies and children. It's literally swarming with small human beings, intent on their play and their games of imagination. Venice changes every moment for each of us, according to the light, the time, and the atmosphere. But now it's *they* who are creating the change, these little ones who seem to have been born overnight.

Apparently at this time every day, if the sun is shining at all, they take over the campo, they crowd the stage, turning it from funereal to living, moving, and gay. And as anywhere else, they're followed around by their mothers, grandmothers, baby-sitters, every now and again a father — the bartender, newspaper vendor, or waiter . . . But it is they, the tinies, who are in command; it's an occupation. They climb all over everything, changing the stones, statues, windows, gratings, monuments, lampposts, and pedestrians' legs; they transform the railings of the canals, the doors of the churches, the *caffè* tables, marble borders, hands and feet of the stiff old man with his books, the cornices of the pigeons, the refuges of the cats. The stones come alive, speak and respond. This is not a separate park, a walled-in garden, a campus "for them," but a tract of the city, the "gravitational center" of Venice that they've taken over, bringing it back to life, crowding it with color, sparking it with hope.

As far as I can see, there are many, many more infants and very young children than older ones; most of them seem to be somewhere between a few months and six or seven years old. I've noticed before that there seem to be more children in Venice than youths. Maybe the demographic curve is changing; or maybe it's just that the ones at the lower end of the curve all end up here. It's an effort, but a happy one, to wade through this crowd of small beings; most of them couldn't care less about me, but every once in a while one of them stops to study me: the alien. Meanwhile I'm seeing the situation turned upside-down, as if I were looking at a photograph of myself in this exact same spot when I was a tiny young boy, standing under this very statue more than half a century ago. I came here infrequently then, because I was poor; at the time this was a campo for rich kids, and we went to Santa Margherita, San Polo, or the Zattere instead. Now it's not like that anymore; a general affluence has seemingly leveled society's strata, so that there are either no more poor or they're much better hidden. At that time, however, people felt these differences very strongly, and the various classes and ages mingled only on the shores of the sea. Even rich boys (we thought they were funny) came down to the Riva delle Zattere to watch the big ships; even a foreign boy now and then. We heard other languages and made fun of them; the Venetian dialect we had learned at home was the only language we knew. I never did bring my young daughter here to Campo Santo Stefano, partly because we lived on the other side of the city, but partly for the old reasons that lingered within me. Yet today, half a century later, it's like it was then on the shores of the sea: everyone's here, all much more alike than we used to be, and almost nobody "funny." Or, wait: maybe everyone funny.

Now I sit down on the same steps as were in my imaginary photo and am immediately surrounded by a flock of human beings about this high, all of them extraordinarily open and amicable, *simpatici*. Some stand sturdily on their small legs, others are still crawling around on the stones, their eyes fixed on the intruder. Right away one of them begins talking to me, and then they all start to talk at once — asking questions, explaining things, crying, laughing, interrogating, as if continuing a conversation that had begun quite a while ago: the first, the previous conversation, the ongoing conversation, the conversation everyone knows. Don't you remember, you silly "big"?

I don't remember or understand it all; but it's this sense of the *continuation* of the discourse that counts, which they keep offering me, one after another. For what are we if not a continuation of each other? We *are* them, and recognize ourselves in them — much more, of course, than they recognize themselves in us; but the years will pass and that will change. Or maybe it's not that simple; maybe some of them see themselves in us and others don't, just like adults. What matters is that there are a lot of them, fortunately for us. Or at least, there seem to be a lot of them at the moment.

Statistics, I know, don't confirm this. Despite the crowd here today, there are only six to seven thousand children in all of Venice. How many were we when I was a boy? At least four times as many — perhaps thirty thousand. In those days we were a little city of kids; now they're a village.

—❧ 96 ❧—

But it's just in this moment, when you feel so strongly your continuity with their village, that you can delude yourself. Proof to the contrary: Martino shows up, and we go off together to look over the situation in other neighborhoods — the Zattere, San Polo, and San Giacomo.

On the Zattere it's hard to tell, since restorations on the riva block everyone, adults and children alike. A couple of little boys gaze down from the bridge, attracted by the great works-in-progress on water and land. San Polo, on the other hand, is packed to the bursting point with running kids. (They all seem to be running, no matter where they are, in Campo Santo Stefano, at San Giacomo, everywhere — from one campo to another, they seem to be running across the whole city.) As soon as we sit down at the outdoor *caffè* among the troops of mothers and grand-mothers — and the occasional father here, too — a large ball flies through the air, landing directly between my mineral water and Martino's spritz. The women discuss money, jobs, sicknesses, and responsibilities, chatting among themselves as they keep an eye on the little ones playing in everyone's communal campo.

"If we could just double it," I say wistfully to Martino, "this little crowd of children, there wouldn't be so few of us anymore. And we could feel secure about the next few years here in Venice."

"Doubling it," laughs Martino, "sounds pretty hard to me. Maybe we should set our sights a little bit lower. How about an imported increase? All it would take is the reopening of a few offices, the 'transplant' of some organization . . ."

I recall how we lost the International Agency for the Environment a few years ago. It moved out of *Venice*, by nature a capital of the environment, and ended up I-don't-know-where: in some unimaginable city that neither Martino nor I can remember the name of.

As I gaze out at this sea of children, it becomes clearer to me that with some kind of "transplant," some sort of international agency like the one we lost or some similar organization, we could augment not only the number of adults in Venice but, more important, the number of children. The Dutch and the Africans, the Germans, the Danish and Asians all tend to have three or four times the number of children that we do. And all of them would be happy in Venice, in the great city-playground par excellence, kids and grown-ups alike. The children would have a whole world to discover: the campi and calli, the sea, the lagoon, the cats and the seagulls, the bridges and boats. And their parents could relax, since the entire city is safe and available (remember, no traffic) starting right under the house. No need to drive miles to take the kids to the playground!

To put it very simply (we say to each other across the boys and girls who have by now taken over our table), it's the same old problem it's always been: the years pass by but the houses are lacking. Venice needs livable houses, new or old; preferably old and restored. There are so many that have been closed and empty for years! Residence, usage, restoration: everyone's talked about them forever, and almost nothing's been done. We need to make up our minds, as well, to utilize the huge spaces that lie empty and waiting: the Arsenale, for instance, that "city within the city." Also, I insist, we have to find a way to establish some kind of international *something* that finally makes sense.

"It's your obsession," laughs Martino.

"But just think of Strasbourg," I say, "or Brussels, or Lyons . . . We both saw it, in all those places. Wherever there was an influx of a certain number of 'officials,' or whatever you call them, it's been followed by an increase of wealth, new human resources, new blood. In other words, it's helped — even in those places that didn't need any help. We don't have anything like that here, even though Venice is infinitely more attractive, and probably needs new blood more than any other city on earth."

As we're talking, the little Armenian girl goes by, the one who knows four languages and works as an interpreter once in a while. She's so diligent, so intelligent, that she embarrasses me when I run into her. And now she has a new little brother; soon they'll learn even more languages in that family.

Martino and I begin reminiscing about the Venetians we've met in America, Africa, and Australia: two or three families from the Giudecca, a few from Castello, one from Cannaregio, another from Dorsoduro . . . The sestieri of Venice scattered around the globe, with four or five children per family, works out to thousands of kids per sestiere. The families we encountered were cordial and kind, warm and good-humored, as everyone used to be in Venice at one time. In other ways they varied, of course, being either rich or poor, cultured or ignorant, sly or straightforward. But most of them were dogged workers, salt of the earth, and often more knowledgeable about the countries they lived in than their native neighbors. They all spoke their new languages with a Venetian accent and couldn't wait to come home, perhaps just for a while, but maybe forever. We talked about Venice all night long, with the young and the old, in Adelaide (Martino laughs), in Wellington and Johannesburg . . .

"Is Venice as beautiful as she used to be?" they would ask us, devouring us with their eyes. "Do you still go fishing at the Punta della Dogana, on the Riva degli Schiavoni, from the breakwater on the Lido? Do people still talk and gossip and laugh at all hours of the day and night down in the calli? Does the *acqua alta* still sneak up the stairs, and the cat warns you by scratching at the door? Is it true, do you really still tie your boat up under the house? Write to us when you get back, write to us every day . . ."

These and infinite other things, too — more or less what I've written about in these pages — were what they asked us about, sitting there in their lovely, impossible suburbs, where everyone has a big car, and no one talks to anyone else.

If they returned, if some of them came back home with those endless families — Martino and I tell each other — in just a few years the population might increase, who knows? by 50 percent. What we need to do is give them a hand, help them come back; some of them are desperate to return. Maybe it's possible; maybe all it would take is some help, an incentive, a house . . . a word, a letter, a book . . . This is no more than a letter for them, a hundred-day-long letter. Who knows what can help? Everything, anything. New blood could flow into Venice from anywhere in the world, and wherever it came from it would be welcome. I'm envisioning the city as an international magnet for children — children who later grow up. I don't know; are these thoughts of mine, invoked by the little ones, good ideas? Or are they crazy? The children — I feel inadequate, always, when I'm among them.

Here and there on the Zattere, on the Punta della Dogana, some little boy is still fishing — with his father or older brother, as we used to do. And the boy is better at it than his father; that's how it's always been. Children feel the fish, the water, everything, with a sixth sense that we, with the passage of years, working in the cities or aspiring cities, have lost.

Others are leaping onto all the available boats — never available enough, for us or for them. We used to be able to set them free, when we were kids. We'd take a wonderful trip around the lagoon and then bring them back; no one ever said anything to us. Now they're all chained, secured with a couple of padlocks. However, I see that some of the little ones, on the lookout, as always, for the kingdom of heaven, have learned to beat the system: they unlock the boat and take off, on their first adventures in the home sea. The city, the labyrinth, the basin, the sea — all of it's only a step away from the house. This is our riva, waiting with us, no matter what age we are. Without being too obvious, trying not to be seen, we wait for the children to come skimming home, back across the lagoon.

acqua alta   "High water," at the peak of high tide, when the Adriatic has been flowing into the lagoon for six consecutive hours.

alla valesana   A method of rowing in which the oars are crossed.

andata e ritorno   Round-trip.

i Bàcari   Old-fashioned Venetian taverns traditionally frequented by men only.

bagonghi   Venetian dialectical word meaning "goofy/demented/reeling," like a clown in the circus.

bauta, bautta   Dating from the eighteenth century, the *bauta* consists of a black cape with a hood topped by a tricorn, and a particularly blank, white, rather sinister, half mask or *domino*. It is one of the most popular costumes during Carnevale.

calle   One of the innumerable narrow, traffic-free streets (never called *strade*) in Venice, traversed by human pedestrians, cats, dogs, pigeons, seagulls, and sparrows; in plural, *calli*.

campanile   Bell tower.

campiello   A small, intimate campo or piazza.

campo
Literally "field," it is the Venetian version of piazza, or square. The only public space called a piazza in Venice is Piazza San Marco.

Ca'
Short for *casa* (house), the title *Ca'* almost invariably precedes the name of any Venetian palazzo.

Dogana
The Dogana da Mar is the customs house, topped by two bronze Atlases supporting a golden ball and a weather vane of Fortuna, overlooking the basin of San Marco at the mouth of the Grand Canal. Just behind it stands the famous church of Santa Maria della Salute, built as a sign of thanksgiving after the devastating plague of 1630.

fondamenta
An exclusively Venetian word, *fondamenta* refers to a paved quayside street, usually wide and airy.

foresti
(Uncouth) outsiders, foreigners.

in secca
"In dry water," when the tide is at its lowest and the inner canals are almost emptied.

in dosana
"Waters going down," during the six hours the lagoon empties its waters back out to the sea.

in restauro
Under restoration, under repair.

Marghera
"Sister" city to Venice, Marghera is the port of the municipality of Mestre. Directly across the lagoon from Venice, it is the largest industrial center in the whole of southern Europe. The industrial pollution and toxic wastes it spews into the skies above Venice and the waters of the lagoon, as well as the deep channels dug into the lagoon itself to accommodate

countless oil tankers and other large ships, have destroyed a delicate ecological balance maintained for thousands of years, literally devouring the city's stone, eroding its foundations, and causing dangerous disturbances in the tides, as well as poisoning a large percentage of marine life in the Adriatic, long a mainstay of the Venetian diet. Unfortunately, due to high rents and the exorbitant costs of maintenance and renovation, many Venetians who formerly lived and continue to work in Venice have been forced to move to Marghera or Mestre and commute to their own city each day across the lagoon.

molo Jetty, wharf, pier.

morto d'acqua "Death of the water," the moments of peak high or low tide when the waters seem to stand still.

osteria Tavern.

piscina The word means "swimming pool" and refers, in Venice, to a former pond that has been filled in and paved over.

ponte Bridge.

ponticello Little bridge.

rio Any one of the innumerable small canals winding through the interior of the city.

rioterrà A rio that has been drained of water, filled, and paved over to form a street.

riva Generically, a *riva* is a shore (as of the sea or the lagoon) or bank (as of a canal). Specifically named *rive* (plural of *riva*) in Venice overlook the *laguna*, such as Riva delle Zattere (Shore of Rafts), Riva degli Schiavoni (Shore of Slavs), Riva dei Sette Martiri (Shore of the Seven Martyrs), and so on. Facing the Riva delle Zattere across the lagoon is the long, curved island of the Giudecca; facing the Riva degli Schiavoni is the tiny island of San Giorgio Maggiore, site of the famous church designed by Andrea Palladio.

ruga   Uniquely Venetian, the *ruga* is a street lined with shops.

salizzada   Uniquely Venetian, the *salizzada* is a paved alley.

Serenissima, la Venice was a republic for centuries, known as the Most Serene Republic, la Serenissima Repubblica. She is often referred to even today as la Serenissima.

sestiere   Venice is divided into six distinctly and very sharply drawn districts: San Marco, San Polo, Cannaregio, Dorsoduro, Santa Croce, and Castello.

squero   A *squero* (plural *squeri*) is a boatyard devoted to the construction and repair of gondolas. At the present time only three squeri remain in the whole of Venice.

traghetto   There are a handful of *traghetti*, or ferries, that cross from one bank to the other of the Grand Canal at appointed locations. They are shaped like gondolas but lack the six-toothed *ferro* on the prow representing the sestieri of Venice. Each boat is manned by two *traghettatori*. Much used by Venetians, they are cheap and pleasant shortcuts from one side of the canal to the other.

vaporetto

A *vaporetto* is a form of public transportation: a water bus. Various vaporetti crisscross the lagoon and growl up and down the Grand Canal, zigzagging from bank to bank and making frequent landings.

vera da pozzo

Since ancient times, every campo and campiello — even the tiniest — has had its own well in the center, most of which is underground. These wells filter rainwater through layers of sand in a sophisticated system that has rendered Venezia's drinking water — straight from the tap — the purest in Italy, even now. The top, or cap, of these wells is visible and forms the centerpiece to every Venetian campo. Curved and exquisitely carved and bas-reliefed, each wellhead, or *vera*, is a unique piece of sculpture. The well itself is called a *pozzo*. The visible wellhead is the *vera da pozzo*. They are as indigenous and famous to the city as its bridges.

zattere

Rafts.